PERSONALISING PUBLIC SERVICES

Understanding the personalisation narrative

Catherine Needham

First published in Great Britain in 2011 by

The Policy Press
University of Bristol
Fourth Floor
Beacon House
Queen's Road
Bristol BS8 1QU
UK

Tel +44 (0)117 331 4054
Fax +44 (0)117 331 4093
e-mail tpp-info@bristol.ac.uk
www.policypress.co.uk

North American office:
The Policy Press
c/o International Specialized Books Services (ISBS)
920 NE 58th Avenue, Suite 300
Portland, OR 97213-3786, USA
Tel +1 503 287 3093
Fax +1 503 280 8832
e-mail info@isbs.com

British Library Cataloguing in Publication Data
A catalogue record for this book is available from the British Library.

Library of Congress Cataloging-in-Publication Data
A catalog record for this book has been requested.

ISBN 978 1 84742 759 5 paperback
ISBN 978 1 84742 760 1 hardcover

Cover design by The Policy Press
Front cover: image kindly supplied by www.alamy.com
Printed and bound in Great Britain by Hobbs, Southampton
The Policy Press uses environmentally responsible print partners.

FSC
www.fsc.org
MIX
Paper from
responsible sources
FSC® C020438

Contents

Acknowledgements

This book owes its completion to the support and encouragement of many people. Grateful thanks must go to all those who were interviewed for the research, who willingly gave their time and experience. Thanks go to Sarah Carr, Josie Kelly, Kevin Morrell, Emilie Whittaker and Charles Leadbeater for comments on the draft manuscript.

Thanks to the School of Politics and International Relations at Queen Mary, University of London for granting me a sabbatical and for contributing to research expenses. Thanks to all at The Policy Press for making the editorial and production process so smooth.

My thoughts on personalisation were shaped in large part through exposure to the ideas of its advocates, such as Simon Duffy and Jon Glasby, and those who have problematised some of its aspects, such as Marian Barnes and Peter Beresford. I am grateful to them all for their provocative scholarship. The work of John Clarke and Janet Newman has been a broader source of inspiration in undertaking critical social policy. Thanks in particular to Janet Newman for reassuring me that it was ok to hold on to ambivalence.

Many of the ideas in the book were tried out in conferences, seminars and workshops and have improved immeasurably as a result. I would like to thank all those who provided comments and suggestions at these events. An earlier version of parts of Chapter 4 appears in 'Personalization: From Storyline to Practice', *Social Policy and Administration*, vol 45, no 1, pp 54-68, February 2011. Thanks to the Public Management and Policy Association and the Centre for Public Service Partnership for collaborating on the Commissioning for Personalisation project which helped to map out the current practice context.

Thanks to my parents, Jim and Yvonne, for providing all manner of support over many years. Thanks to Ray for being a welcome distraction, and to Jean for not arriving until the manuscript was submitted. The biggest debt is to Blake Woodham as always.

CHAPTER 1

Introduction: problematising personalisation

"I don't think we need to talk about the why, I think we all accept that. The big question is where else, where next. And the how." (Chair's summing up, round table on direct payments, London, 2009)

"No one here disagrees that personalisation is a good thing." (Chair's summing up, seminar on personalisation, London, 2010)

The language that policymakers use can be meaningful in many different ways. Language can be a tool through which to make clear the implications of a new policy, or a device to make those implications all the more opaque. The choice of one set of words over another set, or the replacement of accepted terms of reference for new vocabularies, can be indicative of important shifts in the policy terrain. There is a danger in assuming that words are in themselves equivalent to action. Yet it is also problematic to assume that language is just words, with no value to observers of policy analysis. Words carry meaning, shape possibilities, close down alternative courses of action and create coalitions of actors.

This book developed from an interest in the way that a new policy vocabulary was emerging during New Labour's final term in office, and was being picked up and echoed by the other major political parties. The most high-profile term used was personalisation, although related terms such as tailored and individualised services were also utilised. Together they conveyed a sense that public services were being reshaped around what the individual service user wanted – not around the interests of professionals or the performance targets of managers. What was striking about this discourse was its reach – personalised approaches were being talked about across all public services: in social care, health, employment services, housing, criminal justice and education. As Beresford reflected, writing in 2008, 'A term that had been little more than a vague idea in a 2005 Green Paper now seemed to have gained unstoppable force' (2008, p 8).

This was an agenda to which central and local government were committed, and one that New Labour, the Conservatives and the Liberal Democrats seemed to share (Keohane, 2009; 2020 Public Services Trust, 2010). In the former Labour government's call for a 'cross-government push towards personalisation' (DH, 2008a, p 3), and also David Cameron's vision of a 'post-bureaucratic age' (2009), could be found a shared call for services that transferred control to individual service users.

A report from the New Local Government Network set out the cross-political appeal of personalisation:

> For Conservatives it is an expression of choice and confidence in market mechanisms, emerging from a long-held libertarian tradition and belief in state retrenchment with individuals assuming greater responsibilities and the public sector fewer; for Liberal Democrats it has become a driver for fairness. For Labour, the agenda also draws on the radical left's language of democratic models that originate from collective movements of social justice, dignity and self-determination and the current Administration's advocacy of 'Progressive Universalism'. (Keohane, 2009, p 22)

The difficulty of finding anyone to speak out against personalisation (aside from a few sceptical academics and trade unionists) implied the emergence of a new policy orthodoxy. That public services should be tailored to the needs of individual users had become self-evident. The inadequacy of earlier models, which had attempted to serve 'the "average citizen"' (DH, 2008a, p 3), seemed irrefutable. A number of interviewees for this book noted the extent to which personalisation was difficult to argue against, and was here to stay. As one interviewee from the local government sector put it, "all parties are signed up to this which is refreshing. It is essentially apolitical". The quotes from (different) chairs of personalisation events at the beginning of this chapter sum up the mood.

To anyone with an interest in policy analysis, this rapidly emerging orthodoxy suggested a series of research questions: how had personalisation become such a high-profile approach to public service reform, apparently the only fair and politically viable reform option? Furthermore, stemming from this first question, how had alternative approaches, those based on risk-pooling, professional expertise, managerial enforcement, even market efficiency, been eclipsed, or become acceptable only if rebadged in personalised terms? How had the post-war welfare state come to be so discredited that the only plausible account of it was as a 'monolith', offering 'one-size-fits-all' services to an imaginary 'average citizen'? Was it possible that the political differences between the major parties had collapsed into a common agenda of user 'empowerment' and 'joined-up public services', as the New Local Government Network report on personalisation optimistically concluded (Keohane, 2009)?

Looking in more detail at the policics that utilised the personalisation label, the puzzles intensified. What did personalised learning in schools have to do with self-directed support for people with social care needs? How did personalised conditionality for those on Jobseeker's Allowance relate to personal health budgets for people with diabetes and asthma? There were two related issues here: the first was what, if anything, was the essential core of personalisation, which held across all of these services. The second was how was personalisation spreading between policy sectors, and what were the mechanisms and channels of polıcy transfer? How had a policy with a direct impact on only a small number of social care users (at the time that thc rcscarch began, in the spring of 2009) come to redefine the whole public policy terrain? How had social care, the 'Cinderella service' and 'poor relation' of the NHS, come to lead the field in policy innovation?

A further issue centred on the rationale for personalisation: what question was personalisation the answer to, and what problem did it seek to solve? By 2009, the preoccupation within public services was on saving money and preparing for major cuts. Personalisation was frequently positioned as a vital cost-cutting tool, harnessing the creativity of users to help target resources most efficiently. Yet its ascendance in social care had occurred during times of relative plenty under New Labour, and appeared to be driven more by a sensc that higher spending was not being matched by improved outcomes. In its early manifestation, personalisation was best understood not as a cost-cutting mechanism, but as one of a string of interventions that sought to improve front-line practice, a response to the perceived failings of other approaches: bureau-professional control, outsourcing, performance management and market choice.

Efforts to answer these puzzles, to explain where personalisation came from and how it was being used in contemporary policy debate and policy practice, quickly indicated that personalisation could not just be defined and the puzzles solved. Reading policy documents and talking to people involved in public services – across different sectors, levels of government and political parties – it became clear that personalisation was not a worked-out set of policy prescriptions that spanned different services and levels of government. Rather than seeing personalisation as something complex that needed to be explained, it came to seem like something apparently self-evident that needed to be 'problematised' (Foucault, 1991; Fischer, 2007). Instead of seeking to answer the 'What is personalisation?' question, it seemed more interesting and fruitful to inquire: what do different policy actors (politicians, civil servants, managers, front-line staff, service users) take personalisation (and its associated reforms) to mean? How and why do they use it? What values to they attach to it? Why has it caught the imagination of so many people?

Through this method of inquiry, personalisation came to be understood by the author not as a policy device like, say, outsourcing. Nor was it a script, as Leadbeater (2004) calls it, since that implies a fixed content. Rather it was a set of stories that were being told about public services and the people who use and work in them, that together constituted a narrative of public service reform. Personalisation was a term that helped to summarise all that was perceived to be wrong with existing public services and all that could be done to improve them. The process through which personalisation was spreading was by telling compelling stories about the personal, about the individuals whose lives had been transformed through new ways of thinking about public services. So powerful and authentic were these stories, so full of win-wins – more satisfied service users, more fulfilled staff, lower costs, reduced dependence on the state – that it seemed impossible to challenge them, except as an apologist for an unsatisfactory status quo. Underneath the compelling narrative, new puzzles suggested themselves: how had a small number of powerful testimonies of personal transformation come to have a system-wide effect on a large welfare state? How had alternative perspectives – those of trade unions, for example – been so successfully discredited? There was a clear imperative to understand more about the ways in which the personalisation narrative was deployed.

Approaching personalisation as a narrative is not to demean or discredit it, as though stories are trivial and simplistic. As Cowburn puts it, 'The use of the words "narrative" and "story" are not intended to belittle or relegate certain accounts to the realms of fantasy or fiction. Rather, such usage highlights the constructed nature of all accounts' (2007, p 143). A stress on storytelling is not, as Bevir and Rhodes affirm, 'academic whimsy' (2006, p 105). Narrative approaches to policy-making move away from an essentialist search for policy definitions, and look instead at 'meaning making' (Yanow, 1996). Narratives contain storylines which 'suggest unity in the bewildering variety of separate discursive component parts of a problem ...' (Hajer, 2005, p 56). They 'condense large amounts of factual information intermixed with the normative assumptions and value orientations that assign meaning to them' (Fischer, 2003, p 87). Narratives do not straightforwardly 'reveal the past', but 'through interpretation they do reveal truths about narrators' experiences and how they want to be understood' (Patterson, 2008, p 31).

Approaching policy analysis through the lens of narrative fits with a tendency among politicians and political commentators to frame their activity in terms of a narrative. As Squire et al put it:

> Politicians or policymakers suggest they are doing their jobs well because they pay close attention to people's everyday 'narratives', or because they themselves offer a joined-up 'narrative' of what they are doing. Journalists claim a good understanding of events by spelling out for their audience the underlying 'narrative'. (2008, p 2)

Thus the focus on policy as a good story fits not only academic concerns to understand better how policies change, but also the terms in which policymakers talk about their own behaviour.

Within policy analysis, attention to narratives and problematisation also coheres with the growing significance of interpretive approaches to policy, which give a central role to meaning-making and indeterminacy in policy discourse (see eg Yanow, 1996, 2000; Fischer, 2003; Bevir and Rhodes, 2004a, 2004b, 2006; Hajer, 2005; Stone, 2005; Peck and 6, 2006). Approaching personalisation from the perspective of meaning-making offers the prospect of understanding and explaining it, rather than simply describing its apparent impacts. More 'rational' approaches to studying personalisation – defining, measuring, evaluating – face a number of problems, which this author considers to be insurmountable. First, personalisation cannot be defined without reference to the different ways in which policy actors frame it. Problems of definition attach to both the problems that personalisation aims to solve and the solutions it offers. As Yanow puts it, in reference to policy more generally, 'there is no single, correct solution to a policy problem any more than there is a single correct perception of what that problem is' (1996, p 3). Second, personalisation cannot be measured in a way that looks across public services, because its interpretation and application in different services, and by different stakeholders, is so different. Third, it cannot easily be evaluated because its definition and goals are too fluid to allow a formal test of whether or not it has 'worked'. More useful, as Bevir and Rhodes suggest, is to undertake a critique, which 'consists less of an evaluation of its object, than in unmasking its object as contingent, partial, or both … showing it to be just one among several possible narratives' (2006, p 97).

This is not to say that there is no role for evaluation, particularly in relation to particular programmes to which the personalisation label is attached. Indeed, existing evaluative data will be discussed in the book as a way of understanding how far personalisation has advanced as a policy agenda. Rather, it is to reject the notion that evaluation tools will provide an adequate answer to the question of whether or not personalisation itself 'works'. It is also to argue that this is not the only, or even necessarily the most interesting, question to ask about personalisation. More can be learned about the policy process, and the actors within it, by asking why, how and with what effects personalisation has become such a high-profile approach to public service reform.

In order to do this, the book examines the storylines embedded in a range of primary and secondary texts. Sources include a literature review, textual analysis of primary documents (issued by government and by the broader policy community), dialogue with stakeholder groups and 80 semi-structured interviews with policymakers, service managers, front-line staff, users and carers. Taking an interpretive approach to these data, the book explores how policy actors use and interpret personalisation in texts and dialogue.

Chapter 2 sets out why an interpretive approach, based on the use of narratives within public policy, is the most appropriate way to study personalisation. It discusses narrative approaches to public policy and the elements of narratives that make them particularly compelling as accounts of policy change. In relation to personalisation, it examines some of the existing accounts of personalisation, such as Beresford's distinction between 'liberatory' versus 'managerial' personalisation (2008), and Leadbeater's continuum of shallow and deep personalisation (2004). Recognising the ambiguity surrounding what personalisation means, the chapter avoids using spectrums or dichotomies to capture its distinctive elements, and argues instead that ambiguity is a key element of what has made personalisation such a potent narrative of change. Rather than searching for an essentialist notion of personalisation, the chapter makes the case for examining how policy actors use and interpret personalisation. Finally, the data-collection and analysis methods used in the book are set out at the end of the chapter.

Chapter 3 takes stock of the reforms undertaken in the name of personalisation, which thus far have focused on health and social care, education, employment, housing and criminal justice. Specific reforms that have evoked a personalisation narrative in their development include self-directed support and personal budgets in social care, personal health budgets and more accessible services in the NHS, individual learning plans for schoolchildren, personal development plans for students, and family intervention projects and personalised conditionality for those using welfare services. The distinctive features and histories of these policies will be discussed, alongside consideration of their policy traction, recognising the key role of the social care sector as innovator and disseminator of personalised approaches. The focus is on England where personalisation is furthest advanced and has a higher policy profile than in Scotland, Wales and Northern Ireland. The other parts of the UK are at different stages in developing a fuller agenda of personalisation for social care (see eg Scottish Government, 2009; In Control Cymru, no date). It is as yet unclear whether the other regions will 'catch up' with England or develop their own version of, or alternative to, personalisation. By taking stock of the development of personalisation in England, the chapter helps to provide a benchmark for future comparative work.

Chapters 4 and 5 examine how personalisation became a mainstream approach to service reform, focusing in particular on the social care sector as the key site of innovation. Chapter 4 draws on textual analysis of ministerial speeches, government documents, so-called grey literature (think tank and voluntary-sector reports) and interviews to present the key themes of the personalisation narrative. It shows how the narrative deploys the testimonies of social care service users alongside formal evidence of service improvement and claims that the benefits of personalised approaches are self-evident. It highlights five storylines that are embedded in the personalisation narrative:

1. personalisation works, transforming people's lives for the better;
2. personalisation saves money;
3. person-centred approaches reflect the way that people live their lives;
4. personalisation is applicable to everyone; and
5. people are experts on their own lives.

The chapter also explores how the personalisation narrative interacts with the past and constructs the present and future. Narratives contain an account of time passing: 'an "original state of affairs", an action or event and the consequent state of events' (Czarniawska, 1988, p 2). Thus personalisation can be interpreted as a narrative of transformation based on the failure of older or alternative approaches. It is important to explore why prior and existing welfare state formations are framed in particular ways. It is also necessary to consider how previous waves of reform (such as care management) are subsumed by new approaches or required to mutate into new forms.

Chapter 5 focuses on the people and organisations that have promoted personalisation and established its strong hold on the political imagination. It traces the history of personalised approaches within social care and the role of different actors, including disability activists and politicians, in bringing personalisation into the policy mainstream. It also highlights the importance of the broader socio-political context, in which new configurations of individuals and communities, and new participative technologies, have reshaped the citizen's engagement with the state. The chapter goes on to consider the mechanisms and dialogues through which the personalisation narrative has migrated from social care into other service areas, mutating as it did so. Drawing on interviews with civil servants and analysis of speeches and government documents, it applies the theory of policy translation (a modified account of policy transfer) to the personalisation case (Yanow, 2004; Lendvai and Stubbs, 2007; Freeman, 2009).

Having explored how a new narrative of public service transformation has emerged and gained currency, Chapter 6 looks in detail at the experience of social care, where the implementation of personalised approaches is furthest advanced. It considers what the messy complexity of front-line experience can tell us about the relationship between a transformational narrative and the practice context. It considers how initiatives such as personal budgets in social care are shaping practice. Although personalisation is an approach mandated by national policy priorities, the chapter draws out the variability of local practice within statutory as well as voluntary and private-sector bodies. It highlights the ways in which personalisation intensifies the importance of front-line practice to policy development, since services are not only delivered but also brokered, commissioned and managed at the frontline. The fiscal context is also important here: at a time of major cuts in public service expenditure, commissioners must resolve tensions between rationing resources and offering bespoke services. Bringing in interview data from staff and users, the chapter considers how personalisation is being experienced by those charged with implementing it.

Chapters 7 and 8 consider two of the major alternative narratives that have been used to challenge the dominance of personalisation. The first critique is that personalisation is a mechanism for individualising, privatising and consumerising the welfare state. The second is that it is a tool that valorises the service user at the expense of professionals, devaluing an important source of support and expertise, and depressing wages and working conditions to unacceptable levels. Neither set of arguments is new: both have been made against the broader set of welfare reforms introduced by governments since Margaret Thatcher, and formed part of the early criticisms of direct payments in social care. The focus of the chapters is not simply to rehearse the arguments and the evidence to date in relation to personalisation (for a useful summary of those (in relation to social care), see Glasby and Littlechild, 2009). Rather the chapters aim to explore how the personalisation narrative engages with these two critiques, finessing the tensions at times, while at others making them more explicit.

Thus Chapter 7 examines the broader implications of personalisation for the relationship between the state and citizens, probing its claims to be the basis for a 'new social contract' (ACEVO, 2009, p 5). Rejecting a binary distinction between citizens and consumers, it considers the problematic nature of the 'personal' and different ways in which the personal may be framed and appropriated within a personalisation narrative – as well as how it links to the 'social' (Barnes, 2008). It considers the sorts of 'persons' who are constructed through personalisation, and the emphasis on behaviour change and responsibilisation that is implicit in the narrative. Day centre closures are highlighted as a site in which the tensions between the personal and the social take paradigmatic form.

Chapter 8 considers the framing of staff in the personalisation narrative, examining two key themes. The first is that professional expertise must be challenged, and claims to privileged status resisted, to ensure that the promise of user empowerment is not subverted. The second is that personalisation requires close collaboration between front-line staff and users based on co-production principles. The chapter explores the complexities of the staff–user interface within which these dual accounts play out, recognising the key role played by staff not usually encompassed by the term 'professional' (care staff, personal assistants) and the emergence of new roles (brokers, navigators). It considers how trade-offs between staff and user interests are framed and negotiated in local settings.

Bringing together the arguments in the rest of the book, the conclusion in Chapter 9 makes explicit the ambiguities underpinning the personalisation narrative. Personalisation promises to finesse the tensions in earlier policy narratives, such as those around consumerism, responsibility and community, but questions about equity, risk, vulnerability, exploitation, isolation and commodification continue to have purchase. The chapter revisits the meaning of personalisation and assesses how far it can be understood as a stable and portable term within public policy. It also looks forward to future directions for personalisation, both within social care and across other public services. It explores which types of personalisation are likely to find favour with policymakers in a context of major spending cuts, and how far there remains space for a progressive personalisation based on equity and social justice.

Like other interpretive works, the book takes the form of a critical review of personalisation by an 'active reader' and meaning-maker, not an authoritative or independent account (Maynard-Moody and Musheno, 2003; Fischer, 2007; Yanow, 2007). The author aims to 'tease out the argument implicitly embedded in the story', and to give a credible account of the personalisation narrative, while recognising that 'different people construct different arguments out of the same narrative' (Fischer, 2003, p 181). Based on a commitment to reflexivity in the research process, the author aims to be alert to the ways in which policy actors interpret and shape meaning, but also to the ways in which the researcher interprets those meanings. As Yanow puts it, '[W]e have a vision of a policy world that is made up of interpretations – and researchers themselves are also interpreters, making sense of policy documents along with oral policy language (e.g. speeches, interviews) and policy relevant acts' (2007, p 116).

What became clear from an 18-month immersion in literature, interviews, round tables, seminars and conferences was that it was impossible, and unnecessary, to write a book in favour of or against personalisation. Such works can already be found. Glasby and Littlechild (2009) offer a thorough and broadly supportive account of personal budgets; Keohane (2009) provides a broader review of the background to personalisation and its potential future, again from a sympathetic viewpoint. More critical accounts are also available, such as Ferguson (2007), Scourfield (2007), Barnes (2008, 2011) and Beresford (2008). Nor was it adequate to list the features of personalisation and summarise the case study evaluations – again, such works exist and are multiplying (see eg Glendinning et al, 2008; OPM, 2008, 2010; Tyson et al, 2010). What prompted and sustained the work was the author's own ambivalence about personalisation. Attending one event in which personalisation was rubbished as a Trojan horse for cuts, privatisation and de-unionisation, followed by another (the same day) in which disabled people explained how their lives had been radically improved by personalised support, it became important to unpack these different accounts of personalisation. It was necessary to understand what these different voices (which broadly shared a place on the progressive left) meant by personalisation, how they placed it in a historical trajectory and how their own organisations were responding to it. As Hajer argues, for the researcher it is essential to draw out the ambiguities and contradictions, rather than discarding them in order to create a coherent story: 'it is precisely in the contradictions in written and spoken statements that we [begin] to see policy change materialize' (2005, p 5). There are policy puzzles within personalisation – 'How did it emerge?', 'How did it spread?', 'How is it being implemented?', 'Is it working?' – and political puzzles – 'Will it develop as a policy of the left or right?', 'Will it advance or diminish social justice?', 'Will it sustain or destroy the welfare state?'. This book attempts to lay out these features of the personalisation story, and to probe if not solve the puzzles.

CHAPTER 2

Interpreting policy narratives

Personalisation is a term that dominates discussions of public service reform in the UK: it is hard to find a policy area into which it has not yet reached. So far-reaching are its implications that it has been discussed in terms of a new state–citizen contract and a rewriting of the post-war Beveridge settlement (Duffy, 2008; ACEVO, 2009; Glasby et al, 2010). This policy reach makes the drive to understand its meaning and implications somewhat urgent. Yet how is it possible to study a term that is ubiquitous, but elusive? Personalisation is being implemented through a range of policy tools – self-directed support, individual budgets, budget-holding lead professionals, personal advisors, personalised learning pathways, behavioural contracts – yet these terms themselves often lack specificity. Formal techniques of policy evaluation can be applied to the implementation of particular programmes – and indeed have been in several cases, as outlined in Chapter 3 – but they struggle to do justice to the diversity of local programmes that share the personalisation label.

The claim being made in this book is that personalisation has spread because it is a potent story that is told about public services, with all the discursive advantages that stories have over other forms of communication. This chapter outlines what it means to describe personalisation as a narrative. The first section locates the approach within interpretive approaches to policy analysis. The sections that follow explore narrative approaches to policy, and make the case for studying personalisation through the lens of narrative. The chapter concludes by setting out the data-collection and analysis methods that are used in the research, consistent with its concern for meaning and interpretation.

Policy and interpretation

The approach taken here follows the 'interpretive turn' in policy analysis. Rejecting universalist and context-free research, interpretive approaches instead explore how policy is rooted in particular settings (Yanow, 2007). Drawing on the tools of 'policy epistemics' (Willard, 1996), interpretive approaches seek to understand 'how people construct their policy arguments', by exploring 'the interplay between specific statements or claims' (Fischer, 2007, p 105). As Yanow (1996, pp 8–9) puts it:

> An interpretive approach to policy analysis is one that focuses on the meanings of policies, on the values, feelings, and/or beliefs which they express, and on the processes by which those meanings are communicated to and 'read' by various audiences.

Approaching personalisation with interpretive tools means abandoning the assumption that policies have fixed meanings. Policy itself is an unstable word, meaning at times legislation, while at other times a set of practices (Yanow, 1996, pp 18–19). Monistic accounts of a single, unified and authoritative government will expressed through policy have been challenged by a range of approaches, including those rooted in governance, network and systems theory (Newman, 2001; Sullivan and Skelcher, 2002; Bevir and Richards, 2009). Policy is not something that proceeds in one direction, from centre to periphery, rather it is also made in the interactions of local staff, and in the communications they make back to central policy actors (Pressman and Wildavsky, 1973; Lipsky, 1980; Yanow, 1996; Barrett, 2004; Peck and 6, 2006). Nor are service users inactive in this process, relegated to insignificant or subservient roles as clients and 'lay' citizens (Fischer, 2007, p 106). As Yanow (1996, p 26) puts it, 'In the context of policy analysis and implementation ... we may no longer see clients (for example) as passive recipients of a policy's meaning, but as active readers themselves of legislative language and agency objects and acts'. A study of policy as meaning-making must, therefore, incorporate not only those traditionally recognised as policymakers – the central and local politicians and bureaucrats, the policy entrepreneurs and consultants – but also front-line staff and service users. These latter groups are readers of policy, but also translators, making it meaningful for their own context.

Thus policy analysis is best approached as an attempt to understand how a wide range of actors use policy to convey certain meanings, how far meanings are shared, how some meanings come to be dominant and how they shape practice. Policy is here taken to be part of 'the world of rhetorical practices designed to persuade', rather than a product of instrumental rationality (Yanow, 1996, p 60). This is not to say that policy cannot have substantive and material impacts; rather it is to argue that policies 'have recourse only to symbolic representations to accomplish their purposes, and these purposes can be understood only by interpretations of those representations' (Yanow, 1996, p 12).

By recognising the constructed and contingent nature of policy, it becomes easier to examine the normative elements of discourses that are ostensibly empirical and value-free (Fischer, 2007, p 100). Through looking at these 'unexamined assumptions' (Gusfield, 1976, p 32), the 'silent norm[s]' (Yanow, 1996, p xi), the ostensible 'facts of the case' (Baldwin, 1995, p 369), it is possible to know more about the policy communities that share and promote such assumptions. It also helps to identify alternative interpretations and policies that, as Gusfield puts it, 'would otherwise remain unnoticed and unavailable' (1976, p 32).

An interpretive approach – a search for constructions of meaning and normative assumptions – requires attention to the symbols and categories used by policy actors (Stone, 2005). As Fischer notes, drawing on the work of Maynard-Moody and Kelly (1993), the policy process can be described as 'a struggle over the symbols we invoke and the categories into which we place different problems and solutions, because ultimately these symbols and categories will determine the action that we take' (Fischer, 2003, p 59). According to Schön:

> When we set the problem, we select what we will treat as the 'things' of the situation, we set the boundaries of our attention to it, and we impose upon it a coherence which allows us to say what is wrong and in what directions the situation needs to be changed. Problem setting is a process in which, interactively, we *name* the things to which we will attend and *frame* the context in which we will attend to them. (1983, p 40, emphasis in original)

Framing is a key element in the construction of meaning, a way of transforming 'fragmentary information into a structured and meaningful whole' (Van Gorp, 2001, p 5, cited in Fischer, 2003, p 144). Within this, '[T]he categories used by policy makers cannot be taken for granted or ignored but should always be questioned as an important part of problematising policy overall' (Britton, 2007, p 61). As Barnes puts it, citing the work of Crossley (2002):

> frames themselves can be a site of struggle – contention over who has the power and authority to define the nature of the 'problem' is evident in such diverse contexts as environmental campaigning, the growth of the disability and mental health user movements, and AIDS activism. (2009, p 37)

Part of this book's intention, therefore, is to explore the assumptions and processes – the symbols, frames and problem setting – that underpin the shift to personalised public services. Often these are tacit elements of policy. Reliance on unspoken understandings and forms of indirect communication that deploy them – symbols, metaphors and so on – are key elements of language, and do 'not necessarily reflect an intent to deceive or a conspiracy of silence' (Yanow, 1996, p 215). However, for the researcher, it does demand consideration of the ways that tacit norms can veil relationships of power or ideological agendas (Habermas, 1973; Fischer, 2003). As Finlayson (2004, p 154) puts it: 'Political movements develop a particular interpretation of the world and attempt to secure the victory of that interpretation over others so that it ceases to appear as an interpretation and looks to be the truth.' Recognising how such truth claims come to be constructed and interpreted is a key part of understanding how and why certain policies come to take precedence over others.

Policy as narrative

From a focus on indeterminacy and meaning-making in policy comes an interest in the way that policies are constructed and communicated. Newman and Clarke (2009a, 2009b) have usefully deployed the concept of 'assemblage' in policy, drawing on the work of Callon (1986) and Latour (2005). Assemblages draw on 'the idea that the institutionalisation of specific projects involves the work of assembling diverse elements into an apparently coherent form' (Newman and Clarke, 2009a, p 9). The concept of assemblages 'helps to highlight the complex flows of power and resources, the enrolment of different ideas, interests and agents, the potential instabilities embedded in the apparent coherence, and the ways in which contestation is masked, reworked, silenced or accommodated' (Newman and Clarke, 2009b, p 68). However the same authors note the extent to which the concept of assemblage 'risks flattening the spatial and temporal dimensions' of contested aspects of contemporary governance, and they therefore highlight the need to consider 'narrative framings' (2009b, pp 68–9). Narratives locate policy, providing a sense of place and of temporal ordering, rather than an ad hoc assembling of ideas. Moreover, they are storytelling devices, with all the discursive advantages that stories have over other forms of communication.

There is a growing literature on narrative approaches to policy analysis (see eg Kaplan, 1993; Riessman, 1993; Roe, 1994; Atkinson, 2002; Maynard-Moody and Musheno, 2003; Bruner, 2004; Ospina and

Dodge, 2005; Stone, 2005; Morrell, 2006; Van Eeten, 2007; Morrell and Tuck, 2010). Squire et al describe narrative as a 'popular portmanteau term in contemporary western social research' (2008, p 2). They find parallel antecedents to narrative social research in post-war humanism (focused on holistic, person-centred approaches) and in French post-structuralist, postmodern, psychoanalytic and deconstructionist approaches, emphasising 'multiple, disunified subjectivities' (2008, p 3). They recognise the value of working across (though not ignoring) the contradictions of these approaches, allowing for 'maintenance of a humanist conception of a singular, unified subject, at the same time as the promotion of an idea of narrative as always multiple, socially constructed and constructing, reinterpreted and reinterpretable' (2008, p 4).

Not all forms of policy analysis that deploy the term narrative take an interpretive approach: some narrative approaches draw on realist ontologies or on positivist methodologies (see eg Roe, 1994). However, the notion of policy as a story that is told fits comfortably with the assumptions of interpretive analysis that policy involves the construction of shared meaning, rather than the implementation of fixed legislative mandates. Narratives have 'internal logics' (Bevir and Rhodes, 2003, p 20), they are a key part of 'sensemaking' (Weick, 1995; Boje, 1991). Policy actors tell stories and listen to the stories of others, translating meanings to fit their own context. As Fischer (2003, p 162) puts it, 'Narratives create and shape social meaning by imposing a coherent interpretation on the whirl of events and actions around us'. Roe describes narratives as, 'those stories – scenarios and arguments – that are taken by one or more parties in the controversy as underwriting and stabilizing the assumptions for policy-making in the face of the issue's uncertainty, complexity and polarization' (1994, p 3, cited in Van Eeten, 2007, p 251). Thus, by focusing on the narratives that are used to shape and promote particular policy reforms:

> we are able to investigate not just how stories are structured and the ways in which they work, but also who produces them and by what means; the mechanisms by which they are consumed; and how narratives are silenced, contested or accepted. (Squire et al, 2008, pp 1–2)

Narrative analysis is closely linked to the study of discourse – 'A discourse refers to a set of meanings, metaphors, representations, images, stories, statements and so on that in some way together produce a particular version of events' (Burr, 1995, p 48, cited in Cowburn, 2007, p 141). According to Howarth (2000, p 9), 'discourses are concrete systems of social relations and practices that are intrinsically political, as their formation is an act of radical institution which involves the construction of antagonisms and the drawing of political frontiers between "insiders" and "outsiders"'. 'Each discourse allows certain things to be said and impedes or prevents certain other things from being said' (Purvis and Hunt, 1993, p 485, cited in Cowburn, 2007, p 142).

The focus on narrative is indicative of a somewhat narrower approach than the overarching category of discourse. As Morrell (2006, p 372) points out, 'the term discourse is often used rather vaguely.... There is more consensus as to what narrative analysis involves, partly because it is so clearly linked to everyday notions such as stories and story-telling'. Indeed, much of the interest in narrative has come from literary theory, with its interest in form, rhetoric and semiotics. Some policy scholars have pursued an interest in narrative form – for example, Morrell and Tuck's (2010) work on folk tales and Russian Formalism in policy analysis. However, most interpretive policy analysts have tended to take a more functional view of narratives as shared stories through which policies are shaped, ordered, placed in historical context and used to effect substantive change. In some accounts, the use of narrative is relatively 'thin', deploying the concept to convey a category of ideas, 'traditions' or frames (Bevir and Rhodes, 1999, 2003; Orr, 2005; Needham, 2007; Sullivan, 2007). Following Fischer (2003), Hajer (2005) and others, this book focuses on a thicker account of narratives, as modes of storytelling, rather than merely categories of ideas.

Although the policy literature on narratives is diverse, most authors affirm that stories are particularly effective in bringing about policy change. It is possible to distil from this literature six themes that together explain the potency of storytelling. First, stories are compelling, utilising techniques such as defamiliarisation to draw in the reader. Second, stories offer an account of the past, present and future, imposing a temporal structure on events. Third, stories appeal to values and emotions as drivers of change. Fourth, storytelling is social, helping people to make sense of a shared experience. Fifth, narratives simplify complex and contested terrains to make action possible. Sixth, narratives are purposive – promoting certain kinds of action and delegitimising others. These elements of policy narratives are looked at in turn.

First, then, the storytelling mode attracts the attention of the reader or listener, drawing in those who were on the margins of reading or listening. As Ospina and Dodge (2005, p 143) put it, 'Stories are compelling. When someone tells us a story about his or her experience, we become alert, tuned in, curious.' Of course, some stories are more compelling than others. According to Barry and Elmes, 'What the story revolves around, how it is put together, and the way it is told all determine whether it becomes worth listening to, remembering and acting on' (1997, p 433). To be credible, as Fischer (2009, p 198) points out, drawing on the work of Fisher (1989), narratives must offer a storyline that is logically coherent, consistent with 'narrative rationality' and delivered by a reliable narrator. Novelty – or 'defamiliarisation' – is also an important feature of a compelling narrative, one that 'causes us to see things in new and different ways' (Barry and Elmes, 1997, p 438).

Second, narratives provide an account of the past, present and future (Bevir and Rhodes, 2003, p 20). According to White, narrative is a 'form of human comprehension that is productive of meaning by its imposition of a certain formal coherence on a virtual chaos of events' (White, 1981, p 251, cited in Yanow, 2000, p 58). Stories not only provide a temporal ordering, they also help to explain the links between the past, present and future, offering a sequence of events that leads to the transformation from one state to another (Van Eeten, 2007, p 252; Squire et al, 2008, p 10). Morrell (2006, p 381) explains how a narrative can offer 'a justificatory framework'. As Peck and 6 put it:

> The sense-making process must encompass stories about the past – because it is important to define what is believed to be causing a problem, and often who is to be blamed – and also stories about the future, in order to define aspirations, fears, opportunities and threats, as well as standards or models of behaviour. (2006, p 18)

Third, stories are designed to elicit emotional, value-based responses. Emotion helps to establish the 'moral imperative to reform' that underpins a policy narrative (Morrell, 2006, p 381). As Fischer (2009, p 191) puts it, 'Narrative storytelling, unlike the giving of rational reasons, is designed not just to persuade people intellectually but emotionally as well'. Stories involving personal tales of triumph or media representations of disasters – 'moral shocks', as Jasper (1998, p 409) puts it – are known to be effective at driving policy change, even where the policy environment itself is relatively static. According to Jasper, 'Emotions give ideas, ideologies, identities, and even interests their power to motivate' (1998, p 420). As Grant (2009, p 570) puts it, in a discussion of policies towards badger culling, 'some account has to be taken of the role of emotion in the policy process, the specification of blame and the generation of villains and the extent to which notions of injustice come into play'. In a different example, Moe has discussed the ways in which the discourse of Clinton's National Performance Review involved 'heavy reliance upon active verbs – reinventing, reengineering, empowering – to maximize the emotive content of what otherwise has been a largely nonemotive subject matter' (Moe, 1994, p 114, cited in Du Gay, 2003, p 673). In such cases, 'It is not that the facts do not play a role; rather it is that they are embedded – explicitly or implicitly – in narrative accounts' (Fischer, 2003, p 169).

Fourth, storytelling is a social activity, through which shared meanings can be constructed. As Fischer (2009, p 194) puts it, 'All of the elements of a story – plot, structure, meaning, resolution, and so forth – are created by people conversing and arguing with others'. According to Stone, 'Shared meanings motivate people to action and meld individual striving into collective action' (2005, p 11). As well as being constructed collectively, stories tell something about the social context in which they are told, unlike the purported neutrality of scientific explanation:

> It is through storytelling that people access social positions in their communities, understand the goals and values of different social groups and internalized social conventions.... The meaning of the story is, in short, determined by the social context in which it is interpreted. (Fischer, 2009, pp 195, 197)

Some stories are explicitly social, generating macro-narratives that help groups of people to understand their shared experience. Yanow, for example, defines a myth as 'a narrative created and believed by a group of people which diverts attention from a puzzling part of their reality' (1996, p 191). Other stories focus on the experiences of individuals. However, even these micro-narratives are told in a social setting, facilitating 'intersubjective bonds', with the credibility of the story established through appeals to 'general values or common experiences' (Schriffin, 1990, cited in Fischer, 2009, p 203).

Fifth, narratives simplify complex and contested terrains in order to make action possible. They 'provide actors with a set of symbolic references that suggest a common understanding' (Hajer, 2005, p 62). According to Fischer, 'Connecting actions and events into understandable patterns, the narrative is a cognitive scheme' (2009, p 194). Once expressed and endorsed, storylines provide a point of reference – a heuristic – so that people need to make reference only to the storyline and not to the complex bundle of arguments that underpin it, and make sense of new information and ideas by fitting them into the storyline (Fischer, 2003; Hajer, 2005). Hajer talks of 'discursive closure': 'The point of the story-line approach is that by uttering a specific element one effectively reinvokes the story-line as a whole' (Hajer, 2005, p 62). He goes on:

> as they are accepted and more and more actors start to use the story-line, they get a ritual character and give a certain permanence to the debate. They become 'tropes' or figures of speech that rationalise a specific approach to what seems to be a coherent problem. (Hajer, 2005, p 63)

Fischer (2003, pp 79–80) draws a link here with Laclau and Mouffe's (1985) notion of 'nodal points', which must be established in the discursive field for a specific discourse to become stabilised, facilitating discussion about some things and not others.

To achieve this simplification, narratives may be vague on some points, and contradictory on others (Fischer, 2003, p 106). Hajer (2005) makes clear that one of the functions of policy narratives is to be 'multi-interpretable', able to accommodate the value commitments of a range of different actors and to achieve multiple policy goals. Whereas ambiguity in policy-making may be seen as a source of weakness and likely failure – something in need of repair – it is also possible to observe the potency of ambiguity in policy-making (Eisenberg, 1984). As Yanow (1996, p 129) puts it, 'Ambiguity, in fact, may at times be used strategically in the political and policy worlds to accommodate multiple and conflicting values and meanings'. This claim links to the argument of Laclau (1996) about the function of empty signifiers in allowing policy change to take place. As Griggs and Howarth (2002, p 110) put it: '[P]olicy change will actually only occur when groups construct empty signifiers that enable the group to cover over its internal differences and show the dependence of its own group identity upon the opposition of other groups'.

Sixth, narratives are purposive: they seek to promote certain kinds of action and to delegitimise others. As Stone (2005, p 9) puts it, in a broader context: 'Political reasoning is metaphor-making and category-making, but not just for beauty's sake or for insight's sake. It is strategic portrayal for persuasion's sake, and ultimately for policy's sake.' Narratives may not rely explicitly on persuasive argument: as Fischer (2009, p 200) puts it, 'narratives are primarily designed to deal with an "is".… When it comes to making the case for an "ought" we offer arguments.' However, 'narratives are often constructed in ways that rest – implicitly or explicitly – on arguments' (Fischer, 2009, p 201). As Hajer (2005, pp 64–5) puts it, using the related language of storylines:'Story-lines are devices through which actors are positioned and through which specific ideas of "blame" and "responsibility" and of "urgency" and "responsible behaviour" are attributed.' Thus, a narrative is not a mere chronicle, a listing of events: it is a way of seeing events and of legitimising certain kinds of responses (Fischer, 2003, p 163).

Studying personalisation as narrative

Approaching personalisation as a narrative evokes a sense that it is a story about how services can and should change (and are changing), which itself draws on a range of storylines to assure its plausibility and authenticity. Personalisation is primarily a way of thinking about public services and those who use them, rather than being a worked-out set of policy prescriptions. As Carr (2010a, p 67) puts it, personalisation involves 'thinking about public services ... in an entirely different way – starting with the person rather than the service'. This guide to action makes personalisation highly mutable when translated into specific policy agendas, being applicable to a range of different ways of reforming the welfare state. Indeed, a recurring complaint about personalisation in the literature is its ambiguity and elasticity as a term (Leadbeater, 2004; Parker and Heapy, 2006; Cutler et al, 2007; Ferguson, 2007; Beresford, 2008; Carr, 2008; Pykett, 2009; Duffy, 2010). Generally, there is an assumption that this ambiguity weakens the case for personalisation, and is a problem to be solved through tighter definition or more comprehensive categorisation of different types of personalisation.

Leadbeater, for example, offers a personalisation continuum, which at the 'shallow' end involves 'modest modification of mass-produced, standardized services to partially adapt them to user needs' (2004, p 20). He favours an approach called 'deep personalisation', or 'personalisation through participation', at the other end of the continuum, in which people 'devise their own bottom-up solutions, which create the public good' (2004, p 26). Parker and Heapy develop a similar approach in which personalisation can be a process of 'mass customisation' or 'co-design and co-creation' (which they favour) (2006, p 87). Beresford takes a dichotomous approach that distinguishes between personalisation as new freedoms for supported service users (emerging from the independent living movement), and personalisation as 'a process of rebadging, where the language of consumerism and control does little more than overlay arrangements that remain essentially the same' (2008, pp 11–12). Keohane develops an alternative categorisation that positions personalised approaches on two axes: '"Depth" refers to gradations of personalisation through different modes of choice, voice and influence ranging across the where, who, what, when and how. "Devolution" is the scale to which decisions should be made simply by individuals or by communities' (2009, p 10).

Thus, there have been various efforts to develop spectrums or dichotomies of personalisation in an attempt to pin down its apparent ambiguities. However, Cutler et al highlight the limitations of these approaches. They point out, for example, that Leadbeater's spectrum approach suggests that 'all points on the spectrum are forms of personalisation and hence variants on the transition to person-centred services', whereas in fact 'the implications of different "points" are radically different' (2007, p 853). They draw on Du Gay's (2003) work to argue that personalisation is an 'epochalist narrative', which embodies a 'level of abstraction' that helps to generate an 'aura of inevitability' (2007, pp 847, 853). Hence, rather than the ambiguity of personalisation being an inadequacy that can be overcome through effective one- or two-dimensional mapping, ambiguity becomes a key element of its success as a catalyst for reform. Ferguson, similarly, claims that ambiguity is not a weakness of personalisation, but rather one of its core features: like one of Raymond Williams' (1975) 'warmly persuasive' keywords it is 'capable of incorporating multiple meanings' and its connotations are 'overwhelmingly positive and … therefore very hard to be "against"' (Ferguson, 2007, pp 388–9). He concludes that 'the current popularity of the notion of personalization amongst politicians and policy makers in the UK derives precisely from its ambiguity' (2007, p 389).

Cutler et al (2007) suggest that ambiguity can be effective in setting a political agenda, but suggest that it is likely to inhibit effective implementation. They argue that the level of abstraction in epochal forms of argument contributes to difficulties in defining the concept and hence developing a coherent approach to policy implementation (Cutler et al, 2007, p 847). They cite Du Gay (2003, p 671): '"epochalist narratives provide a simple and easily digestible set of slogans through which to catalyse the demand for change" but "problems invariably arise when it comes to the nitty-gritty of actually effecting practical changes within governmental institutions"', and conclude, 'Such a judgment would appear appropriate to the New Labour project of "personalizing" public services' (Cutler et al, 2007, p 847).

However, from a narrative perspective it is possible to argue that ambiguity plays a key role not only in shaping the policy agenda, but also in the implementation process (March and Olsen, 1976; Matland,

1995; Peck and 6, 2006). Implementation can be facilitated rather than impeded by ambiguity. As Yanow puts it:

> To see ambiguous policy language as a problem to be solved in order to improve implementation chances is to ignore the reality of purposive ambiguity: it temporarily resolves conflicts and accommodates differences, allowing contending parties to legislate and move on to implementory actions. (1996, p 228)

Yanow cites examples of policies where it was their very vagueness that was key to their widespread adoption. As she puts it, 'In this view, implementation success or failure may ride on the construction of meaningful, believable myths or other symbols and their associated ambiguities, rather than on the direct pursuit and achievement of explicit policy goals' (1996, p 206). Fischer makes a similar point: 'the ambiguity of symbols helps coalitions form where pure material interests would divide potential members' (2003, p 64). Such arguments have resonance in relation to personalisation, highlighting the importance of a policy context in which a wide range of divergent interests can sign up to and advance it without needing to reconcile internal tensions. As Hartley (2007, p 637) puts it, personalisation is a 'very elastic concept.... [T]his very imprecision also means that it cannot easily be targeted for critical analysis. It is not easily decoded and it will not easily be dismissed.'

Data collection and analysis

Approaching personalisation as narrative demands a methodology appropriate for interpretive policy analysis. As Bevir and Rhodes (2004b, p 134) put it in relation to their own research: 'To tell stories about other people's stories, we have to recover their stories and explain them.' There is a tension here, which runs through interpretive research, between rejecting meta-narratives as ideologically suspect and distorting (Davies, 2008, p 5), and recognising that the very attempt to develop coherent themes from many different stories is to offer a meta-narrative. According to Bevir and Rhodes, 'we deliberately use narrative to describe both what we offer and what we study ... we offer narratives of narratives' (2004b, p 159). As Yanow puts it, reflecting on her own research, 'These continue to be second-level constructs, my representations of participants' interpretations' (1996, p 128).

Given this book's focus on 'understanding the stories public servants [and others] tell to make sense of their situation' (Van Eeten, 2007, p 252), it was necessary to combine a range of sources. Those used were documents, participant observation and interviews. Policy documents on or relating to personalisation were drawn from the government and from the broader policy community (think tanks, voluntary-sector bodies, private consultancies). As well as formal statements of policy, these included committee minutes, training documents, calls for evidence and annual reports. These documents were useful in identifying the key themes of the personalisation narrative as formally set out by the government and as stated by its advocates. They also provided examples of practice and evaluations of policy studies.

To supplement the documents, the author made use of field notes drawn from participant observation in meetings, seminars, round tables and conferences relating to personalisation. At a time when personalised approaches were gaining an increased profile, such events were plentiful. It was instructive to take part in such events and to note the ways in which the personalisation story was framed (often in terms that suggested that the evidence was more compelling than it appeared to be from the documentary analysis), how gaps in the story were finessed (eg on what the large budget cuts in local government were likely to do to the personalisation agenda) and how opposition was silenced from the chair by a presumption that there was no point discussing the 'why' of personalisation when it would be much more worthwhile to focus on the 'how'.

As well as the documents and observations, the project drew heavily on interviews, with the author interviewing 80 people, face to face or over the telephone. Interviews offer an opportunity to explore how people talk about policy change, and how they position their own experience in relation to broader policy narratives. They help to identify gaps and silences in formal policy positions, and to highlight examples from practice that problematise the apparent simplicities of the narrative. Interviewees were selected to provide reflections from practice: they are neither exemplars of best practice nor a representative sample. Rather they were chosen to produce accounts of the lived experience of people involved in the personalisation process. They were selected using a purposive sample to identify relevant spokespeople from the various types of organisation and service sectors affected by personalisation. Participants include politicians, civil servants, local authority managers, front-line staff, service users, carers, trade union representatives, academics, consultants and staff from private- and third-sector providers.

In order to identify people to interview it is necessary to categorise them. However, as discussed earlier, such categorisation is itself a contested process. While the research sought to speak to 'policy-relevant publics' (Yanow, 1996, p 50), categories such as front-line staff and service users are not self-evident, and some people belong in more than one category (McLaughlin, 2009). The language of 'service user' is potentially problematic, defining people according to their dependence on a particular state service (McLaughlin, 2009). However, its connotations are more neutral than the possible synonyms – client, consumer, customer – without being so broad as citizen, or so awkward as 'people who use services'. Thus, service user is utilised here as the best available term, without denying its limitations as a way of labelling and categorising people.

Some of the interviews were what might be described as 'elite interviews', others were with more 'ordinary' people working in or using public services. However, following Neal and McLaughlin (2009), there was no assumption that these gradations reflected simple differences in the power relations between interviewee and interviewer. Power did not flow downwards or upwards in stable ways. Rather, the experience was similar to that which Neal and McLaughlin describe: 'untidy and emotional research encounters in which power moved in mobile ways across interview landscapes' (2009, p 703). However, the interviews were conducted in recognition of Neal and McLaughlin's point that 'researchers always inhabit a place of considerable power and authority given that they design and "direct" the project, they hold the interpretative power over the data collected and they make decisions as to what then happens to it' (2009, p 700).

An effort was made to observe the different phases of the research process – problem identification, data gathering, analysis, writing up – while recognising the iterative relationship between these phases and the 'often chaotic and unplanned nature of social research' (Davies, 2008, p 29). Thus, the project began with a research question – 'Why had personalisation become such a high-profile approach to public service reform?' – and a list of potential interviewees and documents, but the list shifted as the project went on and new people, publications and avenues of inquiry appeared to offer insight. Effort was made to analyse the data at the same time as gathering new material, to ensure that the right questions were being asked, and important themes recognised. The 'sharpening' of the questions and gradual refinement of theoretical categories allowed by this 'interplay between theorizing and collecting data' (Davies, 2008, p 34) was seen as a key element of the research process.

The aim of the interviews was to discuss the same policy initiatives and changes with different people, in order 'to construct a "thick description" (Geertz 1973) of what transpired, (re)presenting an event from different angles' (Yanow, 1996, p 42). Initially, the author started interviewing by asking a set of open-ended questions. However, it quickly became apparent, particularly over the phone where discussion was more stilted, that respondents saw their role as to 'supply answers directly' (Davies, 2008, p 57), often finishing by saying things like 'Is that what you wanted?' and 'Have I said enough?'. Thus, after the first few interviews, the researcher adopted a more conversational approach, asking people to reflect on their work and experiences of personalisation, using follow-up questions to probe at appropriate times to ensure relevant areas of inquiry were covered. Of course, such interactions are not conversations or free-flowing discussions since they are largely one-sided, but they did seem to allow respondents to talk in a way that was somewhat less artificial. Following Tietel (2000), there was 'a recognition that research interviews are "relational spaces" where the researcher and the narrator co-construct interviews' (Phoenix, 2008, p 66).

Most interviews were digitally recorded and professionally transcribed, although in some cases transcribed notes were used. Interviews were conducted on an off-the-record basis, allowing anonymised quotes to be used. Where transcription was done by an external agency, the transcripts were checked for accuracy by the author. The interview transcripts, along with the policy documents and field notes from the observations, were coded using the computer programme NVIVO. The use of computerised coding helps to avoid some of what Davies (2008, p 247) calls 'the idiosyncracies of human memory' when dealing with large amounts of data, thereby allowing a systematic analysis of the text. The coding system developed gradually over the life of the project, with initial overarching categories being filled in by more detailed themes.

The breadth of people interviewed, and the multiplicity of methods used, were designed to secure a convincing study of personalisation as a policy narrative in England during the 2009–10 period. The research endeavoured to maximise within-study reliability, following Davies' advice to 'return to the same topic, even asking the same question, under varying circumstances, and checking verbal assertions with observations' (2008, p 97). The researcher was sensitive to Dowding's objection to interpretive approaches, namely, 'Actors can be wrong about their own actions, the nature of their practices, institutions and so on' (2004, p 142) – and to Howarth's warning 'to be aware of the ways in which social subjects retrospectively construct narratives in particular ways' (2000, p 140). However, the author proceeded on the assumption that the ways that actors choose to interpret their own actions and the meanings they ascribe to policy are constitutive of that policy. The aim of the project was not to get to a pre-existing truth about personalisation, but to develop a composite and accurate picture of how it was being interpreted and applied as a policy reform. The author did not seek 'to uncover the underlying meanings of social practice that are somehow concealed from actors' (Howarth, 2000, p 11). However, the research aimed to do more than 'simply seek to recover the interpretations actors give to their practices' (Howarth, 2000, p 11). Rather, as Howarth endorses, the aim was 'to provide new interpretations of social practices by situating their meanings in broader historical and structural contexts' (2000, p 12).

In the chapters that follow, the author draws on extracts from the interviews and documents that were studied. Given the wealth of data generated, only a small amount is presented in the text. However, this is based on what Davies calls 'reasoned selectivity in presentation of evidence', presenting data as accurately as possible (2008, p 238). Stability over the course of an interview project is hard to achieve. As Davies (2008, pp 42, 115) notes, the researcher may adopt variable personas within and between interviews, and interviewees may draw on different social identities at different points in an interview, generating different perspectives. In addition, the potential universe of interviewees for the topic was extremely large, and it was possible to interview only a small portion of those. Efforts were made to ensure that it was a balanced portion, in relation to roles and viewpoints. However, it may be that a different study, interviewing different people and looking at different documents (or indeed the same people and documents), would come to different conclusions – particularly at a later date when the personalisation agenda has advanced further. As Yanow (1996, p 135) puts it, 'From an interpretive point of view, the possibility of reinterpretation always exists.' It is hoped that the interpretations offered here present an account of policy that meets interpretive standards of credibility, dependability and confirmability (Dodge et al, 2005). It aims to offer an informed starting point for future studies, one that will contribute to a clearer understanding of a key area of policy change.

CHAPTER 3

Personalised public services

The discussion so far has established the value of narrative approaches to policy analysis, and highlighted some of the *prima facie* ambiguities of personalisation as a narrative of reform. Attention now turns to some of the reforms that have been undertaken in its name. Through identifying key policy commitments and common themes it is possible to draw out some of the distinctive elements of personalised approaches to public services. This chapter gives a sector-by-sector account of how personalisation has impacted on public services to date.

There are at least two challenges to this type of overview. First, a snapshot of reforms always overstates the simplicity and coherence of a set of reforms and risks being quickly outdated. Reforms are ongoing and the change of government in 2010 makes for a more volatile policy environment. However, it appears that the Conservative–Liberal Democrat government is not abandoning any of the personalisation reforms discussed here, since they fit with their own approach to service restructuring (HM Government, 2010a). If anything, the Cameron-led government looks set to take the personalisation agenda further and faster than New Labour, a point developed in the concluding chapter. Other sources of potential instability in describing personalisation reforms – the disputed genealogy of the reforms, the contested evidence base, the variable implementation – merit further discussion and are key themes of later chapters.

There is also an issue of boundaries: what to include and not include as an example of personalisation. Some of the people interviewed for the research described personalisation as a new word for an approach that they had always taken, with which government was now catching up. There are various initiatives going on outside the state sector that could be described as examples of personalisation (see eg some of the projects run by Participle [Cottam, 2009]). However, the discussion here encompasses service tailoring that has been promoted or endorsed by government, consistent with the focus on personalisation as a narrative of policy change.

Within government-sponsored approaches, it is still a challenge to identify what counts as an example of personalisation, since the word itself may not always be used. Definitions offered in government documents are often vague: the Prime Minister's Strategy Unit, for example, defined it as 'the way in which services are tailored to the needs and preferences of citizens' (2007, p 33), a definition that could be applied to the efforts of the welfare state at any period since the Second World War. The focus here will be on public service delivery mechanisms that aim to modify the service to meet the specific circumstances facing individual users. Such mechanisms could include individual budgets, personalised assessment mechanisms and new forms of conditionality. While some texts have pointed to community and collective forms of personalisation such as community asset schemes (see eg Keohane, 2009), their inclusion seems to rely on too expansive an understanding of the term personalisation, losing its orientation to the person. Here the emphasis will be on how services are tailored to the person, with the individual as the unit of analysis. This does not preclude individuals working with others to commission and share group services, but it does assume that services cannot be personalised to a community.

Reforms that are premised on the provision of individually tailored approaches include self-directed support and personal budgets in social care; budget-holding lead professional (BHLP) models and family intervention schemes for children, young people and families; personal health budgets and more accessible services in the NHS; personalised learning for schoolchildren; learning and skills accounts for further education; personal development plans within higher education; personal advisors in employment services; and new payment and choice mechanisms within housing. There has also been some talk of taking more personal approaches to offender management and rehabilitation in the criminal justice system, although such approaches remain underdeveloped. The key features of each of these policies will be sketched out in turn, highlighting the breadth and influence of the personalisation agenda, but also the extent to which its principles remain somewhat vague and sector-specific.

Adult social care

Personalisation is furthest advanced within adult social care, reflecting the extent to which its emergence and apparent success in that sector has been a catalyst to broader implementation. Soon after entering office, the Conservative–Liberal Democrat government confirmed its intention to support the personalised approaches to social care developed by its Labour predecessor. The Care Services Minister, Paul Burstow, said: 'I want to put a greater focus than ever on personalisation ... I'm clear there can be no slipping back to the days of one-dimensional, like-it-or-lump-it services. Personalisation must remain a guiding principle for long-term care' (Dunning, 2010a).

Personalisation within social care encompasses a broad agenda of approaches that come under banners such as person-centred planning and self-directed support. It is often associated with the payment of direct payments or personal budgets to those with social care needs, or their carers. However, the agenda is broader than devolved budgetary control. As a 2008 Department of Health document put it:

> Central to the transformation of social care ... is the concept
> of personalisation as an approach to the delivery of public
> services, self-directed support as a manifestation of this
> concept in health and social care and personal budgets as
> the operating system that will deliver choice and control
> to citizens requiring social care support. (DH, 2008a, p 9)

Although personalised social care is about more than devolved budgets, it was the introduction of direct payments legislation in 1996, following years of campaigning by disability organisations, which marked a key policy change. It allowed some people with disabilities to receive a budget to manage their own care needs and purchase appropriate services (Leece and Bornat, 2006). The legislation was later extended to include older people, disabled children, mental health service users and carers. In Control, an organisation that promotes self-directed approaches, and which describes itself as a 'social innovation network', worked with local authorities to encourage the extension of direct payments into individual budgets that could be spent more flexibly and drew together monies from a range of sources (Poll et al, 2006). In 2005, the Department of Health piloted individual budgets in 13 councils. Evaluation of the pilots found that the initiative was generally welcomed by participants, who reported feeling they had more control over their daily lives (Glendinning et al, 2008). Mental health service users, physically disabled adults and people with learning disabilities were more positive about the scheme than older participants. However, attempts to integrate multiple budget sources, derived from different government agencies, were recognised to be problematic, and implementation shifted back to a focus on budgets for social care. These were labelled personal budgets to distinguish them from the more expansive individual budgets.

The Right to Control initiative, based at the Department for Work and Pensions (DWP), did revive the idea of a broader approach to pooled budget streams, focusing on disabled jobseekers (DWP, 2008).

Legislation in 2009 introduced Right to Control Trailblazer pilots, designed to integrate resources from a range of funds, including Work Choice and Access to Work. Right to Control also supports the integration of funds to make it easier to live independently in the community, expanding its remit beyond labour-market entry.

In 2007, the *Putting People First* concordat, signed by central government, local government and the social care sector, widened the agenda, emphasising that personalisation should not just be seen as personal budgets or direct payments (HM Government, 2007). Personalisation was to be about choice and control for the individual, with a number of strands including early intervention and prevention, social capital, and improved access to universal services. The Department of Health has made clear that better service integration is central to the personalisation agenda: 'The expanded use of personal budgets needs therefore be accompanied by the further progression of integrative developments such as care pathways, expert patients, practice based commissioning and similar development in education, employment, housing and leisure' (DH, 2008a, p 7). To better integrate health and social care services, local authorities and Primary Care Trusts (PCTs) were required to undertake a Joint Strategic Needs Assessment (JSNA), looking at the health and well-being needs of local populations, and how to improve outcomes and reduce health inequalities. Personalisation is seen as entailing better access to universal services as well as better tailoring of care services. As the Social Care Institute for Excellence (SCIE) put it, 'Personalisation ... means ensuring that people have wider choice in how their needs are met and are able to access universal services such as transport, leisure and education, housing, health and opportunities for employment regardless of age or disability' (SCIE, 2009a, p 1).

A three-year, £520 million Transforming Social Care Grant was allocated to local authorities from 2008 to assist in the move to personalised care. National Indicator 130 required local authorities to have 30% of eligible service users on personal budgets by April 2011. Care Services Minister Paul Burstow indicated that he expected all eligible users to have a personal budget by 2015 (Brindle, 2010). There were also a series of milestones that local authorities must reach on the way to these longer-term targets, which included setting up a user-led organisation in each local authority and engaging with service users and the wider community. A survey undertaken by the Association of Directors of Adult Social Services (ADASS), published in May 2010, found wide variety in the progress that local authorities were making towards the milestones. Targets on preventive services were the least likely to be met (see www.adass.org.uk).

Many local authorities are putting in place a resource allocation system to calculate how much personal budget should be allocated to a user. Once a budget is allocated, users can choose to manage the money themselves as a direct payment or to have it managed by the local authority or a third party (as an Individual Service Fund). The user (along with their carer, where appropriate) and a support planner (who may be a social worker, another local authority employee or a third party) then work to put together a support plan. Plans must be linked to approved outcomes and signed off by the local authority, but users are encouraged to be creative in how funds are spent. This may be something very different from a traditional package of care services. Service users can choose to employ a personal assistant and/or to spend money outside the formal care sector. The Care Quality Commission (CQC), which regulates the sector, is encouraging councils to find creative uses for budgets, so long as they are outcome-based.

At the end of 2010, Jeff Jerome, the National Director for Social Care Transformation, announced that 250,000 people were in receipt of a personal budget, a quarter of care service users (Pitt, 2010). Many of these will be younger disabled people who were in the vanguard of the movement for more choice and control. The extension of personal budgets to older people, who form the vast majority of eligible social care users, has been slower. Take-up among people who use mental health services is also low (MIND, 2009a). It is not yet clear how far the personalisation agenda will have an impact on people living in residential care homes or in receipt of nursing care since these people may not have much scope to vary the service (SCIE, 2009b).

Children and families

Although some of the early work on personal care planning and budgets was done with disabled children, much of the recent focus on personalisation in social care has been on adults, and there is a perception that it is proceeding in a less focused and more ad hoc way in children's services. In Control has worked with local authorities and the central government to develop more personalised approaches for children, young people and families (Crosby, 2010). In May 2007, the then Department for Education and Skills (DfES) announced pilots to provide individual budgets for disabled children and their families through the Aiming High programme (DfES, 2007). At a regional level, Yorkshire and Humber have supported work improving the experiences of young people at the point of transition to adult services, including working with special schools to support person-centred planning (Cowen, 2010).

For children with additional needs, which may include having a physical or learning disability, speaking English as a second language, or being at risk of abuse or neglect, there have been pilots of a BHLP model. This approach builds on the longer-standing role of lead professional, which has been seen as a key to delivering more focused support for children and families (HM Government, 2003). Preliminary evaluation of the BHLP pilots found that lead professionals could help to coordinate a wide range of services and to work creatively with families and other staff to access resources, 'creating a can do culture from the bottom up' (OPM, 2008, p 34). A national evaluation by Newcastle University was less positive, however, finding that front-line staff did not have the necessary commissioning skills and that budgets from different sources were not being integrated effectively (Walker et al, 2009).

Much of the experimentation in the children's sector has been driven by the person-centred planning rationale that is reshaping adult social care. However, there are other interventions that involve state-led tailoring of services, such as the family intervention projects developed by the previous government, which could be seen as an example of personalisation. The projects, overseen by the Home Office's Respect Task Force, were part of a broader approach to tackling anti-social behaviour. They are intensive programmes, offering tailored support for 'problem families' to tackle recurrent issues associated with the co-occurrence of factors such as mental health problems, behavioural disorders, substance abuse, educational underperformance and anti-social behaviour (DCSF, 2008). Often run by the third sector, the projects provide a range of intervention strategies, including support in the family home and the provision of specialised short-term housing facilities. Most providers stress the importance of voluntary participation by the families, so that they are committed to collaborating with professionals to improve outcomes, although there are usually sanctions for non-compliance. Evaluation of the initial pilots found positive results; however, key elements of the project (small caseloads, well-trained and supported staff) were proving hard to maintain as the project was rolled out nationally (White et al, 2008).

National Health Service

In addition to responding to the needs of adults and children with an assessed social care need, there have been efforts to expand the personalisation agenda within the National Health Service (NHS). As Prime Minister, Tony Blair made a commitment 'to change the National Health Service into a personalised health service for each individual' (Blair, 2004), and introduced a programme to increase patient choice of hospital. An Expert Patient Programme enabled patients with chronic conditions such as diabetes and asthma to make choices about their treatment and to improve skills for managing their conditions (DH, 2004, ch 3). In one of two reports commissioned by Gordon Brown into the future of the NHS, the then Health Minister, Lord Darzi, argued that much of the personalisation agenda had been achieved already, through greater use of information technologies (including the online/telephone enquiry service NHS Direct and the Choose and Book system for hospital treatment) and longer opening hours for GP surgeries (Darzi, 2007, p 12). Everyone with a long-term health condition was promised a personal care plan, setting out a tailored programme of support.

There have also been efforts to offer more tailored solutions to people who use the NHS as a result of lifestyle-related health factors, such as obesity and smoking. Government guidelines emphasised the importance of a 'person-centred approach' and supporting the individual to make appropriate behaviour changes (NICE, 2006, p 7). As Prime Minister, Gordon Brown explained.

> The responsibility of Government, and wider society, is to make sure that individuals and families have access to the opportunities that they want, the information they need in order to make healthy choices and exercise greater control over their health and their lives. (DH, 2008a, p iii)

The Conservative–Liberal Democrat Coalition government has since indicated that it takes a stronger line on personal responsibility for conditions such as obesity, expecting individuals to make appropriate choices to improve their lifestyles (Lansley, 2010).

The most radical change in the health sector, launched by New Labour and supported by the Coalition government, is the introduction of personal health budgets, similar to the budgets used in social care. The introduction of such budgets into the NHS had been ruled out by a 2006 health White Paper (DH, 2006, p 85). However, the

Darzi (2007, 2008) reviews of the health service revived the idea of individual budgets within the NHS, drawing inspiration from their perceived success in social care. In early 2009, Darzi published a report announcing the launch of a pilot scheme for personal budgets in the NHS (DH, 2009a). The appetite for such budgets among Primary Care Trusts (PCTs) appeared to be great, with 75 PCTs involved in pilots for a range of services including mental health, maternity, end-of-life care and substance abuse. Patients can opt to manage the money themselves, following new legislation on direct payments in health. Alternatively they can work with health professionals or a third party to identify how to allocate a notional or managed budget. According to the Department of Health, such budgets 'could support innovative services, potentially including those currently outside the scope of traditional NHS commissioning practice' (DH, 2009a, p 45). 'Personalised purchasing' is seen as a way to create a dynamic provider market, allowing 'popular and successful services to grow, and others to adapt, shaping the available services to meet individuals' needs' (DH, 2009a, p 9).

One of the key elements of the pilot evaluation will be to look at how individual budgets have been allocated for particular conditions and patients. It may be that individual budgets are particularly appropriate for the non-clinical elements of care, where personal preferences and experience are particularly salient. In June 2010, Paul Burstow announced the first direct payments in health as part of the personal health budgets pilots, stating 'This is an important step towards putting patients at the heart of everything the NHS does' (DH, 2010b).

The Coalition government's health reforms, replacing Strategic Health Authorities and PCTs with GP-based commissioning consortia, will shape the future development of personalisation in health (DH, 2010b). The reforms may make it easier for creative GPs to commission services that deal holistically with people's needs, allowing personal health budgets to be spent on services that are not part of core NHS provision. However, they may also make GPs more conservative in their spending, and less willing to allow patients to commission their own services. The wariness of the British Medical Association's response to personal health budgets – citing concerns that patients will choose to spend money on inappropriate services – indicates professional nervousness about the changes (Smith, 2010).

Housing

Personalisation is reshaping housing provision in a number of ways. The first is through addressing the housing needs of people in the social care system, to ensure that accommodation is not left out of the care agenda. As Jeremy Porteus from the Department of Health's Putting People First team put it, 'Decent and appropriate housing is also a way of providing more personalised care, giving individuals more control over how they live their lives' (Porteus, 2008). According to SCIE:

> Housing and the local environment can make a critical difference to someone's ability to live independently.... Housing providers need to be able to offer people a choice in how and where they could live and to ensure that homes are well designed, flexible and accessible. (SCIE, 2009c)

As part of the government's Think Family initiative, targeted at families at risk, housing is one element that can be included in an individual budget (Taylor Knox, 2009, p 17). Local authorities can also draw on Supporting People funds, which provide housing support for vulnerable people, to offer personalised support (Audit Commission, 2009). The government has noted the possibility of using personal budgets to provide options for 'some marginalised groups including the small numbers of people who have slept rough for many years and have, up to now, been unwilling to accept the help on offer' (Department of Health Care Networks, 2009).

However, there are some concerns about the viability of using individualised funding to pay for collectively allocated services such as housing. Supported housing is usually provided to groups of people and funded on the basis of a fixed number of people using the service. For that reason, some housing providers have been nervous about how personal budgets would undermine the viability of their funding base if one or two people wanted to opt for different sorts of support. The Housing Associations' Charitable Trust (HACT) is undertaking a three-year project, Up2Us, looking at service user purchasing consortia for people with individual budgets and/or direct payments. The aim of the project is to explore new approaches to collective purchasing through mutual cooperation in order to 'maximise their purchasing power, increase independence and improve service quality and demand for new services' (HACT, 2010). SCIE have called for greater flexibility in relation to specialist housing, even in a context of collective funding:

'it is possible to develop a core service offer and a menu of options available for purchase either as individuals or jointly' (SCIE, 2009c).

For social housing tenants and those in receipt of housing benefit there have also been efforts to make services more personalised over the last 10 years, through initiatives such as choice-based lettings and the local housing allowance. Piloted in New Labour's first term in office, choice-based letting schemes are operating nationally. People can choose from a range of properties available in an area, rather than having a property allocated to them, with local authorities then deciding which applicant should have priority in relation to a particular property. The schemes are designed to 'enable people to balance their own "felt" need, as measured by the time they felt able to wait, against the availability of the properties they might be able to secure' (DETR, 2000, §9.20).

For people living in private rented accommodation and eligible for housing benefit, local housing allowances have been available nationally since 2008. The allowance is determined on the basis of a local authority rate (set at a median average of local rental rates by New Labour, but reduced to 30% by the Coalition government). Like personal budgets in social care, the money goes directly to the tenant, rather than the landlord. If tenants are able to secure a cheaper rent they can keep the additional money, or they can top up the rent to access more expensive accommodation (DWP, 2006).

Employment

The employment sector has also seen the introduction of more personalised approaches, particularly targeted at the long-term unemployed. The Jobcentre Plus initiative, launched in 2002, incorporates a commitment to personal advisors for jobseekers (Ben-Galim and Sachrajda, 2010). However, an Institute for Public Policy Research (IPPR) report into personal advisors found that the caseloads were too high to deliver effective support to individual clients, and that more training and career progression was required to raise the status and effectiveness of advisors (McNeil, 2009). Services continued to be delivered on a block contract basis with inadequate differentiation between the different needs of jobseekers.

The Gregg report (2008) introduced the language of 'personalised conditionality' for people out of work, combining holistic personalised support with conditionality to incentivise behaviour change. The Department for Work and Pensions Green Paper, *No One Written Off: Reforming Welfare to Reward Responsibility* (2008), developed this agenda, stating its intention to 'provide support that is tailored to each person's needs and to give everyone the opportunity to develop skills so they can find, and get on in, work' (DWP, 2008, p 11). Through such schemes people are to be enabled 'to become the authors of their own lives' (DWP, 2008, p 11). A key thrust of this agenda was the introduction of Flexible New Deal providers: private- and third-sector organisations working under contract to place people in work. According to a civil servant, these are "Specialist and niche providers, catering for personalised problems of those clients" (interview with the author). However, the interviewee clarified that this is quite a different form of personalisation to that found in other services: "Unlike social care, we don't give people the money to buy a package that meets their needs, rather we give money to the provider if they get that person into work."

The Coalition government is continuing with personalised approaches to facilitate entry into the workforce, offering tailored interventions earlier than was the case under the previous government and making it more difficult for people to remain on benefits (Conservative Party, 2010, p 15). A 'Work Programme' has been introduced to simplify the existing range of employment programmes, which is designed to provide 'personalised help for people who find themselves out of work regardless of the benefit they claim' (DWP, 2010).

Education

Just as one of the uncertainties in relation to supported housing is how a collectively provided good can be allocated on a personalised basis, there are challenges in applying the personalisation model to education, which is traditionally provided in a collective school setting. The norm of mass learning within a school setting has been described as 'Fordist' (Hartley, 2007, p 629). This reflects not only the physical aspects of provision and economies of scale, but issues relating to the socialisation of children and learning within a peer group (Campbell et al, 2007).

Alternative movements offering more personalised and differentiated approaches, such as home schooling and child-centred learning, have existed for a long time. However, their impact has been peripheral and their value highly contested (Hartley, 2007; Pykett, 2009). It was David Miliband, as Minister for School Standards in 2004, who brought the notion of personalised learning into the educational mainstream working with New Labour advisor Charles Leadbeater (2004). Miliband defined personalised learning as: 'High expectations of every child, given practical form by high-quality teaching based on a sound knowledge and understanding of each child's needs' (Miliband, 2004a). He was also keen to emphasise what personalised learning was not: 'It is not individualised learning where pupils sit alone at a computer. Nor is it pupils left to their own devices, which too often reinforces low aspirations' (Miliband, 2004a).

After Miliband's endorsement, there came a range of educational documents that focused wholly or in part on how to develop personalised approaches to learning. These include the Nuffield review of 14–19 provision (Hayward et al, 2005), the Economic and Social Research Council (ESRC) Teaching and Learning programme (Pollard and James, 2004), the National College for School Leadership special supplement (NCSL, 2004), the *Higher Standards, Better Schools for All* White Paper (DfES, 2005) and the Gilbert report (Gilbert, 2007). Together these reports aimed to fulfil Miliband's requirement that 'the system is moulded around the child, not the child around the system' (Miliband, 2006a, p 30, cited in Pykett, 2009, p 385). However, there was emphatic distance from older approaches to child-centred learning, and a commitment to personalisation within the national standards regime:

> Some people might see personalised learning signalling a move away from the standards agenda. But this isn't so. Neither is it a return to child-centred theories or letting pupils coast along at their own pace or abandoning the national curriculum. (NCSL, 2004, p 7, cited in Pykett, 2009, p 386)

The Children's Plan published by the Department for Children, Schools and Families (DCSF) in 2007 announced £1.2 billion over three years to support personalisation, including support for children with special educational needs. It stated: 'Personalised teaching and learning will become the norm in every early years setting and classroom, stretching and challenging the able as well as ensuring no child falls behind' (DCSF, 2007). The 2009 *21st Century Schools* White Paper set out a pupil guarantee with an entitlement to personalised support for every child (DCSF, 2009). It created a national expectation that all schools would have an individual learning plan for each pupil, with tailored support for students that fall behind on literacy and numeracy.

Diversity of education providers is a key element of personalised learning, allowing students to choose a range of pathways. As Campbell et al put it, describing personalised learning: 'Schools and teachers would no longer prescribe the content and pace of the curriculum, but would form partnerships and networks with other schools and other agencies so as to broaden the resources and learning opportunities available to students' (2007, p 138). An Office of the Third Sector report noted the valuable role of the third sector in relation to supporting pupils outside mainstream schools and in bringing additional creative skills into schools (McGuire, 2010a). The Specialist Schools and Academies Trust (SSAT) has been very supportive of personalised learning, and some new academies have experimented with more creative approaches to school buildings and timetabling (SSAT, 2010). Three *Kunskapsskolan* academies are opening in England, funded by the same company that has developed innovative approaches to pupil-led learning in Sweden.

However, at a national level the personalisation learning agenda has remained somewhat peripheral, clashing with a focus on standardised testing to a national curriculum. Campbell et al have suggested that personalisation may be incompatible with an emphasis on parental choice, which encourages schools to be as alike as possible (2007, p 144). As one interviewee from the education sector put it: "[Personalisation] is a concept which appeared, shone brightly and has now disappeared again. It still has a place in government narrative but quite a minor place." There is certainly no evidence of the focus or steering from central government that is driving personalisation in social care. As one civil servant from the then DCSF noted in an interview with the author, "The 21 Century Schools White Paper is very heavy on personalisation, although people don't talk about it a lot in the department, if I'm honest."

The Coalition government's plans for individual funding to be more clearly delineated through the pupil premium for disadvantaged children may make it easier to move to personalised budgets in the future (Gove, 2010). However, there is no indication yet that schoolchildren (or their parents) will be given control of real or notional budgets to shape their own learning. The DCSF interviewee confirmed that personalisation for children's services was not yet about individualised commissioning, focusing instead on how to encourage schools to commission more creatively and get the third sector involved in tailoring services to pupil needs.

In the further education sector, catering primarily for 16–19-year-olds, the idea of learning pathways and diversity of provision has a long history (Campbell et al, 2007, p 145). There has been a revival in the idea of devolving budgets to further education students through individual 'skills accounts', which give adult learners an indication of how much funding is available to them to spend on courses (ACEVO, 2009, p 11). However, the experience of Individual Learning Accounts, which were poorly devised and led to widespread fraud, indicates the need for careful quality control and monitoring (Committee of Public Accounts, 2003).

Higher education funding is already more individualised than many other sectors, given that students make a direct and substantial financial contribution to their tuition. In preparation for a large rise in tuition fees, government ministers have encouraged students to see fees in terms of a consumer purchase and to demand more control over the quality and format of their education. This could include the option to undertake intensive two-year degrees and have increased contact time with academic staff (Hurst, 2009). The Quality Assurance Agency for Higher Education (QAA) is committed to the increased use of personal development plans for students, describing them as 'a structured and supported process undertaken by a learner to reflect upon their own learning, performance and/or achievement and to plan for their personal, educational and career development' (QAA, 2009).

Criminal justice

Personalisation is currently underdeveloped in the criminal justice system. An interviewee in the Ministry of Justice reported that there may be some scope to devolve budgets to offender managers, on the BHLP model, although there are no immediate plans to do so. He noted: "Where we're at [with personalisation] is we know it's important but we're not sure how it fits and how it works." However, he also noted: "Our customers aren't necessarily compliant, they don't always want to be customers." A number of interviewees pointed out that personalisation is a bad fit for a system that has existed to depersonalise the individual. As one put it:

> The criminal justice system is set up to degrade, disempower, depersonalise.... The personalisation agenda is set up to do the opposite. It is very hard to assert yourself as an individual in that system. We've got a lot of unpicking to do to achieve that – among prison officers, but also the legal profession.

The development of more personalised approaches to criminal justice has so far focused on how the third sector can be more involved in offering tailored approaches to offender management and reducing reoffending (ACEVO, 2009; Concilium, 2009; McGuire, 2010b). An Office for the Third Sector report identified the contribution that the third sector could play in offering personalised support for rehabilitation, noting that it may be easier for the third sector to build up trust with ex-offenders than it has been for the probation service (McGuire, 2010b). The voluntary sector body ACEVO has suggested using social impact bonds to incentivise the private and voluntary sectors to develop personalised approaches to rehabilitation, with returns to investors based on improved social outcomes (2009, p 51). A Conservative Party policy paper, *Prisons with a Purpose* (Conservative Party, 2008, p 72), suggested that funding for individual prisoners could be disaggregated and paid to a prison and rehabilitation trust, with additional funding available to trusts if they stop prisoners reoffending. However, there are no proposals to involve prisoners and ex-offenders in determining how the money is spent, on the individual budget or BHLP models.

Prisoners with health and social care needs – for example, relating to mental health problems or substance abuse – are (in theory) eligible for personalised approaches, as other social care service users are. However, health and care support for prisoners has traditionally lagged behind practice in the mainstream sector, and plans for a more personalised approach are at an early stage (Moore and Nicoll, 2009). The frequency with which offenders are moved between prisons inhibits the potential for a personal assessment and a long-term support plan, or even consistent prescribing of medicines, making the prospect of personalised care for short-stay prisoners a major challenge.

Conclusion

Personalisation, defined as mechanisms that tailor services to the specific circumstances of the individual, encompasses a wide diversity of initiatives. The range of personalised services described here is broad, including some that can be seen as largely transactional – for example, when people book hospital appointments online or purchase a walk-in bath – and others that are more relational, such as improving support networks for care users or vulnerable families (Leadbeater, 2004). In some cases, personalisation is being done with professionals, as in social care assessments, whereas in others the emphasis is on self-management and peer support, as in the Expert Patient Programme (Leadbeater, 2004).

Across the sectors and types of personalisation, there are cross-cutting themes, including the disaggregation of budgets to users or to front-line staff; and new staff roles as personal advisors, brokers and advocates. An expanded range of organisations is becoming involved in providing services and supporting users, many of which are from the private and voluntary sectors. Personalised approaches share a common focus on outcomes rather than processes or outputs, often encompassing less quantifiable aspects, such as befriending, building relationships and broader quality-of-life issues (Burns and Smith, 2004, p 48; Boyle et al, 2006, pp 37–8; Hunter and Ritchie, 2007a, p 17; 2007b, p 153). Prevention is also a recurrent theme, evident in relation to health, social care and criminal justice.

As would be expected in the current financial climate, cost-cutting is an important, if sometimes implicit, agenda in all sectors. In an extremely tight fiscal context it is unsurprising that personalisation is expected to deliver demonstrable value for money. Most of the reforms discussed here have been promoted on the basis of offering efficiency as well as improved outcomes, although in some cases increased expenditure may be required during the transition phase. Auditors have expressed concern, however, that individualised budgets will contribute to reduced financial control and predictability for public bodies, which will run counter to the tight control required to deliver massive budget cuts (Audit Commission, 2010a).

As well as common themes across sectors, there are disparities in some aspects of the agenda that inhibit its overall coherence. For example, there are tensions between those reforms that emphasise user choice and control and others that emphasise behaviour change and conditionality. The promise of choice and control for the users of social care services is rather different to the tailored interventions and 'personalised conditionality' offered by family intervention projects and the Flexible New Deal. The Coalition government has indicated that disabled people will be subject to more stringent tests of eligibility for benefits, indicating a growth in conditionality (DWP, 2010). Keohane's (2009) distinction between 'self-tailoring' and 'state-led tailoring' may be one way to differentiate services based on user choice and those based on state-imposed conditionality. However, state-led tailoring may be hard to distinguish from the 'traditional' welfare state, in which individual circumstances always played some element in determining what was offered, despite the tendency to caricature the post-war model as 'one size fits all'.

The extent of penetration into different service sectors is clearly very varied. Most of the reforms to date have focused on welfare services, although there have been proposals for personalised approaches across the full range of public services, including transport and recycling (Keohane, 2009, p 111). It is in social care that the agenda has been furthest developed. Personal budgets in social care look set to become the mainstream of provision as part of a 'revolution' and 'transformation' in adult social care services (Glasby and Littlechild, 2009, p 181), whereas personalised learning appears to have low resonance in an educational policy environment characterised by conflicting demands (Campbell et al, 2007, p 144).

In an attempt to improve coherence between the various personalisation initiatives, recognising the extent to which effective approaches to social care and health or care and housing are interlinked, the previous government established an interdepartmental group on personalisation based in the Cabinet Office (HM Government, 2010b). Bodies such as the Office for Civil Society (previously the Office for the Third Sector) are playing a key role in supporting integrated approaches to personalisation across a range of sectors.

The review of service sectors in this chapter suggests that, despite its diversity and indeed incoherence in places, personalisation has become a new 'norm' in the provision of many public services. From this conclusion a number of research challenges take shape. The first is to explore how such a norm emerges and gains currency. This puzzle is the focus of Chapters 4 and 5, which look in particular at social care: the sector in which personalisation has been most fully institutionalised and that is most frequently evoked as the exemplar for personalisation in other sectors. Two key themes are identified as driving innovation in that sector. The first, discussed in Chapter 4, is the emergence of a coherent personalisation narrative, allying user testimonies of transformation with 'hard' data showing service improvement and claims that personalised approaches are intuitively convincing. The chapter identifies the key themes of the personalisation story and looks at the ways in which the past, present and future are framed within the personalisation narrative. The second driver of innovation, discussed in Chapter 5, is the people and organisations that together propelled personalisation into the social care mainstream. The chapter examines the interplay between campaigning user groups, policy entrepreneurs and the broader socio-political context within which policy change was effected. It then looks at the channels through which personalisation has migrated from social care into other service sectors and how the narrative has mutated over time, leaving some of its early advocates bemused about the initiatives undertaken in its name.

A key element of the personalisation story has been the importance of keeping focused on the broad prize of transformation and not getting 'bogged down in the complexities of the system change required' (ACEVO, 2009, p 4). Chapter 6 ignores this invocation and looks in detail at how personalisation is developing in the social care sector, where the evidence base is best established, to consider what can be learned about the relationship between a transformational narrative and the practice context. Chapter 7 examines the broader implications of personalisation for the relationship between state and citizen, including equity and the appropriate balance between the individual and the collective, drawing again primarily on social care and looking in detail at the debate over day centre closures. Chapter 8 examines how the relationship between staff and users is framed in the personalisation narrative, noting the ways in which front-line staff are both valorised and problematised in relation to personalised services. Although the chapters focus on social care, the themes discussed indicate the sorts of issues that other sectors will face as they move towards making public services more personal.

CHAPTER 4

The personalisation narrative

The breadth of reforms described in Chapter 3 convey the extent to which personalisation has been established as a new orthodoxy in public services, influencing change across a range of sectors, albeit in different ways. A central puzzle to explain, therefore, is how personalisation came to hold such a dominant position. This chapter explores the ways in which argumentation is used within the personalisation narrative, as part of understanding how it has established such a pre-eminent role. It is an examination of the internal logics of the narrative, and the role of ideas in shaping policy change. The chapter focuses on social care where the personalisation narrative has been most fully articulated, with its compelling story of improvement for care service users providing the rationale for personalising other sectors.

The first part of the chapter aims to distil the key features of the personalisation narrative from an examination of the claims made in documents, speeches and interviews that are supportive of personalisation. It examines how the personalisation narrative deploys the various tools of storytelling – involving the reader, and telling a simple, purposive story with powerful emotional content. The second part of the chapter discusses how the narrative engages with time, discrediting past approaches to delivering services, but engaging in an ambivalent relationship with change and continuity.

Little is said in this chapter about the agents and interests that have promoted the personalisation narrative and the broader political culture within which it has flourished. Those aspects of policy change are the focus of Chapter 5. The chapter also says little about critical readings of the narrative from practitioners and commentators who contest and problematise its storylines. These alternative readings are discussed in Chapters 7 and 8.

Distilling the narrative

A great deal has been written on personalisation, explaining what it is, why it is important and what its likely impacts will be. Much of this has emerged from the social innovation network In Control, which played a key role in developing personalisation in social care, and from Simon Duffy, one of the founders of In Control (for details of publications, see www.in-control.org.uk and www.centreforwelfarereform.org). However, there have also been extensive accounts and evaluations of personalisation published by academics (Spandler, 2004; Scourfield, 2005, 2007; Rummery, 2006; Cutler et al, 2007; Ferguson, 2007; Barnes, 2008; Beresford, 2008; Glendinning et al, 2008; Glasby and Littlechild, 2009); government departments and government-funded organisations (HM Government, 2007; DH, 2008a, 2009a, 2009b; DWP, 2008; Cabinet Office, 2009; Carr, 2010a); think tanks, for example, Demos (Leadbeater, 2004; Bartlett, 2009) and the New Local Government Network (Keohane, 2009); voluntary-sector bodies (ACEVO, 2009; NCVO, 2009); and professional organisations and trade unions, such as Unison and the Public Management and Policy Association (see eg NHS Confederation/Mental Health Development Unit, 2009; Land and Himmelweit, 2010; Needham, 2010); as well as many publications from individual charities and local authorities. Most of this literature focuses on social care, where implementation and evaluation of personalised approaches are furthest developed.

Through analysis of these texts, and the interview data collected for the project, it is possible to identify not a simple or one-dimensional definition of personalisation, but a set of related stories about public service reform. These are based on ostensibly common (and common-sense) diagnoses about what is wrong with existing policy and a set of self-evident assumptions about how services can be improved. They feature a cast of professionals (usually bad) and service users (often heroic), and a simplified set of assumptions about how complex policy tools can achieve desired results.

While recognising that categorisation is always imperfect, it is possible to identify five recurrent themes that are used in the texts to justify personalisation. These can be understood as separate storylines, which weave together to form an overarching narrative of personalisation. They operate in ways equivalent to the 'nodal points' identified by Laclau and Mouffe (1985, p 142), providing signifiers that together contribute to a new discursive configuration. Through looking at the five storylines in turn, it is possible to identify common themes in the way that the narrative is explained and justified. Together these shed light on the effectiveness with which personalisation has established itself as a new orthodoxy, despite its relative newness, variable manifestations and uncertain impact.

1. Personalisation works, transforming people's lives for the better

There is a growing evidence base, particularly within social care, showing that personalisation is linked to improved service outcomes. In a meta-study of direct payments and personal budgets, Glasby and Littlechild note the wide range of evidence showing that they have expanded choice and control for service users (2009, pp 111–16). The 13 individual budget pilots set up by the Department of Health were evaluated by Glendinning et al (2008). The evaluation found that the initiative was generally welcomed by participants, who reported feeling that they had more control over their daily lives. In a review of personal budgets from 2005–09 by In Control, 'more than two-thirds of people using Personal Budgets reported that the control that they had over their support (66%) and their overall quality of life (68%) had improved since they took up a Personal Budget' (Tyson et al, 2010a, p 140). Reflecting on such data, Duffy notes that while there may be some debate about the level of improvement that personalised approaches to social care can deliver, there is no disagreement that it does lead to improvements (2010, p 5).

Formal policy evaluation is supported by powerful testimonies of individual transformation, what Scourfield (2007, p 113) calls 'narratives of achievement'. Case studies and vignettes are regularly deployed in government documents and reports from other organisations promoting personalisation (Mansell and Beadle-Brown, 2005; Beresford, 2008). A senior member of In Control explained that stories have been a key part of promoting personalisation:

> "One of the things that we did very early on was start to tell positive stories about self-directed support and how it was working, and that's what's captured the imagination. That's what sells newspapers.... That's what people are really interested in. We're human beings, aren't we?"

One director of adult social care said, "We are focusing on what people are doing with their direct payments, gathering stories, publicising those stories. It's about marketing what's happening." As Glasby and Littlechild (2009, p 99) put it: 'there can be no stronger "evidence" [that self-directed support and personal budgets work] than the stories of people who have received personal budgets'.

Alongside the formal evidence base and individual testimonies, the 'it works' storyline is supported by claims to self-evidence and common sense. Morrell (2006, p 379) highlights the ways in which 'a self-evident need for change' is a key device through which narratives establish credibility. This is clearly evident in relation to personalisation. As Duffy (2010, p 13) puts it: '[T]he power of personalisation will continue to lie primarily in its inherent effectiveness. Approaches which make better use of people's abilities, communities and natural positive motivation will always have some advantage even when political and financial circumstances prove challenging.' According to another personalisation advocate, working with In Control, "people say things like personalisation won't work for everyone, but if it's personalised to you of course it will work". Thus, there is a 'common-sense' rationale that can be used to head off claims that personalisation only works for certain types of service user or in certain circumstances. As Glasby and Littlechild (2009, p 80) put it: 'the fact that personal budgets were taken up so quickly and with such enthusiasm is in one sense a triumph of common sense'.

2. Personalisation saves money

A second key theme of the personalisation narrative is that improved outcomes need not come at a higher cost, since personalisation is likely to save money. As Glasby and Littlechild (2009, p 125) put it, '[T]he emerging evidence suggests that this way of working may also be more cost-effective than the previous system, largely because it helps to unleash the creativity of people who have previously been passive recipients of services'. Although the Department of Health expects personalisation to be cost-neutral, there are a number of studies demonstrating the potential for savings. Duffy (2010) provides evidence from a range of local pilots to show that personalised approaches such as personal budgets have cut costs. As the *Independence, Well-being and Choice* White Paper from the Department of Health puts it:

> the ability of people to 'buy' elements of their care or support packages will stimulate the social care market to provide the services people actually want, and help shift resources away from services which do not meet needs and expectations. (DH, 2005, p 35)

Again, this formal evidence base is supported by individual stories of the cost-savings that have been achieved through personalisation – for example, by ending expensive out-of-borough placements and developing local alternatives at a much lower cost. As one In Control interviewee put it, "for the same amount of money, and actually probably in a lot of cases a lot less, families were getting far better outcomes in individuals". In another example from the same interviewee:

> "people were saying the respite unit only takes people in on a Friday and you can only come out on a Monday. All I really want is a baby sitter on a Saturday night. So [with personal budgets] people will use the money in a far more effective way."

The interviewee makes the same claim to self-evidence that is deployed elsewhere: "Now there's only so much money to go around, but surely if the money that you've got is spent better on people in a way that makes sense for them, that's got to be better." According to a local authority care manager:

> "People aren't necessarily just wanting the same amount of money to be spent on them, they actually just want a better service. If that costs less then all the better. It's about not treating them as ... you know, sharing all the information with them to say look we're spending this much money on some of these services, do you feel that's good value? And most people say well 'no'."

There is partly a 'wisdom of crowds' rationale here (Surowiecki, 2004), which again draws on common sense. According to the *Independence, Well-being and Choice* White Paper, 'Self-directed services work because they mobilise a democratic intelligence; the ideas, know how and energy of thousands of people to devise solutions rather than relying on a few policy makers' (DH, 2005, p 35). This 'wisdom of crowds' metaphor has become widely accepted in an era of open-source software and peer-led innovation. Leadbeater and Cottam (2007) see it as a key element of future public service improvement in a 'user-generated state'. As they put it, 'by turning people into participants in the design of services, they become innovators and investors, adding to the system's productive resources rather than draining them as passive consumers waiting at the end of the line' (2007, p 98). Although framed as an assertion of common sense, the 'wisdom of crowds' approach can also be understood as a radical challenge to long-established norms of professional expertise and fears of 'mob rule' (for an alternative view, critiquing the 'cult of the amateur', see Keen, 2007).

Together the 'it works' and 'it saves money' rationales are the key 'hard' indicators that justify personalisation, and are used to indicate that improved outcomes need not be dependent on increased spending. The appeal of this message at a time of severe budget cuts is itself self-evident.

3. Person-centred approaches reflect the way people live their lives

A third key theme of the personalisation storyline is that support for people with care needs cannot be contained within service sector boundaries, because that is not how people live their lives (Duffy, 2010). '[T]he boxes which government uses to categorise us such as *health, social care and physically disabled* are not how we think of ourselves – at best they describe one aspect of our lives', as an In Control report put it (Tyson et al, 2010b, p ii, emphasis in original). According to a Cabinet Office interviewee: "Personalisation couldn't stay with one department, because personalisation is about the whole person."

Thus, there is an impetus to expand personalisation beyond social care into health, since people's care needs are not neatly divided into health and social care segments. Similarly, housing must be personalised in order to ensure that people have control over their lives (Porteus, 2008). Services for ex-offenders must recognise and attend to the drug, alcohol and mental health issues that are common in the prison population (Duffy, 2010, p 10). Universal services, including schools, transport, libraries, leisure centres and so on, must also take account of the personalisation agenda because, as one consultant put it, "Personalisation, unlike consumerism, focuses on life, not on services.... There will be lots of services that I need – health, education, employment – which are not paid for by a personal budget, but which need to be personalised."

Indeed, the focus on services that characterises welfare provision is itself rejected in place of a focus on outcomes, in which there is maximum flexibility about how those outcomes can best be met. As the Social Care Institute for Excellence (SCIE) puts it, 'Self-directed support, as one element of personalisation, is not principally about money or services; it is about enabling people to become active citizens' (2009a, p 10). This holistic approach requires local authorities to develop system-wide approaches to personalisation, rather than seeking to locate it wholly within adult social care. Here again people's stories play a key role, focusing attention on the lived experience of individuals and away from sectoral approaches to welfare. There is also a strong common-sense element to this strand of the narrative (people's needs cannot be segmented into bureaucratic silos), alongside the use of data to show the interlinking of various health and care needs (for example around dementia) and the transformative impact of integrated approaches (DH, 2009a).

4. Personalisation is applicable to everyone

A related point to the one just made is that personalisation is not only about recognising the multiple and interacting needs of people who require care, but is a relevant policy for all users of public services. This theme relies on stretching the arguments about personalisation in social care into other sectors. Thus, the introduction of personal health budgets – which were rejected for the NHS in 2006, and then revived in 2008 (DH, 2006; Darzi, 2008) – was driven by an assumption that the transformational potential of personal budgets in social care can also be achieved in health, despite the substantial differences in funding and service provision.

Duffy is convinced that personalisation can transform the welfare state as a whole. Indeed, given that implementation in social care has been rather slow, he notes, 'It is also possible that personalisation, while born in adult social care, may actually not come to maturity in social care at all' (2010, p 9). For example, he discusses the prospects for family-led education and tax–benefit reform, noting that the key insights of personalisation are not limited to particular sectors of government: '[T]he efficiency of Individual Budgets lies primarily in the way it enables the individual to be an effective citizen, taking responsibility for their own life and integrating support into the framework of their own personal and community resources' (2010, p 9). Again, there is an assumption of common sense here (people can meet their own needs best), as well as an appeal to formal social care evidence.

5. People are experts on their own lives

A fifth element of the personalisation story is that users are best placed to know their needs, as 'experts on their own lives' (Poll, 2007, p 53). One of the successes of disability campaigners has been in establishing a norm that service users must play a key role in shaping services (Evans and Hardy, 2010, pp 59, 67), challenging the 'professional gift' model in which people are kept in a state of dependence (Duffy, 1996). There is a strong assertion of personhood underlying the personalisation agenda, with people with disabilities recognised as individuals, rather than groups with a 'generic "need"' (Hutchinson et al, 2006, p 74). Tyson explains the importance of personalisation to personhood:

> Older and disabled people are no longer passive recipients
> of the 'gift' of care or welfare. They are active citizens, with
> gifts themselves and a contribution to make, people who
> take risks and have a life within – not apart from – their
> communities. (2007, p 26)

Hutchinson et al (2006, p 74) make a similar point: 'direct payments
not only give [people with disabilities] a new way of obtaining
assistance, but also offer them a whole new type of life'. One local
government interviewee highlighted the basic affirmation of dignity
that underpins personalised approaches to care: "Trite examples get
trotted out – money to buy season tickets or what have you – but this
is about people not having to be put to bed at 5pm." According to an
interviewee from In Control:

> "I think in basic form, for me, it's about people being able
> to live a decent life, a life that makes sense to them, and
> that's regardless whether you have support needs or not....
> You're not just talking about something that's superficial
> here. You're talking about massive, very big changes for
> individual people."

Alongside an assertion of personhood, there is also a redefining of
expertise, to recognise that it can be held by the service user, or carer,
as well as the professional. User expertise is seen as trumping the
view of professionals as having special claims to knowledge. There is
a reassertion of the value of 'knowledge-based practice' or 'standpoint
knowledge', incorporating the 'lived experience' of service users,
rather than assuming that professional practice should be shaped only
by formal norms of evidence-gathering (Glasby and Beresford, 2006;
Evans and Hardy, 2010). A Department of Health report published in
2009, which called for pilots for personal health budgets, includes the
following exchange: 'As one carer said to a professional: "You may be
the expert professional but I am the expert carer"' (DH, 2009a, p 23).
User-experts are expected to put that expertise into practice through
taking a more active role in meeting their own needs. According to
Tyson, 'In fact most of the "work" [of personalisation] will be done
by older and disabled people themselves who will make choices and
bring their new purchasing power to bear' (2007, p 21). A report on
personalisation from ACEVO describes citizens and communities as 'the
primary agents of change' (2009, p 3), stating, 'We should see people not
as "service users" but as "service helpers" and change agents' (2009, p 5).

Key to achieving this shift of power is the transfer of budgetary control to the user (either through a direct payment or a managed personal budget), so that user-experts can shape service provision. As a recent report on housing and personal budgets put it, 'We must understand that at the heart of the personalisation agenda is a cultural shift which requires providers and professionals to be accountable to customers or risk losing their business' (Taylor Knox, 2009, p 4). Some interviewees expressed the view that monetary control itself was a side issue on a journey to person-centred care. Indeed, as the National Director for Social Care Transformation, Jeff Jerome, put it at an In Control conference, "The issue is not having the money. It's can you get the care and support you want in the way that you need it?" However, it was clear that the best mechanism for making that happen was perceived to be giving users the 'purchasing power' (Tyson, 2007, p 8). Again, the explanation here drew in part on self-evidence: as one of the In Control team put it:

> "Until I've got hold of the money, or at least I'm directing the way that that money's spent, that provider is never going to listen to me. It's the power of the pound, the power of having the money is the bit that makes the difference."

These five storylines of personalisation are weighted differently in different texts, but together they constitute the core claims that support the personalisation narrative, recurring throughout the documents and interviews: personalisation works; it saves money; it reflects how people live their lives; it is applicable to everyone; and it recognises that people are experts on their own lives. The three sources of evidence (formal data, individual stories and self-evidence) provide the narrative of personalisation, the story that is told about public service transformation. Formal evaluative data remains important, as might be expected in an era in which ministers demand 'evidence-based policy' (Cabinet Office, 1999). However, when compelling findings have proved somewhat elusive – for example, in relation to improved outcomes for older people (Glendinning et al, 2008) or cost-savings (Audit Commission, 2006; Carr, 2010b) – appeals to common sense and/or resonant stories about individual transformation are deployed to fill the gap. The narrative is therefore 'self-supporting' (Morrell, 2006, p 382).

This interlocking support base in part explains why personalisation has become a new valence issue in British politics, since all five of the propositions are hard to refute. Tensions that have emerged in relation to other welfare reforms – for example, between user empowerment and user responsibility, between effective outcomes and cost-cutting, between producer failure and the valorisation of front-line staff – are finessed within the personalisation story or dismissed as false dualities. Personalisation was described by one interviewee as an "aerosol word – you can spray it over anything and it looks better".

Chapter 2 highlighted six elements of policy narratives which help to explain their reach and impact. First, stories are compelling, utilising novelty and defamiliarisation to draw in the reader, presenting what may be familiar issues in a new way. Second, stories offer a credible account of the past, present and future. Third, stories appeal to values and emotions as drivers of change. Fourth, storytelling is social, helping people to understand a shared experience. Fifth, narratives simplify complex and contested terrains to make action possible. Sixth, narratives are purposive – promoting certain kinds of action and delegitimising others.

It is possible to identify all of these elements in relation to the personalisation narrative. The stories of individual transformation offer compelling before and after accounts of change, with an emphasis on the disjuncture with previous welfare approaches (defamiliarisation). The telling of individual life stories – 'self-narratives' – adds to the credibility of the story and fosters a sense of shared identity, but also contributes strong emotional resonance to the narrative (Ibarra and Barbulescu, 2010). There is an interaction between personalisation as what Bruner (1990, 2002) called a 'canonical narrative' (defined by Phoenix as 'narratives of how life ought to be lived in the culture, i.e. normative cultural expectations') and the 'personal narratives' of the people whose lives have been changed by it (Phoenix, 2008, p 66). The frequent invocation of individual testimonies highlights the extent to which narratives of political change continue to be sustained by personal stories, despite the supposed ascendancy of evidence-based policy and 'hard' data.

Changes are rooted in the struggles of the disability movement and individual families to fight for inclusion and control – the social aspect of the narrative. The storylines offer relatively simple messages of change. In the construction of the personalisation narrative, ambiguity, incommensurability and counter-evidence is silenced in the reporting, in favour of the presentation of certain approaches to welfare as self-evident and natural. The narrative is also purposive, promoting an agenda of welfare state reform, and linking it to claims of social justice, economic efficiency and improved outcomes.

The past, present and future

One of the key elements of a narrative, highlighted in Chapter 2, is the way in which it engages with time. Along with providing a compelling account of the past and present, narratives 'work to create the future' (O'Connor, 2002, p 312). By exploring how this framing is done in relation to personalisation, it is possible to understand better some of the implicit elements of the narrative. Pollitt's (2008) work on time in public policy can be usefully deployed to highlight some of the complex ways in which time is presented. Pollitt describes time as 'a vital, pervasive, but frequently neglected dimension in contemporary public policymaking and management' (2008, p xi). Certainly, it is an approach that is attracting increasing attention (Morrell, 2006; Peck and 6, 2006; Randall, 2009). Randall (2009, p 188) talks of a 'temporal turn' in recent years in the social sciences and humanities. As Peck and 6 put it in a discussion of organisational capability and implementation:

> The capabilities of organisations are ... intimately connected with the narratives about the past that are told, believed and challenged within organisations. Histories are critical in creating commitment, renewing bonds and structuring conflict; they also create the feelings of direction and of momentum that are vital to the shared sense of purpose in organisations. Furthermore, stories about the past, both of continuity and discontinuity, are vital in praise and blame.... Stories about the future – which are the essence of strategy – cannot be made intelligible without closely related stories about the past. (2006, p 51)

To understand the ways in which the personalisation narrative engages with the past, present and future, it is useful to look at three different framings of time offered by Pollitt and others: continuity and discontinuity; cycles and arrows; slowness and speed.

Continuity and discontinuity

It is evident that the personalisation narrative makes a claim to both continuity and discontinuity with the past. Part of the justification for personalisation rests on the assertion that it is timeless. A number of interviewees drew on claims that personalisation was nothing new. Rather than a new innovation, it was a "jargonistic word ... a title for what it is that we're trying to do". As one consultant put it, "It is not about doing something new, it is about doing things all together and in the same place." The phrase 'the Emperor's New Clothes' was used by a number of interviewees to explain how personalisation had caught on despite being nothing substantively different. As one interviewee from In Control put it:

> "self-directed support is a little bit like the Emperor's New Clothes, what we've done is the stuff that's already here anyway, we've just painted it up to look something different. And you, you know that parading the emperor around and everybody's going look at this, and I think that's what's happening at the moment. Actually if people sit down and they really think about it, it's what's already there.... If I'd have stood up and said well, we just looked at the money you'd already got and we rejigged it and this has been a better outcome, that wouldn't have been as powerful as pretending it was something new. And that's what confuses people. But if they really understand it, it isn't anything new. It's about working it out for you in a way that makes sense for you, but give people sight of what money there is."

This account fits with Pollitt's discussion of temporal change, in which 'successful tacticians and policy entrepreneurs frequently use the crisis opportunity (which they to some extent may have manufactured themselves) in order to advance "solutions" that have actually been lying around for many years' (2008, pp 139–40).

Many interviewees drew on the notion of timelessness to indicate that personalisation was something that their organisations or staff had always done, be it as voluntary organisations that were close to user communities, professionals driven by an ethos of care or private-sector providers being customer-focused. In these accounts, the novelty of the agenda came from other sectors catching up with their own to make personalisation a reality: micro-providers were encouraging large voluntary organisations to catch up with the sensitivity to service users that they themselves had long embraced; private-sector providers were urging the voluntary sector to become customer-focused like themselves; the voluntary and private sectors felt that local authorities in general, and professional staff in particular, needed to follow their lead in offering services that were tailored around the user.

Running alongside the claims to timelessness in the interviews was a rival assertion that personalisation constitutes a radical new approach to service delivery. Du Gay (2003, p 676) has noted the ways in which 'epochalist schemas … are established in large part through sets of dualities and oppositions in which the discontinuity between past and future is highlighted'. This can be seen in narrative terms as a process of 'defamiliarization … a different way of viewing things, one that renews our perception of the world' (Barry and Elmes, 1997, p 434). Thus, Care Minister Ivan Lewis described personalisation as 'a revolution in the way we seek to offer services to people in this country' (cited in Tyson, 2007, p 3). Matthew Taylor, Chief Executive of the Royal Society of the Arts and former Downing Street lead strategist, described it as 'the most important innovation in the public sector for 20 years. The question is: how can we take these principles and apply them everywhere else?' (Taylor, 2010). The idea of personalisation as a radical disjuncture from the status quo is captured in the following extracts from the New Local Government Network report on personalisation:

> A top-down politician-driven monopoly on decision-making for service provision is no longer appropriate.… The term 'personalisation' has emerged as a corrective to the previous centralised approach to service delivery. Under the post-war bureaucratic state, entitlement and delivery of service was centrally prescribed and unresponsive to the circumstances of individual users. For too long, services have not borne the needs of the user in mind, in terms of convenience of access, options or alternatives for services.… For too long, services have been de-personalised: the individual relationships that underpinned our health services have been eroded; regulation and uniformity has sapped civic enthusiasm and engagement; a system that has consistently provided too much to some and too little to others has delivered inefficiency and worse. (Keohane, 2009, pp 7, 14, 121)

Alan Johnson, Health Secretary under Gordon Brown, similarly described personalisation as '21st Century social justice' based on 'an active and empowering state, rather than one which is paternalistic and controlling' (cited in Barnes, 2008, p 152).

Discontinuity, therefore, represents a position in which 'the past becomes an accusation' (Wright, 1985, p 151, cited in Randall, 2009, p 196). An interviewee from In Control gave a similar account of the traditional welfare state, to which personalisation was a radical alternative: "You had to ask permission for everything you wanted to do.... I came to the conclusion, that maybe it was broken and wasn't fit for purpose in its current state".

Thus, the case for personalisation rests on both emphasising the timelessness of its ideas and practices, but also foregrounding its claims to be a radical break with the traditional welfare state. It is a narrative of both continuity and discontinuity: of a timelessness, which establishes credibility, but also of an unfamiliarity, which garners attention (Barry and Elmes, 1997, p 438).

Cycles and arrows

A second paired approach to time identified by Pollitt is that of cycles and arrows. He draws on the work of Stephen Jay Gould (1988) to note the distinction between 'time as sequential, moving forwards like an arrow', and 'cycles or alternations' (2008, pp 51–2). He notes: 'It is not hard to see the tensions and paradoxes ... where politicians promise to build trust and stability whilst in the next breath holding out visions of endless, relentless modernization, innovation or flexibilization' (2008, p 63).

Again, it is possible to identify both of these approaches in the personalisation narrative. In the 'arrow' account, personalisation is the end of a long road towards empowerment and justice for disabled people. Claims to innovation and progress, having overcome the problems that beset earlier reforms, are integral to the narrative. Here personalisation fits a broader theme of New Labour policy-making in which 'the case for reform is portrayed in teleological terms, as self-evident; a historic, democratic and technological necessity or *telos* ... an implicit trajectory of improvement which enhances the credibility of the policy narrative' (Morrell, 2006, p 379; see also Randall, 2009). This teleological account of policy change fits with the 'stages' approach that politicians and academics have used to categorise New Labour's time in government (Blair, 2003; Miliband, 2004b; Needham, 2007; Bosanquet, 2008; Greener, 2008; Paton, 2008; Shaw, 2008; Cabinet Office, 2009).

One director of adult social care in a local authority expressed this sense of progressive improvement: "[Personalisation] is a step on the way from closure of old long-stay hospitals to smaller day centres to getting people into the community, mainstream in society." Indeed, it may not itself constitute the end phase. As one interviewee from a user-led organisation said:

"As far as disabled people are concerned, we're talking about personalisation because it's a step along the road to our goal of independent living, which is having choice over how our support needs are met, being in control and taking part in society on an equal basis with everyone else."

There is a concern to avoid the mistakes of the past, which is evident in a number of ways. As one interviewee from the regulatory sector put it: "Personalisation is about solving a problem created by privatisation and marketisation. People are so keen on personalisation because of the failure of privatisation in home care, 15-minute home visits, etc, agency staff." There is a particular concern to acknowledge care management – an earlier narrative with parallels with personalisation (discussed further in Chapter 5) – as a missed opportunity, and to learn lessons from its apparent failure. Interviewees drew parallels between the two reform periods: the same sense of optimism, of a transfer of power down to front-line staff and service users. However, care management is widely perceived to have failed to deliver on this promise (Lewis and Glennerster, 1996; Means et al, 2008). As a result, there is a strong sense that history must not repeat itself. As Martin Routledge from the Department of Health Putting People First team put it, 'I was there in 1993 when care management came in. We simply must make sure that doesn't happen again. It mustn't be like 1993 all over again' (Routledge, 2010).

Similarly, there is a desire to ensure that personalisation does not constitute a merely symbolic change, as earlier reforms had done. One interviewee commented on the *Valuing People* White Paper for people with learning disabilities (DH, 2001) in these terms:

> "So *Valuing People* came out, fantastic. People were promised it would revolutionise services for people with learning disabilities, best thing that's ever happened in 30 years. And you sit and you wait. And two years on after it came out it hadn't made a jot of difference."

In this account, personalisation is located within an 'arrow' view of time, linked to constant refinement and improvement. The past is not wholly discredited within the narrative, however; indeed, it is possible to find expressions of the 'cycle' view of time as well, in the sense of personalisation being a process of 'getting back' to something valuable that has been lost. A recurrent theme in the interviews was that personalisation constituted a return to 'real' social work – 'why so many people decided to become social care professionals in the first place' (DH, 2008b, pp 4–5) – a point repeated by interviewees from a range of sectors in language that was remarkably similar:

> "If you speak to social workers, they tend to find personalisation quite liberating, that's what they came into the job to do." (Policy officer, local government representative body)

> "I think some, particularly in social work, are absolutely dying for this ... they can feel they are actually ... doing the work that they actually went into the profession to do." (Social entrepreneur, In Control)

> "If you speak to social care directors you will find personalisation fits with why they went into the job, how they would like to behave – even though they don't always." (Adult social care director)

This shared and ostensibly common-sense account of how social workers are engaging with personalisation implies recovery of a lost past.

There has also been a sense of recovering community and peer forms of support, which had been squeezed out by a professionally dominated welfare state bureaucracy. The ACEVO interim report, for example, talks of personalisation as a 'Journey of Rediscovery': 'It shows perhaps how managerial and technocratic the debate about public services has become that we have felt the need to reassert the central role of self-help and mutual aid' (2009, p 3). There are clear echoes here of Du Gay's account of other 'epochalist narratives' in which 'The wholeness that the bad old bureaucratic past rent asunder is to be recovered, the disenchantment it brought in its wake reversed' (2003, p 668). Here, then, personalisation is part of a temporal cycle of rediscovery rather than an 'arrow' moving towards a constantly improving future.

There are silences, however, on aspects of the past which indicate that personalisation is repeating failed cycles. One interviewee noted the similarities to past initiatives that came and went: "You can go back to Seebohm and others – put the documents side by side, the rhetoric is the same. The Good Neighbour Scheme, for example, the rediscovery of social capital." Similarly, there are silences about the extent to which personalisation might be intensifying the privatisation of social care that accompanied care management, rather than reversing or refining it. For some critics of personalisation, the reforms are not a rejection of a marketised past, but an intensification of its logics, a theme returned to in later chapters.

Slowness and speed

The ambivalent account of time offered by the personalisation narrative is also evident in relation to the speed of reform. Personalisation has had a long gestation within the disability movement, but there is uncertainty about whether it is now best characterised as an agenda that is speeding ahead or inching along at a slow pace. In some of the interviews the pace of change was described as 'galloping' and 'phenomenal', indicative of a rapidly moving innovation. However, elsewhere the pace has been described as 'glacial', particularly in relation to change on the ground. One interviewee said, "To talk about personalisation you would think it was all being achieved. The way it's often discussed in policy circles. But it's really quite early days in terms of actually achieving things." According to another, "We talk about IBs [individual budgets] as if they are everywhere and they aren't yet." A Department of Health civil servant expressed frustration about the slow pace of change, despite the widespread support for the agenda: "Why, when it's motherhood and apple pie, is it so blooming difficult to do?".

Thus, again, personalisation is hard to locate temporally, apparently characterised by both rapidity and slowness in its implementation. This may reflect a disjuncture between the speed with which a narrative can spread – with stories moving fast between policy actors and across sectoral boundaries, gathering momentum – and the slowness of establishing new mechanisms through which to allocate resources to service users, which may require formal policy change, regulatory approval or professional retraining.

Conclusion

Key to understanding the effectiveness of personalisation is the recognition that it is a story that is told about public services, their history and the roles and experiences of the people who use and work in them. Like other stories it is compelling and emotionally resonant, but also multi-interpretable.

The case made here is that part of the reason that personalisation has established such a strong hold as a narrative of policy change is that it manages to combine a set of interlocking stories and a shifting evidence base in such a way as to deflect criticism. It also offers a compelling, if at times contradictory, account of the past, present and future. In these aspects, it has the features of what Du Gay (2003) calls an 'epochal narrative' (see also Cutler et al, 2007). The way that personalisation engages with the three pairs of time orderings – emphasising continuity at the same time as radical change; drawing on an account of progressive improvement, while also rediscovering valuable aspects of the past; racing along and yet being hampered by the slow speed of implementation, and finessing any contradictions between them – is also indicative of its mutability. It reaffirms the importance of time to narrative accounts of policy, with future changes premised on particular framings of the past and present.

This chapter has focused on the personalisation narrative, and the storylines embedded within it, but has said little about the agents who have spread the narrative and built support for it – the storytellers. To some extent this minimising of the agent role can be seen as itself part of the strategy of establishing a dominant narrative. For example, in Du Gay's (2003) notion of an 'epochalist narrative', there is an implication that the agency of those who construct and promote the story is backgrounded, in favour of a common-sense discovery of the right way to proceed. However, it is also the case that narratives establish their credibility through portraying 'the narrators as credible and competent and their ideas as worthy and good' (O'Connor, 2002, p 312). It is important, then, to look at who those narrators are, and how the narrative has gained such potency. It is to the mechanisms, channels, personnel and broader political contexts that have created a climate conducive to personalisation that the next chapter turns.

CHAPTER 5

Policy translation: how personalisation spreads

The discussion in Chapter 4 highlighted the storylines that are embedded in the personalisation narrative, and explored the ways in which those stories were told through a combination of formal evidence, individual accounts of transformation and claims of self-evidence and common sense. It focused on the way in which the narrative built a compelling account of reform through shifting accounts of the past, present and future.

This chapter examines how personalisation emerged as a narrative of change within social care, and spread into different contexts, establishing a strong hold on the imagination of policymakers. It is of course too simplistic to claim that there is a single line of policy innovation from social care to other sectors. As Chapter 3 sets out, personalised education had its own intellectual roots and developed separately from the social care agenda. Patient choice and the Expert Patient Programme in the NHS developed in parallel with social care reform (DH, 2004, p 42). However, it was within social care that personalisation developed as a transformative policy narrative, offering a rationale and set of policy mechanisms that could be the basis of innovation in other sectors.

Thus, the focus here is on understanding the process through which personalisation became established as a mainstream approach to social care, how it has been influential in other sectors and how it is mutating as it develops. Whereas the agents of change were underplayed in the last chapter, this chapter discusses who those agents were and how they built the case for personalisation. It also focuses on the broader political culture within which personalisation has flourished, highlighting links to other dominant ideas of state restructuring.

The origins of personalisation

As with almost all policy innovation, there was no master plan for personalisation that can be revealed and dissected, and even the label personalisation was only adopted part-way along the process. Within social care it is often described as a bottom-up initiative, emerging from grassroots organisations of disabled people, although it has top-down elements too, particularly in its later incarnation. As one interviewee put it: "Personalisation is best seen as a series of initiatives, not as a thought-through programme at the beginning." Glasby and Littlechild (2009, p 83) note that the language of a 'personalisation agenda' has emerged relatively recently, and 'lacks much of the clarity and practical focus' of an alternative term such as 'self-directed support'. There remains a puzzle to explain how those initiatives emerged and coalesced into something that can plausibly be seen as a new policy agenda, one that its advocates hope will radically reconfigure the welfare state – the basis of a 21st-century rewriting of the post-war Beveridge settlement (Glasby et al, 2010).

Theories of policy change often highlight the ways in which major change occurs slowly, through gradual evolution or the coalescing of a number of strands in the policy and political process (Hall, 1993; Kingdon, 1995). As Paul (2007, pp 140–1) puts it, 'Paradigm shifts are rarely sudden and dramatic…. Insider accounts of the practice of policy making reveal how policy is made and changed through successive iterations of shifting policy visions'. This appears to be the case with personalisation, which emerged as a formal policy commitment – perhaps best exemplified by the *Putting People First* concordat (HM Government, 2007) – following a long campaign. Three themes are most relevant in explaining the adoption of personalisation as a central approach to social care reform: a committed campaign by organisations of disabled people and advocates, which twinned social justice claims with evidence of improved outcomes; dynamic interventions by policy entrepreneurs, both outside and within government; and coherence with the broader context, in which new interactions between the individual and the community were being promoted politically, but also being made possible through technological innovation. These can be considered in turn.

Disability campaigners

Campaigns by disability organisations for more person-centred approaches to care, including devolved budgetary control, is a key element in the story of how personalisation came to be a mainstream agenda. Personalisation within social care really begins with such campaigns, although even here there were (and remain) a diverse set of stories, rather than a single message. It is possible to separate out two key strands of development, while recognising that they spoke to and informed each other along the way. Although there is a danger of *post hoc* simplification and rationalisation, innovation arose from the independent living movement, centred on people with physical disabilities, and from the move to more inclusive approaches for people with learning disabilities, linked to the social model of disability (Oliver, 1990).

The independent living movement began in the United States in the 1970s, and led to the creation of a network of user-led Centres for Independent Living, aimed at supporting disabled people in taking greater control of their lives (Glasby and Littlechild, 2009, p 12). Within the UK in the 1980s, independent living was picked up by people living in residential homes who wanted the freedom to live independently (Morris, 1993). Campaigns for more inclusive approaches for people with learning disabilities were becoming influential at a similar time. Growing dissatisfaction with long-stay hospitals, sparked in part by abuse scandals, was intensified by the emergence of new theories about the potential of people with disabilities to enter education and employment and to live in the community. The work of John O'Brien and others highlighted the importance of inclusion and of involving people in planning their care (O'Brien and Tyne, 1981). In response, formal policy shifted to the relocation of people out of institutions and into small group homes within the community. Group homes themselves then came to be recognised as potentially transitional to a goal of encouraging more person-centred and independent approaches (Cambridge et al, 1994). Professionally led initiatives, such as individual programme planning, were challenged by more radical user- and family-led initiatives such as person-centred planning (Cambridge and Carnaby, 2005). Person-centred planning (as opposed to service-led planning) involved several features that would later be seen as key to the broader personalisation reforms. These included: recognition of 'the authority of the service user's voice'; a focus on 'aspirations and capacities' of the service user rather than 'needs and deficiencies'; and 'attempts to include and mobilise the individual's family and wider social network, as well as to use resources from the system of statutory services' (Mansell and Beadle-Brown, 2005, p 20).

Self-advocacy became increasingly important, facilitated by organisations such as People First and programmes such as Partners in Policy-making (Elwell, no date). Within mental health services, the user and survivor movement challenged dominant psychiatric models of normalisation (Baker et al, 2008). The foundation of Shaping our Lives in the mid-1990s, as the first pan-disability and user group umbrella organisation, marked a shift towards coordinated campaigning. Carers were also able to develop more coordinated campaigns for recognition of their contribution, through the work of organisations such as Carers UK and the Princess Royal Trust for Carers.

These campaigns were ongoing at a time of broader policy change within social care, marked by the passage of disability discrimination laws, the embedding of community care approaches and the shift to care management. The community care agenda was promoted by the Conservative government in the late 1980s (DH, 1989), with an emphasis on moving the provision of care services from the state to the private and voluntary sectors (Lewis and Glennerster, 1996; Means et al, 2008). However, Rummery (2006, pp 646–7) notes that community care was never framed within a discourse of citizenship and cites Lewis and Glennerster's (1996) conclusion that the '"deep normative core" of the policy has been shown to be rationing access to resources' (2006, p 640).

The 1990 NHS and Community Care Act introduced care management, which aimed to devolve greater power to the front line to shape care provision, and involve service users in needs assessment (Means et al, 2008, p 54). One of its objectives was 'promoting individual choice and self-determination' (DH, 1990). However, local authorities tended to focus on the administrative aspects of the reforms, rather than their scope for empowering users, as social workers found more of their time taken up with filling in forms (Lewis and Glennerster, 1996, p 104). Mansell and Beadle-Brown highlight the extent to which attempts at individual planning were hampered by resource constraints, leading to 'the use of standardized procedures for assessment ... the bureaucratisation of management processes and the reservation of funding decisions to higher-level managers removed from direct contact with service users' (2005, p 25). Implementation varied widely between different local authorities. Cambridge and Carnaby (2005, p 11) note that 'even under a central policy spotlight, individual planning and care management developed in a variety of ways, based on ideologies, management and professional imperatives, operational expediency and wider demands from outside the service system'.

Some local authorities were receptive to experimenting with new ways of providing support. The Independent Living Fund, introduced in the mid-1980s, had demonstrated the enthusiasm of disabled people for cash allocations that allowed them to pay for personal assistance (Glasby and Littlechild, 2009, p 14). A few local authorities introduced direct payments for service users in the 1980s, despite their dubious legality, or experimented with alternatives such as independent living funds paid to third parties (Glasby and Littlechild, 2009, pp 26–7). Sustained campaigning by disability organisations, particularly the commissioning of research demonstrating the potential cost-savings of direct payments, eventually caught the attention of the Conservative government (Zarb and Nadash, 1994; Pearson, 2000, p 461; Bornat, 2006, p 7). The passage of the 1996 Community Care (Direct Payments) Act gave local authorities the power to make direct payments. This became a duty in England and Wales in 2001 and in Scotland in 2003. Its passage was described as 'the realization of 20 years of collective advocacy' (Campbell, 1998, cited in Spandler, 2004, p 191).

As direct payments gained a more secure legal footing, the emphasis within learning disability remained on person-centred planning (PCP) and inclusion (O'Brien and Lyle O'Brien, 1998). This was central to the *Valuing People* White Paper (DH, 2001), which also allowed for the commissioning of further research into PCP. *Valuing People* facilitated the growth of national and local training programmes in PCP approaches, and research into how PCP could operate alongside care management (DH, 2002). Interest in the potential link between PCP and devolved budgets was also growing within local authorities such as Wigan, leading to the trialling of individual budgets in six local authorities by In Control, supported by the Valuing People team within the Department of Health (DH) during 2004/05 (Poll et al, 2006). Such budgets were more flexible than direct payments, based on the principle that people should have maximum choice and control over money spent on their behalf, including the freedom to spend it on anything that meets an assessed need (Glasby and Littlechild, 2009, p 76).

The 2005 *Improving the Life Chances of Disabled People* strategy paper can be seen as the coming together of the two movements: independent living for people with physical disabilities, and inclusion for people with learning disabilities (Prime Minister's Strategy Unit, 2005). The paper identified direct payments as a key tool for encouraging independent living. It also required that every local authority have at least one user-led organisation by 2010, confirming the central role of organisations led by disabled people themselves. The adult social care *Independence, Well-being and Choice* Green Paper was also launched in 2005, and promoted self-directed support in general and individual budgets in particular (DH, 2005). In the *Opportunity Age* strategy document (DWP, 2005) the relevance of these ideas to older people was also explored, although people with mental health issues, located in health rather than social care, remained peripheral. Through these various policy papers, individual budgets were promoted in a range of settings. The Office of Disability Issues was particularly keen to explore how budgets from a range of sources could be joined up (including adult social care monies, the Independent Living Fund and Access to Work and Family Funds), and this became the focus of individual budget pilots launched in 13 sites.

Evaluation of the pilots showed that participants welcomed the additional choice and control that was available, but that it was very difficult in practice to join up funds from different sources, given the different legal, funding and reporting frameworks (Glendinning et al, 2008). Thus, when the DH was ready to advance the policy, it focused on social care monies, designated as personal budgets, rather than the broader funds that had been called individual budgets. Better integration of funds from multiple sources was later revived by the Department for Work and Pensions in its Right to Control programme, although legal barriers ensured that social care personal budgets remained separate.

The 2007 *Putting People First* concordat, agreed between the DH, local government and other key social care organisations, set out the direction of adult social care reform over ten years. A Transformation Grant of £520 million was made available to local authorities to promote personalisation, which incorporated the development of personal budgets, alongside more investment in prevention, better access to universal services and the development of social capital (HM Government, 2007). The concordat shaped the policy context in which personalisation continues to operate, with later targets and milestones confirming the direction of travel. An online personalisation toolkit was launched in 2008 to support councils in planning and delivering the transformation of their social care systems.

Although the role of campaigns by disabled people and their advocates is hard to capture, involving thousands of people over many years and lacking coherence as a single movement, it clearly played a crucial part in embedding personalisation as a mainstream approach. As Bornat (2006, p 1) puts it, 'direct payments came into being as a result of decades of campaigning against a society which turns disabled people into dependants without choice, control or independence in their lives'. Centres for Independent Living have been seen as key to the development of personal budgets, as part of a broader move to user-led services and self-advocacy (Davey et al, 2006). According to Glasby and Littlechild, again writing about direct payments, 'More than almost any other policy, this is something that was developed *by* disabled people *for* disabled people' (2006, p 25, emphasis in original).

Advocacy by organisations of disabled people was crucial in building both an evidence base for personalised approaches and a rights–based rationale – something that had been lacking in the community care agenda (Rummery, 2006, p 647). Debates about the rights and responsibilities of the individual and the collective have been central to welfare reform over decades, but one of the achievements of disability campaigners was to reject the dualism of individualism versus collectivism. Personalisation was located in a discourse in which citizenship and personhood were the basis for a legitimate collective (Duffy, 2005). Writing about PCP, Mansell and Beadle-Brown (2005, p 22) note, 'The language of person-centred planning is the language of reciprocity, mutual interdependence and community', which they contrast with the isolation felt by many people with learning disabilities.

Some of the permissive atmosphere towards personalised approaches in the UK came from broader international trends (Carr and Robbins, 2009). Moves towards cash transfers to disabled people or their families have been a feature of care reforms in a number of countries, including the United States, the Netherlands, France, Germany, the Czech Republic and Japan (Izuhara, 2003; Glasby and Dickinson, 2009; Grit and de Bont, 2010; Land and Himmelweit, 2010). This international trend ensured a wider network of support for domestic campaigns to draw on, and a diverse evidence base to support claims of improved outcomes (Lundsgaard, 2005; O'Brien and Duffy, 2009). In many of these cases, however, as in the UK, the evidence base revealed limitations as well as successes. A Help the Aged report on personalised care in France, Germany, the Czech Republic and the Netherlands found, 'Without exception, the introduction of personal budgets abroad has led to increases in the costs of providing care' (2009, p 12). Lord and Hutchinson's (2003) review of individualised funding schemes in Canada, the United States and Australia found that 'where governments promoted individualised funding without resourcing community support networks in the non-profit sectors, it could result in a highly privatised system that limited the choice and control available to individuals' (cited in Spandler, 2004, p 203). Land and Himmelweit cite evidence from Germany and Sweden showing that 'While there is a common aim to increase "choice" and "flexibility" in long-term care services, one of the key objectives of these policies has also been to curb the growing costs to the public purse of social care' (2010, p 40).

Policy entrepreneurs

Although separating out the role of individuals from a broader social movement is problematic and contentious, there was a role for policy actors – located both within and outside government – in crafting and disseminating the personalisation narrative. Entrepreneurs are widely credited with playing a key role in policy innovation. As Kingdon (1995, p 174) puts it, entrepreneurs are people who 'couple' policy solutions to problems, taking advantage of a 'window of opportunity'. In relation to personalisation, they are people who built on the somewhat narrow achievements of the direct payments approach, which had been 'bolted on to traditional and unresponsive systems', and called for much broader transformation based around personal budgets (Glasby and Littlechild, 2009, p 76). The choice and control principles underlying personal budgets, then, themselves triggered demands for a total rethinking, first of social care, and then the whole welfare state in its Beveridgean formation (Duffy, 2010).

Many well-known disability campaigners were active as policy entrepreneurs, making the case for reform over many years. Some of these were what Leadbeater and Cottam describe as 'lead users', innovating in their own care provision and telling stories to others about what was possible. Drawing analogies with user-generated innovation in the technology sector, Leadbeater and Cottam argue that such users:

> tend to have more extreme and intensely felt needs which put them in the vanguard of change in a field. Lead users often have greater knowledge, they use products more intensively and they have skills that allow them to adapt products. (2007, p 97)

Within the social care sector, many individuals and families with high support needs met these criteria. However, there were barriers to people sharing their ideas with other service users. As one 'lead user' explained:

> "You'd meet the odd person who might be a family member who'd managed to achieve some good stuff for their son or daughter, but they were the exception to the rule. And what they never told you was how they really did it. It was almost kept a big secret, because if I rock the boat or tell you, it might rock the boat for me."

Policy entrepreneurship in this sector, although often starting with service users, thus required networks of support to disseminate their experiences outside of the immediate service context. The social innovation network In Control played a key role in doing so. Emerging in the North West, the contribution of In Control and its members included gathering information, setting up experiments, supporting lead users and telling their stories, and creating networks of interested people and organisations. Simon Duffy, one of the founders of In Control, experimented with individual budgets for people with severe cognitive impairment in Scotland and brought those experiences with him to In Control (Poll et al, 2006). An In Control staff member describes how Duffy came to Wigan and did research to show that the audit bill for direct payments was almost twice the amount being paid out in the budgets themselves: "And when you take that information back to this board that we have, to the chief executive, he's just thinking this system's completely bonkers. He'd never had anybody really looking in on the ground so hard before." One newspaper columnist later said of Simon Duffy, 'Pretty much single-handedly, he changed the terms of political discourse on the issue of social care in this country' (Dearden Phillips, 2009).

A key contribution of In Control was to marshal evidence demonstrating the transformative impact of personalisation, particularly in relation to cost-cutting. One interviewee reflects: "[Personalisation] was kicked off by In Control. It was sold to government as delivering 25 per cent savings as people would spend the money better.... In Control were brilliant – it was very well sold." Members of In Control worked closely with the DH in setting up the individual budget pilots and promoting the development of person-centred approaches more broadly, as well as publishing evaluations of their projects. This close relationship between advocacy and evaluation has continued to be a key (and somewhat contentious) element of In Control's work.

At the same time as building national influence, In Control was developing links with local authorities, facilitating pilots of individual budget-type approaches in adult and children's services. The ambiguous role of In Control, working closely with government, but striving to retain independence and a critical edge, proved fractious, leading to internal rows. The DH's introduction of targets for the numbers of people on personal budgets was one source of tension. A member of In Control reflects:

> "[A]s soon as the DH grabbed hold of it, they did the individual budget stuff, and then they launched Putting People First. On one hand you want to celebrate that, but on the other hand they put targets with it. And the targets stupidly have been about numbers. So what you see is anybody trying to tick any box just to fill the numbers."

Within the government, interest in individual budgets from social care ministers and from the Prime Minister's Strategy Unit appears to have been crucial in maintaining momentum during New Labour's third term in office. Civil servants and personalisation activists interviewed by the author noted the extent to which sympathetic care ministers, such as Stephen Ladyman, Ivan Lewis and Liam Byrne, drove the agenda forward. At the Department for Work and Pensions, one civil servant highlighted the importance of John Hutton in promoting the agenda, ultimately leading to the Right to Control initiative. A number of interviewees drew a contrast between ministerial enthusiasm and civil service cautiousness. There was felt to be a tension between the ethos of individual budgets, based on devolved control and transparent financing, and traditional civil service approaches to risk and opaque structures of funding and cross-subsidy.

The importance of supportive ministers is highlighted in an interview with a Cabinet Office civil servant:

> "The best way to explain patchy, stop-go, implementation of personalisation in different departments is to do with the personal commitment of ministers. Some are committed to that and take that with them. Others are nervous, or like it when they are in health, but get worried when they get to the Ministry of Justice that personalisation will be seen as giving money and choices to ex-cons."

Asked to predict in advance what impact the 2010 general election would have on personalisation in social care, one interviewee noted that the most important thing was not which party won, but which minister was allocated to social care. This emphasis on personal relationships and personal champions appears to be a key element in explaining how personalisation became so influential. Recalling how links with ministers were built up through dogged persistence and a series of coincidences, one member of In Control noted: "it's about relationships that, and that's what scares you. Because this could be equally something really bad, that somebody could infiltrate to get into the government, and probably that's how other things have got in."

Beyond the individual connections, the Prime Minister's Strategy Unit was a key institutional force, operating across government and encouraging a range of departments to experiment with individual budgets – driven perhaps by New Labour's restless striving for a new 'big idea' to sustain it in government (Taylor, 2001; Miliband, 2006b; Toynbee, 2006). Charles Leadbeater is often cited as an innovator who translated personalisation into a broad policy programme that could provide a big idea for New Labour. His 2004 pamphlet for Demos, *Personalisation through Participation: A New Script for Public Services*, is widely referenced as the beginning of personalisation as a vocabulary and a broad way of rethinking public policy. It presented case studies where innovative personalised approaches had improved people's lives, and highlighted the scope for personalisation to transform not only personal care services, but also the NHS and schooling (Leadbeater, 2004). Working with Hilary Cottam, Leadbeater promoted personalised and co-productive approaches to service reform that drew on creative participation by users (Cottam and Leadbeater, 2004; Leadbeater and Cottam, 2007). The foreword to Leadbeater's 2004 pamphlet, by David Miliband, then Schools Minister and a key figure in New Labour policy development, indicated the extent to which personalised ideas were gaining attention within the government.

Enthusiasm for the policy among senior ministers and policy advisors seems to go some way to explaining the timetable of change, in which the extension of personal budgets was announced even before the individual budget pilot evaluation was concluded, reaffirming the extent to which a sound evidence base is only part of the story of policy diffusion (Nutley et al, 2007, p 181; Beresford, 2008, p 9). As one interviewee reflects:

> "The biggest piece of evaluation of course which was done around this was the individual budgets pilot and it was completely semi-detached from policy because the evaluation wasn't even completed when the government announced it was going to roll out the policy. And you know if you quiz ministers about that they say 'Yes, it wasn't ever about whether we were going to use the evidence from the pilot to support whether or not we did it'."

It is noteworthy that the adoption of personalised approaches by the government in the mid-2000s coincided with major battles between ministers who favoured Tony Blair's hawkish attitude to user choice within public services (see for example the joint ministerial statement on expanding choice [Ministers of State for Departments of Health, Local and Regional Government and School Standards, 2004]), and other ministers, perceived as close to Gordon Brown, who were concerned about the impact of choice on equity (Brown, 2003). It may be that personalisation appealed to both sides as a more emollient version of choice, legitimised by its deep roots within organisations of disabled people and links to citizenship. Certainly, there was no slowing of pace in the implementation of personalisation when Brown replaced Blair as Prime Minister (Brown, 2008). Indeed, it was Brown as Prime Minister who authorised the piloting of personal health budgets within the NHS, which had been ruled out in a 2006 White Paper. It is possible that the devolution of financial control necessitated by personal health budgets was more palatable to a new Prime Minister in search of policy ideas than it was to a Chancellor of the Exchequer famous for retaining tight Treasury oversight (Rawnsley, 2010; Richards, 2010).

The broader context

Campaigns by organisations of disabled people and advocacy by policy entrepreneurs together played a key role in the establishment of personalisation as a central approach to social care reform. However, it is also important to note the congruence of the reform movement with the broader context within which it was located, and the ways in which that context itself shaped personalisation. As Coleman (2007, p 202) puts it: 'New discourses will emerge and gain widespread acceptance if they are more or less congruent with the prevailing culture into which they are being introduced.'

Thus, the development of personalisation needs to be understood in relation to broader state restructuring, welfare redesign and cultural change over 25 years. Personalisation can in part be interpreted as a reprisal of the political and intellectual critiques of the post-war welfare state that inspired the 'New Right' and 'New Left' movements of the 1970s (Clarke et al, 1987). Both movements problematised the state and sought to re-legitimise a focus on the individual, albeit in very different ways (see eg London Edinburgh Weekend Return Group, 1979; Murray, 1984; Wainwright, 1994; Waldegrave, 1994). The bogeymen of personalisation – bureaucrats, professionals, trade unions – are the same as in that earlier reform period (Schön, 1983). The alternatives to the welfare state encompassed by personalisation – mutualism, co-production, self-help, cash payments – are those promoted by an earlier generation of reformers. Leadbeater and Cottam (2007, p 113) acknowledge the influence of Ivan Illich (1995, 2002 [1970]), for example, whose writings on capabilities provided an alternative paradigm to welfare dependence. Pearson (2000, p 474) notes the extent to which direct payments resemble the cash transfers promoted by Keith Joseph (1975).

The process through which New Left and New Right ideas influenced the governments of the 1980s and 1990s and created a political climate conducive to personalisation is complex and contested. The Conservative governments of Thatcher and Major, and the New Labour governments that followed, appeared receptive to the critique of state power and keen to champion the individual. An emphasis on service user agency, choice and independence was evident in the consumer-oriented politics of John Major's Citizen's Charter and in New Labour's broader public service reforms (Needham, 2007). However, the governments of this period also oversaw the creation of new institutions of regulation and compliance that intensified state power. The top-down managerialism of the target culture, with its distrust of professionals and commitment to standardisation (Barber, 2007), clashed with the sorts of front-line diversity and innovation that advocates of personalisation such as Leadbeater (2004) were promoting.

Thus, rather than a straightforward march towards personalisation, personalised approaches appeared to advance when they could be coupled to broader political strategies. In the early 1990s, disability campaigners and policy entrepreneurs were able to convince Conservative ministers to introduce direct payments by demonstrating that the payments were a move towards reducing the size and cost of the welfare state (Zarb and Nadash, 1994). As Glasby and Littlechild (2006, pp 27–8) put it:

> While direct payments were a victory for disabled campaigners, they were also championed by a Conservative government committed to neo-liberal social policies aimed at rolling back the frontiers of the welfare state and promoting greater consumer choice through the creation of markets in social care.

Pearson also noted continuity with the broader Conservative agenda, describing the adoption of direct payments based on a rationale of enhanced accountability and efficiency as a 'variant of marketisation … underpinned by a notion of "scroungerphobia" that dominated social security reform from the late 1980s onwards' (2000, p 470).

Similarly, personalisation cohered with some aspects of Labour Party political strategy, as it sought to reinvent itself in the 1980s and early 1990s. Influenced by the ideas of the 'New Left', although without its radicalism, the Labour Party under Kinnock, and particularly under Blair, positioned itself as the party that represented consumers as well as producers (Rouse and Smith, 1999; Panitch and Leys, 2001). The work of Leadbeater, Mulgan and other contributors to the 1988 *Marxism Today* special issue on 'New Times', infused the New Labour project with a sensitivity to the demands of a post-Fordist economy and culture in which one size did not 'fit all' (Hall and Jacques, 1989). There was a focus on equipping the citizen to be an active and responsible force within society, bearing risks that for a generation had been borne by the state (Corrigan et al, 1988; Leadbeater, 1988; Mulgan, 1991; Giddens, 1998). Leadbeater called for 'Power to the person', emphasising that this should be a 'democratic individualism' as opposed to the consumer individualism of the Right (Leadbeater, 1988). As Labour leader from 1994, Blair indicated his broad acceptance of the New Times thesis, promoting, 'A dynamic knowledge-based economy founded on individual empowerment and opportunity, where governments enable, not command' (Blair, 1998, p 7; see also Finlayson, 2003).

In government from 1997, personalised approaches cohered with New Labour's broader political strategy in a number of ways. First, the language of personalisation provided a way for New Labour to differentiate its politics from those of earlier Labour administrations. The idea that the welfare state was 'monolithic', 'rigid', 'hidebound', was a recurrent theme of Blair's speeches (Needham, 2007). As Cutler et al (2007, p 848) argue: 'A characteristic feature of statements on public sector reform by Tony Blair has been the postulated link between the need to "personalize" public services and the deficiencies of earlier/existing patterns of provision.'

Second, personalisation appeared to demonstrate that New Labour was attuned to changing public expectations, driven by improvements in private-sector customer care and technological innovation. In Keohane's account of personalisation, he argues that the drive for personalised approaches has come in part from changing public expectations of service responsiveness, experienced day to day as customers of banks and supermarkets: 'We now expect not only to be able to control our own lives, but also for public services to fit around the rest of our activities in terms of convenience, time of access and speed of service' (2009, p 7). Leadbeater and Cottam have highlighted how growing public use of initiatives such as eBay and open source software has reshaped how people expect to interact with public services:

> Imagine what it will be like in ten years' time, as public services seek to serve people who have grown up with Bebo and social networking, MSN instant messaging, buying and selling on eBay, looking up stuff on Wikipedia, getting music via MySpace, playing multi-user games and broadcasting themselves across YouTube and its successors.... A public sector that does not utilise the power of user-generated content will not just look old, outdated and tired. It will also be far less productive and effective in creating public goods. (2007, p 114)

Certainly New Labour shared the perception that a new generation of consumers expected public services to be responsive to them as individuals. As the NHS Plan put it, 'We live in a consumer age. Services have to be tailormade not mass-produced, geared to the needs of users not the convenience of producers' (DH, 2000, p 26). In New Labour policy documents there was repeated emphasis on the ways in which changing experiences of private-sector responsiveness were influencing expectations of the public sector. Health Secretary Patricia Hewitt talked of '21st century aspirations – to be treated as an individual, to get personalised services' (Hewitt, 2006). According to the DH, 'personal health budgets, and personalisation more generally, should be seen in the context of the wider movement to empower people to have more say and more control in all aspects of public life' (DH, 2009a, p 11). The final Darzi report on NHS reform suggests that people want services that 'instinctively' respond to them, in the same sorts of ways that Amazon provides recommendations for books based on previous purchases (2008, p 26).

Third, the emphasis on self-management within personalisation cohered with New Labour's broader policy of transferring risk away from the state and on to the individual, and encouraging people to see themselves as members of communities with responsibilities as well as rights (Driver and Martell, 1999; Finlayson, 2003). Risk transfer has been part of a response to the perceived exigencies of globalisation, equipping workers with the skills to respond to a global knowledge economy while creating a more 'flexible' labour market (Finlayson, 2003; Coats, 2007). Within the welfare state, the shift to asset-based forms of welfare – such as the Child Trust Fund and Savings Gateway – indicated a move from collective to individual provision for future needs in the 'social investment state' (Lister, 2003; Finlayson, 2009). Individual budgets for social care users were encompassed by the same logic, passing the responsibility for the selection of appropriate services and personnel from the state to the individual.

During the 1980s and 1990s, therefore, personalisation campaigners and policy entrepreneurs were able to advance their agenda within a political culture broadly receptive to individual approaches to welfare. However, while all governments after 1979 undertook welfare state restructuring and valorised the individual, it was often in ways that reaffirmed state control and standardisation, rather than permitting difference. Particularly under New Labour, there was an emphasis on how the state could do more for less, using performance management to drive efficiency. Charles Leadbeater and Hilary Cottam (2007) and other personalisation advocates were calling for a state that did *less* and allowed people to develop their own capabilities. Towards the end of New Labour's time in office, faith in targets as a driver of public service improvement seemed to be diminishing in favour of approaches that were more explicitly personalised around the individual (Barber, 2007; Cabinet Office, 2009). The incoming Conservative–Liberal Democrat government made clear that it saw targets as anathema to the sorts of front-line innovation and personalised approaches that it favoured (HM Government, 2010a).

It can be seen, then, that establishing the personalisation narrative within social care involved a combination of pressure from social movements, interventions by policy entrepreneurs and the generation of arguments that were consonant with broader political and socio-cultural changes. These have not always been coherent or easily aligned, requiring unlikely allegiances and the finessing of tensions between elements of the personalisation story. The development of personalisation is usually seen as having bottom–up and top–down elements, suggestive of what Rogers (2003) calls a 'hybrid diffusion system' (cited in Nutley et al, 2007, p 179). The direction of diffusion appears to have been horizontal as well as vertical, spreading from one locality to another, through the networking activities of organisations such as In Control and the National Centre for Independent Living. Parr and Nixon, drawing on the work of Uitermark (2005), note that the significance of such horizontal distribution networks can often be missed:

> While this transfer of knowledge can happen independently from the centre, given that the process of horizontal distribution is marked by the promotion of key concepts and discourses, it can appear to be the case that the strategy has been conceived and implemented at the centre. (Parr and Nixon, 2009, p 110)

However, the direction of diffusion (upwards, downwards, horizontally) has been contested. Beresford writes that its bottom–up elements have been exaggerated:

> a broader picture is emerging ... of service users having had little involvement at local level and none at central policy level in this supposedly 'user-led' development. The same worrying picture emerges with face-to-face practitioners – the group which will be significantly affected by this

development, and will have a pivotal role in making it work. (2008, p 11)

How personalisation spreads: From transfer to translation

Having considered some of the elements that have contributed to the emergence of the personalisation narrative within social care, it is important also to consider how it has moved into other sectors. Chapter 3 outlined the broad policy reach of personalisation, which is reshaping approaches to health, education, housing, employment and criminal justice. This presence in multiple sectors is to some extent intrinsic to the personalisation storyline itself, with its emphasis on the need to treat people holistically, rather than in silos. So, for example, the stretch of personalisation into housing for people with social care needs has been driven by an awareness of the importance of accommodation to providing good outcomes for people (Porteus, 2008). The adoption of personalised approaches for children with disabilities has been driven by the claims of improved outcomes for adults, and the need to facilitate transition from children's to adult services (Cowen, 2010). Within the NHS, interviewees felt that it was people with long-term health conditions who pushed for the introduction of personal health budgets, based on their experiences of utilising social care services.

This migration from social care into other sectors may be explained in part by the distinctive policy problems facing each sector, which led them to import a policy 'solution' from elsewhere. For example, within the NHS there was an increasing awareness that its cost base was threatened by the growth of long-term conditions (Wanless, 2003). Expert patient and self-care approaches were felt to contribute to the continued financial viability of the health service (Alakeson, 2007). Within employment services, the drive to tackle long-term unemployment led policymakers to explore tailored support for individual job-seekers (Gregg, 2008). Within criminal justice there was a sense that rehabilitation was ineffective in reducing reoffending rates and that a personalised approach could be more effective (McGuire, 2010b). In all of these cases, the narrative of personalisation as a success in social care pointed to a ready-made policy solution.

The notion that a policy problem in one sector leads to the borrowing of a successful policy from another sector fits the dynamic of change described in the policy transfer literature. The insights of policy transfer theory, developed by Dolowitz and others, aim to offer an empirically robust approach to explaining how policies utilised in one context emerge in another. They provide tools to interrogate the transfer process, offering testable hypotheses about when, why and by whom transfer takes place (Bennett, 1991; Robertson, 1991; Rose, 1991, 1993; Wolman, 1992; Dolowitz, 1998; Dolowitz and Marsh, 2000; Mossberger and Wolman, 2003). These texts discuss how far such moves are evidence-driven and what the mechanisms and channels of transfer are likely to be.

As a way of understanding the migration of personalisation from social care into other sectors, the neatness of the transfer approach – in which problems couple up to solutions – has limitations. It has been criticised for relying too heavily on the notion of policy as stable and observable (James and Lodge, 2003). Interpretive approaches to policy challenge the assumption that policies have fixed meanings (Yanow, 1996; Fischer, 2003; Hajer, 2005). Policy itself is recognised to be an unstable word, meaning at times legislation, but at other times a set of practices (Yanow, 1996, p 19). It does not generally describe something that is portable, ready to be picked up in one context and applied in another.

Rather than examining the migration of personalisation as a neat process of policy transfer, it is useful to consider the process as one of translation (Yanow, 2004; Lendvai and Stubbs, 2007; Freeman, 2009). Freeman argues that translation can be seen as a rejection of the mechanistic and linear assumptions of policy transfer, in favour of 'a closer attention to the problem of shared meaning and how it might be developed' (2009, pp 439–40). In a similar vein, Yanow (2004, p 15) argues:

> Translating is not the same thing as transferring knowledge. 'Transfer' suggests an objectification or commodification of knowledge, extrapolated from its context.... Even this simple model of knowledge transfer, however, incorporates the problem of 'noise' – a distortion of the original meaning – which recognises the likelihood of altered meaning although treating it as an unintended, and unfortunate, change away from the 'literal' meaning, which should be controlled for.

Lendvai and Stubbs have similarly developed a critique of policy transfer, and opted instead to use the metaphor of translation:

> While the mainstream policy transfer literature with its realist ontology sees 'policy' both in the source and in the

recipient context as a stable, pre-existing and uncontested 'reality', and the transfer as a more or less linear process, a sociology of translation works with a much more fluid and dynamic framework. (2007, p 179)

According to Freeman, 'What is described as translation is often the result of multiple iterations by multiple actors, eroding the distinction between source and target' (2009, p 441).

Thus, the translation literature offers a view of policy that is much less stable and portable than the account offered by the transfer model. It alerts us to the ways in which policies are translated – interpreted, modified – as they migrate from one setting to another. It also draws attention to the role played by policy actors in that translation – foregrounding issues of power, hierarchy and indeterminacy, rather than neutral transmission. A key role in the spread of personalisation – highlighted earlier – was played by policy entrepreneurs who conveyed the message that personal budgets were working in social care and could be exported across the welfare state. Such reassurances downplayed the varied structures and funding systems in different services that might be barriers to successful implementation, and overstated the robustness of the emerging evidence base within social care. Personalisation advocates both outside and within government weaved together a range of compelling discourses, encompassing the dignity of the individual, the rights of the citizen, the power of consumer choice and the failure of bureau-professional welfare states. Driven on by compelling testimonies of individual transformation in social care and an appetite for the next 'big idea', policy actors were encouraged to stretch the same storyline into other sectors. Being primarily a discursive tool, personalisation could be used to build coalitions and silence critics, drawing selectively on a range of validations.

The result is a policy climate in which, according to one Cabinet Office advisor, "whatever the policy issue, the question is: how can we use an individual budget?". A range of policy challenges including the rehabilitation of ex-offenders, long-term unemployment and rough sleeping are being re-examined to explore the potential for personal budgets (DWP, 2008; Department of Health Care Networks, 2009; McGuire, 2010b). This 'normative isomorphism' (DiMaggio and Powell, 1983) is broader than merely a problem looking for a solution, as the policy transfer approach might have it. Nor is it best understood as a solution looking for a problem, an alternative ordering that has been used to explain how policy innovation sometimes occurs (Kingdon, 1995, p 86). The uncertain terms under which it is spreading are best expressed in a quote from a civil servant from the Ministry of Justice, interviewed by the author: "Where we're at [with personalisation] is we know it's important but we're not sure how it fits and how it works." Here is an actor struggling to understand how to make a dominant policy story meaningful for his own policy and practice context – not to import a policy mechanism to solve a particular problem. What is occurring is a process of translation in which, as Freeman (2009, p 437) puts it: 'Meaning is not prior to translation, but is constructed and reconstructed in the process of communication.'

A shifting narrative

Contained within translation is the presumption of adaption and change. As personalisation develops, it is possible to observe it mutating as well as migrating. This is evident not only as it adapts to new sectoral contexts, but also as it becomes deployed in local settings and for different user groups. Here the stories of personalisation, as well as its application, take on distinctive local attributes. As Coleman (2007, p 201) notes: 'The transformation of national discourses (set out in legislation and guidance) to locally acceptable versions of the discourse, which all actors understand and buy into, is key to the successful implementation of public policy.' In Coleman's own work on local authority health scrutiny, the author observes the evolution of different local discourses:

> This was due to those at local levels who were driving the process exploiting the discursive ambiguities of the broad policy in order to accommodate local interests. In order to maintain local claims of progress and development in implementing and operation of the policy, individuals had to work within the government's definitions, fitting their stories into overarching discourses. (2007, p 212)

Although the policy context of personalisation is very different, these reflections have obvious salience. It is a policy that has evolved from the interplay of horizontal and vertical channels of innovation. Its original founders express frustration at the ways in which the meaning and values of personalisation have changed as it has been on this journey. According to one interviewee: "it's taken a life of its own and I think it's one of those unfortunate words like recovery, it becomes anything to anybody really. It can mean many things." Another talked about how it's current implementation and links to cost-cutting "concerns me because that was never the original idea". A member of In Control said, "you've got experts who are coming in almost in the middle without having the fundamental basic understanding of what it's about, and that's where a lot of the language is being twisted". This echoes Jeffares' analysis of how policy ideas catch on, in which he notes that the original entrepreneurs can see them as having been 'stole[n]' by policy officials (2007, p 178). Some expression of this sense of loss is evident in a commentary on personalisation by Simon Duffy, one of the pioneers of individual budgets, in which he notes: 'a term like personalisation is vulnerable to being used and interpreted in different ways…. For civil servants the term is usefully broad and allows sufficient ambiguity to enable any sharp policy questions to be evaded and postponed' (2010, p 2).

A number of interviewees reflected on the sense that personalisation is not something that has been achieved (despite its high policy profile), but rather an ongoing process that can still succeed or fail. As one consultant put it:

> "When I was going around talking to people about the personalisation agenda I got a really strong view from both officers and members in many authorities that this was just a passing fad, and if we just keep our heads down it will just pass over and we can go back to what we did before. So I think there was a lot of foot-dragging and people not really engaging with it. And you can understand in some ways because there have been lots of initiatives after all in social care. Some of which are here today and gone tomorrow."

One director of adult social care talked of: "a radical fringe, represented by In Control, which has a legitimate viewpoint, but which particularly represents adults of working age. We've got to exercise a degree of caution." Such quotes highlight the extent to which personalised approaches continue to be translated and problematised by local policy actors, a theme explored further in Chapter 6.

Conclusion

The personalisation narrative has been influential as a result of the work of social movements and policy entrepreneurs, and also due to its ability to cohere with the broader political climate in which individual rights are twinned with responsibilities in an unstable mix. The ambivalent accounts of citizenship and consumerism within the personalisation narrative are reflected in a broader political culture in which people are expected to pursue their maximal rights as public service customers, but to be active and responsible citizens, exercising restraint as members of communities. The cost-cutting rationale of personalisation – central to early campaigns and taking on a new urgency in the current financial climate – has been deployed alongside claims to be revitalising the welfare state.

In explaining how personalisation has moved into different sectors, the mainstream policy transfer literature is of only limited value. Approaches from the interpretive policy literature that emphasise translation rather than transfer can provide a more nuanced and convincing account of policy migration. Here emphasis is placed on indeterminacy and purposive ambiguity, as well as the role of translators in foregrounding certain translations and disregarding others. This recurring theme of purposive ambivalence is key to understanding personalisation as a narrative. However, it is easy to see that it creates challenges for those charged with implementing personalised approaches in local settings. At the front line, staff and service users must make sense of an agenda that lacks a clear set of parameters, shaping the practice context as they go. The challenge of using an ambiguous storyline as a guide to policy practice is the focus of Chapter 6.

Delivering person-centred services

Approaching personalisation as a narrative, the previous chapters have examined its origins, reach and potency. The remaining chapters consider the implications of personalisation, with a particular focus on front-line practice. Implementation studies are somewhat en vogue, after being out of fashion for some time (Hill and Hupe, 2002; Barrett, 2004; Schofield and Sausman, 2004; Gains and Clarke, 2007, pp 133–8). Although the duality between policy-making and implementation is rejected here, nonetheless there is a difference between policy as it is narrated within a national policy context and the experience of those charged with making it meaningful in a local setting. It is the process through which an ambiguous and overarching set of storylines are translated into tangible resources: staff, services, buildings. As Yanow found in her research into Israeli Community Centres, in the face of ambiguous enabling legislation, local policy actors were nonetheless:

> faced with the necessity of having to hire staff, draw clientele, attract ministry funds, and raise private donations – all of which required the translation of this ambiguity into more concrete terms for a program whose very concept was unknown and whose goals were not obviously and clearly actionable. (1996, p 160)

In this process, local people are not merely audiences receiving national policy stories. They are 'active creators and interpreters of meaning', rather than 'passive recipients of others' meanings' (Yanow, 1996, pp 219–20).

In relation to personalisation, an analogous process is occurring, as an ambiguous narrative is made meaningful in a practice context. One of the storylines of personalisation is that in order for support to be tailored more closely to the users, there will need to be a radical redevelopment of the local service interface. Users will take on new roles in commissioning their own services and front–line staff and local authority commissioners will play a facilitating role in connecting users to markets. Developing new roles and relationships in this context is a profound challenge. In the interviews conducted for the book, making sense of, or acting in spite of, ambiguity was a recurrent theme. This chapter focuses on some of the key points of uncertainty reported by those engaged in this translation process. The chapter focuses on developments in social care, relating in particular to personal budgets, since this sector is furthest advanced in a direction of travel that other services are starting to follow. After briefly setting out the new service context, the chapter focuses on a number of points where roles and relationships still seem highly uncertain: support planning, market-shaping, financing, risk and mainstreaming.

Service users as commissioners

A key theme of personalisation is that services must be shaped by and responsive to users, some of whom will themselves take on the role of service commissioner. Existing local authority commissioners and service managers are being urged to engage users and carers more effectively and also to reach out to the broader community, including potential future users. This requires being responsive to the diverse ways in which users want services to be personalised, with some choosing to manage a budget and others wanting traditional services to be delivered in a more flexible way.

New service users should first be assessed to ensure that they are eligible for local authority support (which may include an element of self-assessment). Eligibility criteria are tight – and likely to become tighter in the current financial context. An Audit Commission (2010b) report highlighted the shortcomings of local authority approaches to needs assessment. Once the assessment is done, most local authorities use (or are developing) a Resource Allocation System (RAS) to determine the financial allocation. Local authority staff then work with users to develop a support plan (replacing the traditional care plan), and to determine what degree of financial control is desired by the user (on a spectrum ranging from a full direct payment to full local authority management of a personal budget). Many local authorities use In Control's Seven Steps to Support in shaping the support plan – the stages are: find out how much money I am entitled to; make a plan; get plan agreed; organise money; organise support; live life; see how it worked (for more details, see the In Control website, available at: www.in-control.org.uk).

Commissioning of services should then be undertaken by a range of actors, rather than remaining the role of local authority specialists. As a Department of Health (DH) document puts it, commissioning is not limited to people 'with commissioning in their job title' (DH, 2008a). The DH envisages a nested set of commissioning functions in which individual commissioning by service users and their representatives links to operational commissioning by local authorities (supporting users and providers to allow individual commissioning to take place, filling any service gaps that may arise), and above that to strategic commissioning, which is the responsibility of senior management and involves bringing together a range of service sectors and planning for future workforce and population needs (DH, 2008a). At all of these levels, commissioning is expected to be a multi-agency function, drawing in partners from different service sectors and from the private and third sector.

This approach constitutes a major shift from the traditional outsourcing models that have predominated since the 1980s, in which commissioning was largely a process of local authorities allocating block and spot contracts to private- and third-sector organisations. This involved bulk purchasing of standardised services in advance, subject to various contractual agreements. Under more personalised approaches, there is an assumption that either users will contract directly with provider organisations to purchase the services that they require (the personal budget model), or that block and spot contracts (for example, for information, advocacy and prevention) will more carefully specify the need to tailor services to the needs of users. The range of services that can be commissioned is expanding to cover anything that can be linked to an agreed outcome for the individual, which may be a traditional type of community equipment, like a walk-in bath, or may be a holiday, a laptop or a massage. A director of social care expressed the aspiration that people with care needs will be removed from the 'ghetto' in which they have been placed: "Less and less will it be possible to talk of a social care market, because people will spend their money in the same way as other people." Another social care manager commented: "We need to stop using the language of commissioning. People won't 'commission' things – they will buy them."

It is the individual commissioning of services by personal budget-holders that has attracted most attention, as it is the most transformative aspect of personalisation, with the potential to be expanded much further within social care and other sectors. The practitioners and service users interviewed by the author raised a number of challenges and uncertainties relating to this new commissioning context, including the role played by support planners, the complexity of shaping the local market, the political challenges of decommissioning, the unfavourable financial climate, the management of risk and the extent to which personalised commissioning could move from the fringes to the mainstream. These are discussed in turn.

Support planning

A recurrent theme in the interviews and literature on personalisation is the importance of the support planning process in which people are helped to navigate the system and make appropriate and empowering choices about their care. The Putting People First personalisation toolkit, published in May 2008, advises:

> effective support planning and brokerage are crucial in enabling disabled people to exercise more choice and control in their lives. Support planning and brokerage, including easy access to information, advice and advocacy, should offer disabled and older people the opportunity to make decisions for themselves that might otherwise be made for them by other people. (DH, 2008b)

The importance of effective information and advocacy was highlighted by most interviewees, and has been the focus of a report from the Improvement and Development Agency (IDeA, no date) and a project by the charity SCOPE. There are a range of approaches on offer at the moment, offering different interpretations of the support planning role. In some areas, support planning is being provided in-house by local authorities, funded through top-slicing personal budgets. Local authority call centres are being set up or co-opted to provide information and support (Jerome, 2010). In other areas, third-sector bodies (including user-led organisations) are being commissioned by the local authority to provide support planning facilities, alongside information and advice. Websites such as In Control's Shop4Support have developed to make it easier for service users and carers to see what services are available. A third model involves the use of professional brokers who provide support planning under contract to individuals – although this option has generated little enthusiasm from commentators on personalisation, anticipating a reassertion of professional control (Dowson and Greig, 2009; Duffy and Fulton, 2009).

Exploring the debate about whether local authorities or third-sector organisations should provide support planning raises a number of themes relating to the legitimacy base of these different sectors. Internal support planning by local authorities was felt by some interviewees to ensure appropriate professional input – rather than relying on 'volunteers' – and to minimise complexity. As one interviewee put it, "It is hard enough to find out what people are actually commissioning with their personal budgets.... Involving external advisors lengthens the information chain back to local authorities as to what current demand is for." The issue of multiple layers of staff and additional complexity was also expressed by a contributor to a *Community Care* (2010) online debate on personalisation:

> The average service user now has three teams involved in their care – the social work team, the support planning team and the support service. It is a nightmare and very confusing as everyone has different ideas of how the new policy works and the service user/family receive very conflicting information.

Some local authorities have opted for a simpler model in which a social worker or other professional undertakes both the assessment and support planning processes. However, this approach raised concerns about a conflict of interest. One interviewee, running a third-sector organisation, was troubled by the fusing of roles:

> "The person doing the assessment – deciding on eligibility – shouldn't be the same person as does your support plan. It's a different kind of power relationship. The person holding the assessment decision has so much power. It shouldn't be about persuading them, playing up to them – while they are thinking I shouldn't tell them their budget, they'll just want to spend it."

Similar concerns led the Social Care Institute for Excellence (SCIE) to observe: 'Complete independence from the agencies which fund and which have hitherto provided services has been identified as the essential characteristic of the brokerage model' (SCIE, 2007, p 14). However, one local authority commissioner reflected that separating staff out into assessors and support planners was not viable: "We can't afford to do that."

There were also concerns that professional care staff such as social workers may be cautious about offering advice on the purchase of external services (particularly non-traditional ones) for fear of litigation if problems arise. In a *Community Care*/Unison survey of social work practitioners and managers, less than half of respondents felt that they had the requisite skills around brokerage and employing personal assistants (Lombard, 2010). A further concern expressed in relation to local authority staff acting as support planners is that they lack an incentive to sell personal budgets to users. According to the Chief Executive of In Control, Julie Stansfield: 'You can't really rely on local authorities to get out the message about personal budgets and direct payments because turkeys don't vote for Christmas' (Stansfield, 2010). Jeff Jerome, National Director for Social Care Transformation, has warned that 'many local authorities have used the managed budget route to direct people away from direct payments' (Jerome, 2010).

The third-sector brokerage model draws on a different base of legitimacy, building on what may well be well-established advice and advocacy services. Users may be more likely to trust these because of the charity 'brand' and distance from local authority control. Whereas in-house brokerage may need to take into consideration complex and lengthy internal procurement mechanisms, external brokers are likely to have more freedom. For these reasons, a number of interviewees felt that advocacy by user-led organisations or other external bodies would deliver more creative approaches than in-house brokerage by local authorities. One observed:

> "We are identifying what is it that you really need a professional to do. There will be some tasks that have to be done by a social worker or one of our professionals, but much of it doesn't have to be done by somebody who is working in the local authority or with the health trust.... The pilot we did [here] showed quite clearly ... when people were supported by somebody who wasn't based in the local council they were getting better outcomes, we were getting more creative support plans."

However, some interviewees from within local authorities were concerned that third-sector organisations have their own conflicts of interest. For example, if they also provide services (such as day centres), there is a financial gain in recommending use of those services. This conflict may be particularly pronounced in cases where the third-sector organisations are managing the budget on behalf of a user (on the Individual Service Fund model), as well as developing the support plan and providing services. According to one interviewee:

> "So I think if [a large voluntary-sector body] are doing provision, they shouldn't also be doing advocating. I think they're compromised. They might be running the best

service in the world but they are compromised if they are doing the advocacy and maybe the brokerage that says if you don't go there it will present you a problem."

Such concerns have led the voluntary-sector umbrella organisation ACEVO (Association of Chief Executives of Voluntary Organisations) to recommend a Financial Services Authority-style model in which users have a clear idea whether advisors are independent or tied to a particular set of services (2009, p 40). Some third-sector organisations are setting up a separate social enterprise, which will enable them to sell services in a way that is not possible as a charity. However, other interviewees rejected the idea that charities ought to move in such a direction, selling services like a financial broker. As a manager from a women's refuge put it:

> "Can you imagine us having adverts on the telly like Tesco? This week in a special offer at the refuge, buy one bed get one free. It's just ridiculous ... particularly if you are a political organisation, with a campaigning arm as well as service delivery then I think it's difficult to play that game.... It's not an environment I'd like to be involved with and I don't think it's what a charity is there to do."

Such anxieties echo longer-standing concerns about the extent to which direct payments have led to some user-led organisations focusing on service provision at the expense of advocacy and campaigning (Riddell et al, 2006, p 16).

Some of the uncertainties here surround the different models that exist within the third sector, in which very large charities operate on business models that can appear little different to the private sector, whereas small local organisations and micro-providers may offer something more distinctive (PASC, 2008). Certainly, user-led organisations are seen as having a distinctive legitimacy and an important role to play in fostering peer and informal support networks that negate the need for formal support planners. As a 2007 SCIE report put it, '"Brokerage" has become an international short-hand expression for the kind of flexible interpreters of systems which recipients may welcome. But a prior question is, why do systems need interpreting?' According to a local authority social care manager:

> "we're really intent that we don't go down the road of having professional brokers because I just think it's a dead

end really. We'd just replicate another professional label. You don't need it. You just need somebody with the right value base and skills."

A local authority commissioner commented:

> "People say, well, we've got to provide all this information to people, we've got to tell them about the services, we've got to talk about that, but again and again I turn round to people and say, well actually when I choose a plumber I go and talk to my friends and say, what plumber have you got, and, have you a good plumber?"

These reflections reaffirm the extent to which the personalisation narrative problematises professional expertise, favouring informal knowledge accessed and controlled by service users.

Shaping the market

Local authority commissioners are expected to take an active role in market-shaping, as more of the direct commissioning passes to users and their advocates. A diverse market of providers is seen as making it more likely that supply can match user demand, while also providing the engine of competition to drive innovation and quality. There are alternative storylines – for example, that a part of the public and professional ethos has always been to tailor services to the needs of particular clients, even within a context of monopoly state supply (Plant, 2003). Indeed, a trade union response to personalisation has been to reaffirm that point – as Unison General Secretary Dave Prentis (2010) put it: 'Personalisation is something our members do everyday, responding with individual attention to user needs.'

However, within the personalisation narrative and the wider disability movement, that argument is not seen as a credible defence of the status quo. Across all policy sectors, personalisation is driving greater involvement by the third and private sectors in the name of increased user responsiveness. Clearly outsourcing of services is not a new initiative – and the rationale for it has evolved as successive governments have pursued different approaches to service reform – but it is now a core part of the personalisation offer. According to a Cabinet Office interviewee, "If you want to personalise, you need to work with partners because no one provider can provide everything someone needs.… There needs to be a multiagency approach". As a private-sector provider of financial services put it: "There is no point in having personalisation if there is a closed shop."

For commissioners charged with shaping and managing this market, the first challenge is to map existing provision. One national policy officer in a voluntary organisation felt that local authorities currently lack basic market knowledge: "You can only stimulate the market if you know what your provider market is, the vast majority of local authorities don't actually know the massive amounts of activity that are going on in their local authority areas anyway." One way for local authorities to proceed is to build on the customer-focused market that may already exist for self-funders (Tyson, 2007, p 13). However, in many local areas there is no vibrant self-funder market to draw on: rather, markets are patchy and unresponsive. Wealthy areas, with high levels of self-funders, may have more active markets than areas with high numbers of people receiving council-run services, and provider services in rural areas may be underdeveloped compared to urban areas. As one social care manager put it, "People say to us it's all very well to have direct payments but there's bugger all to buy", a point echoed by national personalisation head Jeff Jerome (2010). According to ACEVO,

> The experience of self-funders of social care is instructive here, with many carrying on paying for and receiving quite traditional and often inadequate services, either because better alternatives do not exist, or because people lack the information and advice to find them. (2009, p 33)

In some areas, there may be a high number of providers, but the range of services may be limited. As one third-sector representative said of his region: "We've got a lot of providers but it tends to be someone to get you in and out of bed. There is a problem now with the need for people to get more variety." According to another director of adult social services, "Our sense at the moment is that the market is very dysfunctional. There are few incentives for providers to be innovative. I don't know of any authority that can genuinely say otherwise."

A number of interviewees expressed concern about the extent to which commissioners 'get' the personalisation agenda, highlighting cases where block contracting continues to be the norm. As one put it, "Commissioners have taken 10 years setting up block grants etc, so they don't want to get rid of all that." Commissioners themselves expressed concern that they do not have the right skills for market-shaping: "A sophisticated approach is required to manage a market, you need analysis and modelling skills. We don't have that" (local authority social care manager). Another said: "It is quite difficult to stimulate a market in a context of personalisation because there is less security."

Some local authority interviewees felt that effective markets could best be developed on a regional or sub-regional basis, particularly since many providers operate across local authority boundaries. However, a DH regional officer interviewed did not agree that this was part of the regional role. She also indicated that some local authorities were resistant to working with the regional office, seeing it as having an enforcement role on behalf of the national government.

Having identified the market and the sorts of services that users are likely to want, commissioners are expected to work with providers on business development skills, market responsiveness and financial planning, supporting the transition from 'wholesale' to 'retail' provision. In some areas, providers are being offered outcome-focused contracts, in place of task- and time-based contracts. The new contracts are designed to assure quality and supply through the preselection or validation of providers. In domiciliary care, for example, providers in some local authorities have signed up to framework contracts that commit them to providing personalised and flexible services, but with no guarantee of demand (DH, 2009b). Providers and budget-holders agree on the detail of provision, with the contract setting out only the broad outcomes. Quality assurance is then provided on the basis of Care Quality Commission (CQC) ratings and user feedback. This contractual arrangement provides much less security for providers, particularly since the DH is keen to affirm that people should be free to purchase services from outside the framework contract should they choose to do so (DH, 2009b). In relation to personal assistants, local accreditation practices are variable; local authority interviewees indicated that they were still consulting locally on whether to create a register of personal assistants. There are particular challenges in rural areas and issues around employment of migrant workers (Bawden, 2009).

Providers are expected to become more sophisticated at marketing themselves to service users, carers and support planners, rather than relying on established links with local authority commissioners. This involves moving from a model in which the chief executive sells the service to a local authority commissioner, to one in which front-line staff sell the service to individual service users (ACEVO, 2009). Many local authorities have set up provider forums to improve communication with and support for providers in adjusting to the new model. The DH is keen to communicate to providers the benefits that personalisation can bring: 'The beneficial nature of dealing directly with their client base should be emphasised [to providers] – happy customers are a more stable basis for medium to long-term planning than block contracts influenced by political and budgetary concerns beyond their control' (2008c, p 33).

However, relationships between commissioners and providers have traditionally been adversarial and many continue to be problematic. As Tyson (2007, p 19) puts it in a discussion of market-shaping, 'neither commissioners nor providers felt particularly powerful or "in control".... Commissioners and large providers tended to ascribe power to one another.' According to one local authority manager interviewee, "[Providers] want us to tell them what to do. It's a parent–child relationship, we've been their biggest purchaser. The bulk of providers don't even come to our events." A director of adult social care noted, "we're not awash with entrepreneurial spirit here really". Another said: "We wanted the third sector to run a drop-in service, but we had no take-up." A third expressed frustration with his local third sector:

> "The voluntary sector, again in my own personal opinion, are still grappling with the concept of what's coming along and having some difficulties moving forward, so I'd say generally, very, very generally, that our private providers generally get it because that's sort of what they've been for some time but our voluntary-sector colleagues don't all get it at the current time and we're needing to do some work around that."

The third-sector perspective is of course rather different:

> "There's local authorities that I'm aware of that are going out doing these pilot activities and are just not talking to the [third] sector.... They come to the provider market and say you've got to do it, it's adapt or die, and that doesn't really work." (national policy officer, voluntary organisation)

According to another voluntary-sector interviewee: "Local authority commissioners are saying this is not my problem, market development. Even the ones involved in the pilots, the ones you'd expect to be ahead of the game, who've got Aiming High money." Voluntary and private care providers have complained that too much of the Transforming Social Care grant has been absorbed by the local authority, rather than being used to support providers to make the transition to personalised services (English Community Care Association, 2010).

Provider anxieties focus around the unpredictability of organisational financing once more purchasing is done on an individual basis. Problems of instability are being anticipated across the private and third sectors. There will be institutional challenges for providers, for example, around the administrative burden of issuing and chasing hundreds of invoices sent to individual users. As one head of a small-scale social care provider said, "We don't have a finance department or an HR department.... I'm not sure the infrastructure is there if everyone managed their own money, to do all the invoices." The likelihood that back office costs will rise under personalisation, and that there may be an increase in late payment and non-payment of invoices, requires organisations to think creatively about how to resource these elements. This will be a particular challenge for small and medium enterprises and third-sector organisations with low capitalisation. A number of local authorities have opted for pre-payment cards for service users, which can be loaded up with a direct payment allocation and used to purchase services, avoiding a lengthy invoicing process. However, again, there may be difficulties for small organisations, who do not have a Visa platform or other relevant technology.

In the face of these challenges, some providers are optimistic: "If you do what people want they will stay with you. There are some vulnerabilities in it. But generally people like what we do." According to another:

> "If I was a residential care home-owner, and into profit or whatever, I would make my business so good you would buy what you would have off me, and I'd be confident that what I'm supplying is what actually people want to buy."

However, others are worried: "No local authority has thought about the destabilisation and closure, and the impact that will have on staff and users" (director, third-sector umbrella organisation). Another interviewee reflected on the issues: "It's going to take a lot of fleetness of foot and commitment from commissioners, both local authority and health, to make sure you don't idiotically and unintentionally sweep away some really good services" (civil servant, DH). Some providers may choose to exit the market. A civil servant working on personalisation and housing warned: "Larger providers have made announcements that they are not going for new housing. They are saying that personalisation challenges their care and support packages – pensions, employment rights etc." Alternatively, other interviewees felt that it would be the larger providers that would prosper:

"Ironically you might end up with just the big players like the foundation trusts kicking around and sweeping it all up again, because they have size to be robust and survive a storm when smaller sector organisations very often can't."

Financing personalisation

Issues relating to the financing of personalisation were a concern for many interviewees, given the adverse financial climate, with local authorities being required to make savings of up to 25% of overall budgets. Interviewees were concerned about the micro-financing issues – what budgets could be spent on, how services should be disaggregated and costed – and the macro-issues of sustaining personalisation in a context of major cuts.

The first of these challenges – micro-financing – was highlighted as a problem for front-line staff. According to one support planner: "We need more support on knowing what we should be funding and what not, what people should have a responsibility for paying for themselves." Some interviewees felt that staff do not yet have adequate training to work within the support plan model – "they are trained to think in hours, not prices". A manager from a user-led organisation for disabled people commented: "The support planners don't know how to cost things, they don't understand that personal assistants have overheads, like holiday and sick pay." According to a Scottish Personal Assistants Employers Network (SPAEN)/Unison report: 'A large number of employers did not make arrangements for "contingency". This referred to arrangements for staff sickness, holiday cover and unusual circumstances' (SPAEN and Unison, 2008, p 5). This echoes findings in an Office for Public Management (OPM) publication, drawn from research in Essex, which reported: 'Service users and family members explained that while in many cases frontline staff appeared confident in selling the initial idea of cash payments, they felt they often struggled to explain the "nuts and bolts" of how they work' (OPM, 2010, pp 7–8).

Costing and pricing more broadly were recognised to be underdeveloped in many areas. As one third-sector provider put it: "At the moment we can't see the cost of the in-house day centres, so we've got nothing to compare with." Uncertainty about costing is often internal as well as external, with local authority staff themselves not having access to disaggregated costings for in-house services (OPM, 2008, p 40). One interviewee noted that pricing services in advance can be particularly difficult, because the unit cost may depend on how much of that service is purchased. In uncertain markets, providers often charge more to cover the risk of low demand, but the head of one provider umbrella organisation indicated that this route was not being held open to providers: "Local authorities are taking stability away and not allowing a notice period, but also won't allow organisations to charge more than they did before."

There are also problems around ensuring that support plans realistically reflect the costs of external services. As a support planner put it: "Our local authority panel has set a cost for home care that is not enough to afford it through self-management, it doesn't cover the agency rates.... But if people have been assessed as needing a certain amount of home care, that is what they need." In this context there is a disincentive to take the money as a direct payment, even though this is supposed to be the default option for service users.

The relationship between personalisation and cuts – the macro-financing issue – remains unclear. Personalisation is an agenda that developed in a much more auspicious financial context, and is now being modified in anticipation of severe funding cuts ahead and predictions of major staff cuts (Dunning, 2010c). As one local authority social care manager noted:

> "The circumstances are very different than when we had the national pilot here for personalisation. That was very laissez faire, very flexible. It had a lot of money thrown at it. Now for older people, personalisation is costing more and we need to look at that."

In the interviews, there was some cynicism that personalisation is now being used as a label to legitimise service changes that are more about cutting budgets than about enhancing choice and control. As one national policy consultant put it: "Local authorities that are cutting everything, that have massive budget issues, use personalisation and individual budgets to justify anything that they want to do." A local authority chief executive noted: "Councils are hiding behind the deficit reduction plan – it makes it easier to close day centres." This fits with comments made by Andrew Tyson, Adult Social Care lead at In Control: 'There are reported instances of commissioners using the introduction of individual budgets and a new Resource Allocation System as an "excuse" to hold down or reduce fees, or to disinvest in existing services' (2007, p 20). One council interviewee acknowledged that financial allocations were decreasing: "the individual budget is highly unlikely, we would say, to be of the same amount as what they're currently getting, what they're currently spending".

A number of interviewees expressed concerns that the shift to personal budgets would make it easier to cut spending: "I do worry about the decreasing costs. This is what we've had with direct payments. It's very easy to pick off individuals, you give them less and less and less." According to a service user: "Once the RAS kicks in, all of a sudden it will be very easy to alter the amount of money depending on what's in the budget that year." A carer expressed a similar concern:

> "It isn't that I'm against the principle of personalisation of care services.... It's the Personalisation agenda I'm not happy with and the way it's being publicised and implemented in practice.... [T]he process is actually about money and not services. It isn't about what an individual needs but is about rationing.... In this Local Authority, they started quite crudely – putting cost ceilings on the RAS matrices and targeting the 10 most expensive care packages for cuts by crudely incentivising consultants on a pay by cost reductions basis." (Email correspondence with the author)

Retaining the ethos of self-directed support while undertaking swingeing budget cuts will thus be a key issue for all councils. One local authority manager explained the challenge:

> "Personalisation has got to save us money, we've got no choice.... We know we can achieve dramatic savings on individual people. Personalised services will be cheaper in some circumstances, particularly for learning disability and physical disabilities. There's not so much savings to be made on older people because we're stingy to start with."

According to another local authority social care manager:

> "The DH is still saying this will be cost-neutral – which is just not helpful. We'll have loads more people coming through for starters. We'll have to find savings. There will be a greater push to get people onto self-directed support."

There are concerns about the extent to which personalisation may raise demands for services from people who currently do not use state provision. According to one interviewee from the mental health sector:

"Word of mouth is bringing people out of the woodwork. So people who have not really reported to services in the past, because they didn't want anything to do with them are now seeing a much more sensitive and thoughtful approach which includes money, and they're coming out of the woodwork saying actually I'm a chronic depressive or whatever, can I be assessed and can I have a budget?"

This issue of unmet need may be more relevant in the health sector than in social care, where, as one social care director put it, "you have to be pretty vulnerable and fairly poor" to get money in the first place.

Despite these concerns, some local authority interviewees remained upbeat about the cost-savings that personalisation could bring. According to one director of adult social care:

"Personalisation meets the needs of people in the community and that's a whole lot cheaper for us. At the end of the financial year, we said to people can you return any unspent money to us – we got over two hundred thousand pounds returned to us. People are much more frugal with their resources than we would be."

However, this so-called clawing back is controversial. In Control have argued that:

Claw-backs are inappropriate, expensive to administer and counter-productive – when people believe that they may lose money left in their account at the end of a month or a year they are more likely to rush to spend it – often inappropriately. (In Control, 2010)

A SPAEN/Unison report similarly highlighted the perverse incentives created by clawing back: 'Those who retain a contingency fund found that, often, the local authority "clawed back" monies which were "unused" in the employers account' (2008, p 5).

Risk

Personalisation requires commissioners, providers, users and carers to encounter and manage new forms of risk. For providers, there are financial risks posed by the retail model, in which the security of local authority block contracts will disappear. Private- and third-sector providers are faced with managing this new risk profile, and working with local authorities to minimise the risk of market failure (perhaps through accessing preferred provider status as part of an outcome-focused contract). Local authorities and other commissioning bodies are required to manage the risks of market failure, putting in place contingency funding where appropriate. One local authority chief executive observed: "In adult social care – most providers are third sector. A lot are going out of business. They've got large residential properties and they've seen the value of those fall. These are immature, fragile markets."

Commissioning organisations will also need to clarify how far they can (or should) divest themselves of legal liability for the spending choices of people with personal budgets – for example, if there are legal disputes between direct payment-holders and personal assistants, or if people choose to purchase inappropriate support services. An Association of Directors of Adult Social Services (ADASS) publication *Personalisation and the Law* (2009, p 13) – stated, 'the taking of a Direct Payment suspends the authority's duty of care in relation to provision, but not in relation to ongoing care management'. However, this distinction may not provide clear guidance to support planners and care managers advising people on what they can purchase.

There are also issues relating to financial risk, and the loss of control by local authority and national auditors over the use of public money. When direct payments were first introduced, local auditing tended to be heavy-handed, which was encouraged by extensive guidance from the Chartered Institute of Public Finance and Accountancy (CIPFA, 1998). Since then, CIPFA has shifted to recommending a more light-touch approach, and local auditors are less likely to demand that budget-holders produce every receipt for inspection (CIPFA, 2007). The Audit Commission, however, expressed concerns that personal budgets will make it easier for service users or their representatives to commit fraud. It has called for social workers to be given appropriate fraud awareness training, recognising that there is often little communication between counter-fraud teams and front-line social workers (2010a). A number of interviewees reported that it was only a matter of time before a high-profile media story emerged linked to the misuse of personal budgets, and that a robust response would be required to ensure that the broader personalisation agenda was not derailed. As one consultant noted: "There are reputational risks for local authorities when people want to spend their money in creative ways." According to a civil servant working in mental health:

"A number of cases were being cited that were quite recent where you can imagine a horror story in the press, but actually when you did the sums, the course that had been chosen was significantly cheaper to the public purse, and crucially more effective for the individual."

Safeguarding more generally is a key concern within care services, particularly following high-profile failings in child protection cases. The impact that personalisation will have on it remains uncertain. A report of the consultation on the 'No Secrets' guidance for safeguarding adults noted that safeguarding must be built on the principle of empowering the service user (DH, 2009c). However, it also noted that the relationship between safeguarding and personalisation was not yet clear (DH, 2009c, p 5).

Interviewees differed in how far they saw personalised commissioning as increasing or decreasing the likelihood of abuse. One social entrepreneur commented, "actually the starting point is does the current system keep people safe? No, it doesn't, it's screwed up people's lives in the past with all kinds of things. So no, we're not starting from a good place anyway." A director of adult social care observed: "You've got to strike the balance between keeping people safe versus giving them a better life.... We need to make sure managers know what a safe but personalised service will look like."

A number of reports have sought to identify how risk identification can be improved and managed in a context of self-directed support (Carr, 2010c; IDeA, 2010). Creating a culture in which social workers and other front-line staff feel they can take a positive view of risk will require engagement with the blame culture that has surrounded recent media controversies over social work interventions. It will also require greater engagement with service users about what constitutes an acceptable degree of risk. Mitchell and Glendinning's (2007) review of attitudes to risk in adult social care found that service users themselves are rarely asked about their own perceptions of risk.

Mainstreaming personalisation

All of the challenges discussed so far will become more pronounced as personalisation moves into the mainstream of social care, and expands beyond social care into a range of other services. To date it has tended to be an agenda pursued by a relatively small number of 'early adopters'. A Demos report published in October 2009 predicted a 'chaotic transition to personal budgets', noting that more than 20% of care users were as yet unaware of the move towards personalisation (Bartlett, 2009). This creates a number of challenges in evaluating personal budgets to date and in considering their likely future:

> What is known is based on the small number of people who hold personal budgets and have been evaluated, which is just a few hundred. It is not clear how representative they are of the 1.5 million people who will eventually move onto personal budgets; in truth, probably quite unrepresentative because many of them were the vanguard – selected to try personal budgets because they were unhappy with their existing services. This means there is a 'representation bias'. As a result, many of the sample group benefitted from strong personal networks of support, or considerable assistance and guidance from the local authority, combined with a strong urge to change. It is therefore probable that the changes in spending patterns by those with personal budgets outlined above are more dramatic than the norm. (Bartlett, 2009, p 14)

A number of local authorities described their current approach as running two systems in parallel – flexible services for people with personal budgets and traditional services such as day centres for people in receipt of conventional funding. There are clearly question marks over how far dual systems will remain affordable at a time of severe budgetary constraint. The DH expects this dual financing to be phased out as personal budget-holders become a majority of users (DH, 2009b). Indeed, Martin Routledge, National Programme Manager for Putting People First within the DH, explains that the National Indicator of 30% of eligible people on personal budgets by 2011 was expressly designed to move away from this: 'When you have got 3 or 4 people on direct payments you can run two systems. We want to ensure self direct support is the main system' (Routledge, 2010). The OPM has noted the importance of 'tipping points' where sufficient levels of participation in new schemes lead to new patterns of contracting and disinvestment (OPM, 2008, p 38). However, the transitional phase may be a long one. Interviewees reported that three- or four-year block contracts remain common, limiting the scope for personalisation to be anything other than a fringe activity. As one observed:

> "Lots of local authorities have used the Transforming Social Care Grant to set up a personalisation team, and

then the rest of the local authority and the rest of the adult social care department leave it to that team to bring about personalisation."

A local authority chief executive reflected on the slow progress of change, highlighting the difficulties posed by decommissioning some existing services, delivered on the basis of block or spot contracts: "Why is the agenda going so slow? It's redundancy costs, it's fear, organisational inertia, not wanting to close down the day centre, or other service. We need to actively manage decommissioning at the same time as giving out budgets." A local authority social care manager said:

"Personalisation doesn't yet link to decommissioning of services because there isn't yet anything to replace it. We would have thought we'd have a major closure programme for day centres but we aren't because we haven't got a viable alternative offer. Plus people quite like day centres. Some people have been going for 40–50 years; the day centre is a community in itself."

Some interviewees felt that day centres would continue to be part of local authority provision for years to come, in part because older generations tend to be dependent on them. However, others felt that they should not continue to be subsidised if they did not provide a service that people wanted to buy, noting that day centres are much more heavily subsidised than other forms of provision such as home care. One director of adult social care was bullish about their future: "We need to demolish the old buildings, cash in their value, and build state-of-the-art facilities for those people who really need them." In Liverpool, for example, nine day centres are being closed, and replaced by a combination of round-the-clock care facilities and community hubs. According to the journal *Community Care*, 'The council said growing numbers of personal budget holders in Liverpool had led to a huge drop in the demand for in-house services such as day centres, some of which are half-empty' (Dunning, 2010b). The issue of day centre closure raises concerns about the balance between individual and collective provision, a theme discussed in Chapter 7.

Some interviewees expressed concern that the transformatory spirit of personalisation will be lost as it becomes routine and mainstream. The initial creativity and support that has been possible looks hard to support on a mainstream basis, given front-line caseloads. As one local authority support planner observed:

"It is taking a long-time to do a support plan, about 25 to 40 hours per person. That includes going out to get quotes for the services they want and bringing back various options. At the moment that time is agreed by the chief executives, but it can't be funded going forward. I can do 3 or 4 at a time, that is realistic. But that won't continue. Social workers have caseloads of 50–60 older people. They haven't got time to do a support plan."

Such concerns were echoed in a recent report from the OPM that placed emphasis on 'the amount of face-to-face time frontline workers will need to spend with service users to encourage creativity in developing support plans that are designed to have a positive impact on their lives' (OPM, 2010, p 9). Bartlett cites research from Davey et al (2007) showing 'that the support services infrastructure does not currently have the capacity to deal with the number of people who use direct payments currently, let alone the prospective number of personal budget holders' (2009, p 29). However, without effective support planning there are fears that inequities between service users will widen, or that people will continue to commission the same services as before, and the potentially emancipatory spirit of personalisation will be lost (Carr and Robbins, 2009).

Running alongside the risks that personalisation will transform and overload public services, a number of interviewees perceived a different kind of risk: "In the first year [of having a personal budget] most people buy the same thing as before. The biggest risk in all this is that nothing will really change" (local authority social care manager). According to Clive Miller, of the OPM, 'There is a danger that this becomes about how to do personalisation and make sure nothing changes' (Miller, 2010). Glasby and Littlechild raise a similar concern:

As personal budgets have become something of a hot topic, the biggest danger is that they get hijacked by people who do not understand them or who have other motives, allowing the old system to pay lip-service to the concept while essentially recreating itself. (2009, p 86)

Such concerns reflect a point that Nutley et al (2007, pp 182–3) make about policy innovation more generally: 'when the level of [local] reinvention is quite high it can mean that the status quo engulfs the innovation such that the service changes very little and the innovation changes substantially'.

One representative from a financial auditing body reflected on his uncertainty about the future:

> "There is a variety of feeling on how far this will take off. When direct payments came in people said it would revolutionise and change everything. But the volume is not there – although it did make a significant difference to those who took it."

The shadows of the care management reforms of the early 1990s, which were designed to devolve more power to front-line staff and service users, but failed to do so, loom large. As one interviewee put it: "Prescription is starting to emerge [in relation to personalisation] – as it did with care management."

As the numbers of people on personal budgets rise year-on-year, there is concern that care plans are simply being renamed support plans without the transfer of choice and control to the service user that self-directed support envisages. As one director of adult social care said:

> "The question is, is it just a piece of paper saying you have got £100 but nothing has really changed?... The danger is that we will all rush to get the numbers right, but we might have done it in a way that isn't real."

A support planner said, "What will happen is care plans will be converted to support plans – just changing the title." According to another social care director:

> "We've got 4,200 people with personal budgets. The key question is: what does that mean? Most of them are not taking the cash, just cash-quantified services. The rationale for not taking the cash for most people is twofold: first, managing money and employment issues and second what's the market offer?"

Jeff Jerome, speaking at an In Control conference, was clear that:

> We are a bit anxious that people getting managed personal budgets are being told the value of their budget, but not much else is happening.... We want people to focus on the values rather than the national indicator.... The most

important thing is getting the personalised service. (Jerome, 2010)

Rather than a radical shift, one local government interviewee predicted that people would make adjustments at the margins: "Change will be around the edges for people. They don't want to risk change in their crucial service, like their home care." But she went on: "Even if the money is going to the same providers, we want more dialogue between them and service users about what service users want, more flexibility of provision." Another said: "People may only want to tweak services around the edges, but actually those changes may be crucial."

Conclusion

This chapter has examined the practice context of personalisation, and explored the ambiguities facing managers, front-line staff and service users as they 'translate' a policy narrative promoted by national government. It has highlighted the gaps and uncertainties of the agenda, and the extent to which it remains relatively underdeveloped. Uncertainties around financing in particular remain a concern, with staff lacking information about the 'nuts and bolts' of what people can spend their money on and with severe cuts limiting the amount of money that can be allocated to users.

Identifying a gap between the clean certainties of national policy rhetoric and the messiness of local practice is of course a mainstay of implementation literature. Front-line provision will always be a process of interpretation, of filling in gaps and resolving or finessing uncertainties. As Newman and Clarke (2009b, p 78) put it, 'those involved in public work, translating multiple theories and conflicting policy prescriptions in specific sites, or doing the work of maintaining fragile assemblages, find themselves constantly faced with contradictions, dilemmas and paradoxes'. However, personalisation is not merely another challenge to be interpreted by the front line. It redefines the front line itself, as a place where services are not only delivered, but also brokered, commissioned and managed. The experience of staff as they make sense of what this means for their roles and manage the attendant uncertainties is explored further in Chapter 8. Chapter 7 considers the repositioning of the service user, asking 'Who is the person?' in the personalisation narrative.

Who is the person?

A central tenet of the personalisation story is that there is a self-evident legitimacy in focusing attention on the person and being responsive to their self-defined wants and needs. As one interviewee put it: "The nature of personalisation is only the person can decide whether the service is personalised." Such a claim is consistent with broader and well-established principles of liberal citizenship, and resonates with powerful strands of thinking from the New Left and the New Right. It is wholly congruent with the consumer-oriented reform programmes espoused by all governments in the UK since 1979. To argue that the person using services should not have an influential voice in shaping service provision is to defend paternalist, elitist or collectivist positions that are untenable in the political mainstream.

It is immediately obvious, however, that even in a personalised health and welfare system there will be examples of cases where user demand has to be circumscribed. Information asymmetries, rationing decisions, public safety and concerns for user well-being are all used regularly to justify situations where users' 'felt needs' are overridden. What has shifted since the post-1945 welfare settlement is the burden of proof, with the default position now being that a person is the best judge of their own interests unless there is a compelling case to the contrary. This principle undergirds the personalisation agenda, and is its guide to action.

There have been two broad ways in which this principle has been problematised, however, and these are the focus of this and the next chapter. The first critique is that personalisation has the potential to erode the collective principles of the welfare state, promoting atomised consumerism and facilitating privatisation. The second is that personalisation is simply a new route to deprofessionalise front-line staff, valorising the service user in order to fulfil the managerialist project begun by Thatcher. Clearly these critiques are related. They are part of a broader centre-left critique of welfare reforms since 1979, and link to wider efforts to protect the post-war welfare settlement. They have formed part of opposition to social care reform since the 1980s, focusing attention in turn on community care, care management and direct payments (Glasby and Littlechild, 2006, 2009). With such critiques now directed at the broader personalisation agenda, disability campaigners have expressed exasperation. According to one frustrated campaigner, responding to such criticisms at a policy event on personalisation in mid-2010: "How long will the debate go on for? It's been going on since direct payments were first talked about. We need to resolve issues through getting on with it." This echoes the sentiments of another prominent campaigner, expressed during an earlier debate on direct payments, 'all reasonable arguments against it have been demolished ... it would be a foolish waste of time to repeat that process' (Campbell, 1997, p 23, cited in Spandler, 2004, p 194).

However, the critiques have endured and continue to offer a counterpoint to the personalisation narrative. This and the next chapter examine how some of these critiques have been framed and how advocates of personalisation have responded to them. The focus of this chapter is the apparent dichotomy between the personal/individual/consumer and the social/collective/citizenship. The next chapter focuses on staff–user relationships, and the ways in which person-centredness problematises professionals and front-line interactions.

The debate

Chapter 4 set out the key strands of the personalisation narrative. These included an emphasis on the user as an 'expert on their own lives' (Poll, 2007) and an assumption that people would spend money better on their own behalf than the state would do so for them. It is easy to see how such claims have been provocative for people who celebrate a collective and social account of the welfare state. The claims echo arguments made by exemplars of anti-welfarism, from Frederick von Hayek (1944) to Keith Joseph (1975), about the injustice and inefficiency of taking resources away from the individual and giving them to the state. Calls for personalisation to be the basis of a welfare state in which all funding is given to the individual as a personal budget – or conditional resource entitlement (Duffy et al, 2010) – echo the arguments for voucher-based systems advocated by Joseph and others in the late 1970s. A state that does no more than assess people's eligibility and give them cash to purchase services from the private and third sectors appears to constitute the apogee of right-wing thinking.

The result, argue critics, is likely to be a stratified welfare state in which individualised and isolated consumers push their maximal demands, bearing the risks of their own choices, with no concept of or concern for shared welfare. Inequalities will widen as better-off and more knowledgeable users play the system, private companies cherry-pick the most desirable clients, and there is no collective voice to argue for a fairer distribution of resources. Variants of these arguments have been made by Spandler (2004), Ferguson (2007), Scourfield (2007), Barnes (2008), Beresford (2008), Land and Himmelweit (2010) and others. Many of these authors do not argue for a wholesale rejection of personalisation, and it is important not to caricature their positions. Anxieties about the practical and financial implications of personalisation have been expressed by authors who do not necessarily challenge its underlying principles. However, these authors have raised concerns about elements of the personalisation agenda, and contested or problematised some or all of the personalisation storylines presented in Chapter 4. Barnes sums up her 'unease' with the agenda as follows: 'personalisation within social care ignores the "social"', misunderstands the political challenge to state welfare coming from service users, and assumes a rational actor concept of the individual that is incapable of responding to the complexities of needs' (2008, p 153).

As claims and counterclaims about the likely impacts of personalisation have flown about, some academics have attempted to find a stable evidence base from which to evaluate them (see, for example, Glasby and Littlechild, 2009). However, what is quickly apparent from a reading of various personalisation texts is that the rival positionings rest on irreconcilable understandings of welfare pasts and futures, deploy different framings of equity, citizenship and agency, and utilise different reservoirs of service user testimonies. Recognising the incommensurability of the arguments for and against personalisation is not to take refuge in claims that all values and viewpoints are equally valid, nor to deny that evidence-gathering plays a key role in understanding better the likely impact of personalisation. Rather, it is an attempt to make explicit some of the often implicit points of tension within the rival viewpoints, and to explain why the debates appear to have moved on little since the early days of direct payments.

The chapter begins by looking at how equity, citizenship and agency are framed by what are here termed the advocates and critics of personalisation. Such a Manichaean distinction does not of course do justice to the complexity and nuance with which people have set out their interpretations of personalisation, but it does make it possible to extract the key themes that resonate within what Pal called 'contending interpretive communities' (1995, p 202, cited in Yanow, 2000, p 21). The chapter goes on to examine the debate over the closure of day centres as an exemplar of the tensions between the two positions. It then discusses how some of these tensions are playing out in practice, examining how far person–centredness is proving an adequate principle for those charged with implementing personalised approaches.

Equity

As discussed in earlier chapters, a key theme of the personalisation agenda is to emphasise its timelessness while also demanding a clear break with much of the recent past. Chapter 5 set out the diverse coalition of interests that came together to promote direct payments. What these somewhat unlikely bedfellows shared was a rejection of the welfare past, albeit for different reasons (Glasby and Littlechild, 2009, p 135). Thus, in the face of claims that personalisation will increase inequality between users – empowering the most articulate at the expense of others and creating a two-tier system (Leece and Leece, 2006, p 1380) – personalisation advocates have responded by rebutting the claims to equity of the post-war welfare state (Glasby and Littlechild, 2009, p 153). Vast disparities between the funding levels received by people with similar assessed needs are highlighted by Duffy (2008) and Keohane (2009) to demonstrate the inequities of the existing system. There is an assumption that, in the future, increased transparency of financial allocations as a result of personalisation will expose these inequalities, helping to ensure that 'people with equal needs start to receive equal resources' (Glasby and Littlechild, 2009, p 154). There is also an assumption that better tailoring of services itself will be a route to greater equality and fairness. According to Darzi's final report on improving quality in the health service, 'Providing personalized care should also help us to reduce health inequalities, as the households with the lowest incomes are most likely to contain a member with a long-term condition' (Darzi, 2008, p 28). There is here a denial of the potential for conflict between personalising services around the individual and ensuring equity between users. Whereas New Labour's early health White Papers emphasised the need to balance the 'personal' with the needs for national fairness and consistency (DH, 1997, 1999), personalisation was later reframed as a tool to deepen solidarity and equity within the NHS.

However, a broader issue of equality – the extent to which people are receiving enough money in a personal budget to meet their needs – gets less attention, as it is assigned to broader distributive questions that fall outside the ambit of personalisation. It is those sorts of arguments that have been the focus of some critiques of personalisation. As Barnes puts it:

> [A]ny strategy that claims 'empowerment' as an objective
> requires an understanding of the processes and circumstances
> that give rise to disempowerment. People's experiences of

the way in which public services are delivered is one factor in this, but not the only one. Claiming transformational effects from a strategy that focuses solely on this aspect of people's lives simply will not do. (2008, p 156)

Reflecting on similar concerns, Spandler argues that it is in collective manifestations and settings that battles for empowerment will need to be fought, quoting O'Brien: 'it is not as consumers but as political organizers, lobbyists, participants in civil disobedience, defendants ... that people with disabilities and their families influence the level of money available in the current system' (2001, p 6, cited in Spandler, 2004, p 204). Barnes argues that political change requires a view of social action that expands beyond 'making it personal' (the title of a Leadbeater et al [2008] publication on personalisation):

> [W]ithout collective action neither the political analysis nor the interpersonal support necessary for such transformations would have been achieved.... [T]hose who became involved in an increasingly diverse range of activities associated with user movements understood very well that it is not just about 'making it personal', that feeling in control, securing both the services and the support that is necessary to deal with chronic illness, impairment, increasing age and frailty, poverty and other experiences common to users of social care services, is intensely *social*. (Barnes, 2008, p 154, emphasis in original)

A further point of tension between advocates and critics of personalisation is focused on the pooling of risk and resources between individuals. Risk-pooling and cross-subsidy as tools of equalisation, through which monies can be shared in a flexible (albeit largely invisible) way between individuals, tend to be discredited in the personalisation story and associated with a lack of transparency in the post-war welfare state. The more transparent cash allocation of a personal budget may limit opportunities for risk-pooling and cross-subsidisation. The potential tension was expressed by one local authority social care manager in an interview with the author:

> "The [DH] letter this week on managed budgets says that even if people don't take the money as a budget we have to send them a statement at the end of each year saying what we've spent it on, and what we're doing with the

money we haven't spent. But won't we have spent that on someone else?"

Issues relating to risk-pooling and cross-subsidy are likely to become more contentious as part of proposals to integrate health and social care monies into a combined budget (HM Government, 2010a). It was a perceived clash between universal health funding and means-tested social care that was given as the reason for the rejection of personal budgets in the NHS in a 2006 White Paper:

> We do not propose to [extend individual budgets into the NHS], since we believe this would compromise the founding principle of the NHS that care should be free at the point of need. Social care operates on a different basis and has always included means testing and the principles of self and co-payment for services. (DH, 2006, p 85)

However, the Darzi reviews of the health service, published in 2007 and 2008, revived the idea of individual budgets within the NHS. The *Personal Health Budgets* document is explicit that, as a result of the reforms, 'opportunities for risk pooling are reduced' (DH, 2009a, p 33). However, there is little discussion of what the implications of such a reduction might be.

Proposals for integrated budgets are also likely to revive debates over topping up in the NHS, with implications for equity (Richards, 2008; Unison, 2009). As one interviewee noted, "People are not allowed to top up in the NHS. But [with personal health budgets] how do you police that, draw the line, if people just want to pay for a bit more physio?" Hartley has warned that personalisation 'may be about a residualised model in which the state provides the basics and everything else is co-produced and co-funded as personalised "add-ons"' (2007, p 638).

Citizenship

A second set of rival framings circulate around citizenship, and its relationship with consumerism. Some of the strongest advocates of personalisation have positioned its appeal explicitly in terms of a fuller vision of citizenship and a new state–citizen contract (Duffy, 2005; Morris, 2005; Tyson, 2007). Within the personalisation narrative, citizens are promised a more tailored interaction with the state, fostering self-determination, responsive to their diverse needs and alert to real outcomes rather than abstract rights or nebulous targets. According to one interviewee:

> "we would say it's more about a citizenship model. The shift was the participation. So it's no longer, you don't just buy a service. It's not just about having the ability to purchase, it's about having the ability to shape what you are purchasing."

However, critics of personalisation have noted its problematic engagement with citizenship. Prior and Barnes discuss the ambiguity of the status of the citizen and his/her location in the public sphere. They note:

> [M]any public service users, who may be discursively constructed by policies as citizens with public rights and responsibilities are primarily concerned with 'private' matters – their own health and social care requirements, the well-being of their children and other family members, their relationships with their neighbours. (2009, p 194)

Thus, traditional understandings of the citizen as a public figure may not accurately capture the experience of being a user of welfare services. Hyphenated identities such as the 'citizen-consumer' (Needham, 2003; Clarke et al, 2007) may be more appropriate, emphasising the distinctive experience of using public services. However, both citizen and consumer are unstable categories making it difficult to specify exactly what is implied by their hyphenation (Clarke, 2010).

Critics of personalisation have tended to see consumerism as diminishing citizenship, replacing the social rights of citizenship (Marshall, 1992 [1950]) with the logic of market choice. Hartley, writing about education, offers one account of the perceived linkage between personalisation and consumerism:

> Personalisation is strongly associated with the notion of 'choice': that is to say, of choosing that which is thought to accomplish personhood. There is an affinity, therefore, between consumerism and personalisation.... In its 'market appeal', personalisation – despite its current incoherence and vagueness of definition ... – runs with the grain of identity-seeking individuals who are continually on the make(over). (2007, pp 630, 639)

This critique is linked to a perceived recommodification of citizenship, in which personalised public services are increasingly allocated through cash transfers to self-regarding individuals (Ungerson, 1997; Spandler, 2004; Rummery, 2006). Such a process is seen as intensifying the privatisation and marketisation of care services, as 'privatisation by the back door' (Hasler et al, 1999, p 7; Land and Himmelweit, 2010). Service users are required to act as consumers of market services, and to bear the attendant risks. As Beresford (2008, p 12) puts it, 'service users – no longer protected by access to the traditional range of regulated services – will be exposed to financial and personal risk, because of an enforced reliance on unregulated workers and services'.

Such a commodification of care services is seen to diminish the moral and social aspects of caring, replacing a 'relational logic of care' with a 'logic of choice' (Mol, 2008). According to Barnes:

> [T]here are also relational and moral dimensions to [people's] everyday needs for support. A model of service delivery that focuses only on the personal dimension, that works with a concept of care as a commodity that can be planned for, bought and controlled is inadequate in the face of the messy moral dilemmas, and the need to be able to construct and re-construct lives and relationships in the context of pain, hurt and unpredictability. (2008, p 158)

Turning care into a commodity that can be traded and purchased by consumers is thus seen as ignoring something fundamental about what it means to care, distorting the ethical context in which care ought to be located (Williams, 2001). There are a broader set of debates here about the ways in which informal care – usually women's work – is valued and who ought to be paid for caring (Ungerson, 1999).

The notion that personalisation is a route to an atomising consumerism or commodification has been strongly resisted by advocates of personalisation, who argue instead that it provides scope for new forms of citizenship (Leadbeater, 2004; Keohane, 2009). The emphasis is on the achievement of inclusion within the broader community – something that disabled people historically lacked. According to Tyson:

> The model is premised on active citizens living and working in their communities. To make a reality of this, older and disabled people will not have their own territory in day centres and care homes, but will instead engage with their

fellow citizens in the workplace, the pub, the college, the
gym and at the community centre. (2007, p 17)

A key element of personalisation has been helping people to develop
networks of support that are based on friendship and reciprocity,
rather than contract. A strong role is ascribed to families – marking a
shift from assumptions that people need independent professionals to
protect them from families to an assumption that 'family and friends
can be the most important allies for disabled people and make a positive
contribution to their lives' (Duffy, 2005, p 10).

Although there is a denial that personalisation is consumerising,
there are clearly aspects of being a consumer that do belong within
this inclusion agenda. Personalised approaches invoke the freedom of
disabled people to be consumers in the same way that other people
are: spending their money on the same things, using the same services
in the same spaces, rather than relying on segregated and distinctive
provision. Here, being a full citizen includes having the freedom to
consume services and participate in public spaces (cafes as well as day
centres, shops as well as libraries) on the same terms as other people.

In response to claims that personalisation has diminished citizenship
through fostering the privatisation and marketisation of services,
advocates have offered a twofold rebuttal. The first (as in relation to
equity) is to dispute the adequacy of existing state-based care services.
In place of poor-quality segregated state services there has been a
celebration of new forms of provision, particularly those provided by
user-led organisations. Supported by such organisations, people are
seen as more likely to access what they actually need, which might not
actually be a formal care service at all, but rather access to 'mainstream'
leisure and creative activities.

The second response to claims of 'privatisation by the back door'
has been to locate personalisation within broader inevitabilities around
welfare state restructuring, which takes as a given a mixed market
of providers. Du Gay argues that such an approach is typical of an
'epochalist narrative' in which changes 'appear the inevitable outcome
of abstract, nonlocatable impulses and imperatives (the information
and communication revolution, the changing consumer, globalization)
rather than the result of specific (and traceable) political choices' (Du
Gay, 2003, p 670). Du Gay cites the work of Rose (1999, p 467), noting
that personalisation slots into 'a widespread scepticism concerning the
powers of "political government" to know, plan, calculate and steer
from the centre. The state is no longer to be required to answer all
of society's needs for health, security, order or productivity' (Du Gay,

2003, p 675). Personalisation advocates, in this account, can therefore be understood to be working with these new realities, rather than trying to turn the clock back to a non-existent 'golden age' of in-house care.

The relationship between personalisation, citizenship and consumerism is therefore a contested one, due to the instability of the terms and different perceptions of welfare pasts and futures. Both citizenship and consumerism can take individualistic forms, but both too have collective, politicised and solidaristic forms that speak to communities of interest beyond the individual service user. Critics of personalisation have located it in a particular rendering of individualised and risk-taking consumerism, whereas its advocates position personalisation as an approach that enhances inclusion for people as citizens and consumers.

Reflecting on such tensions in relation to direct payments, Spandler notes the problems of trying to suggest that such payments are either a route to democratic citizenship or consumerism:

> it seems clear that neither a simplistic pursuit of direct payments as empowerment, nor a kneejerk reaction against them as merely cost-cutting consumerism is an adequate response. Direct payments are not clearly a 'consumerist' or a 'democratic' approach to social policy, but actually an example of a convergence of the two, a convergence that yields both problems and possibilities. (2004, p 202)

Agency

A related point of tension between advocates and critics of personalisation relates to the scope for users to exercise agency, be it as citizens or consumers. Here, there has been a tension between those who emphasise the capacities of people with disabilities, often hampered by a paternalistic state, and those who emphasise the vulnerability of disabled people, at risk of exploitation and abuse (Glasby and Littlechild, 2009, pp 161–4). A number of interviewees noted that personal budgets raised the potential for disabled people to be treated more like other benefit recipients, eroding the post-war division between social care and social security. As one director of adult social care put it: "We aren't bothered what people spend their unemployment or social security on. When people raise concerns about disabled people misusing funds I just see it as an example of prejudice." However, another director felt that unconditional payments would diminish "the professional raison d'être" and that their implementation "just isn't affordable. We're focusing on what's realistic and being honest with people."

Underpinning the debate between empowerment and vulnerability is uncertainty about how far it is appropriate to reconstitute service users as risk-bearing individuals, willing to take on more responsibility for improved outcomes in return for greater choice and control. The ACEVO report on personalisation stated, 'We recommend ... a new right of control should set out a new conditionality, matching devolution of power with greater clarity over individuals' responsibilities' (2009, p 6). It talked of the need for a 'can do' approach involving 'self-direction' and 'self-control', although without any suggestion that those two imperatives might be in tension. One interviewee from In Control similarly talked about personalisation requiring people to become more active in meeting their own needs:

> "It's also about moving from this dependency model to this participatory partnership model that the world will not come and give you everything. You have got to look.... Putting some effort in gives you far better appreciation of something I think, than it being given to you on a plate."

The idea of giving people the freedom to experiment and learn through practice, links to Bang's (2005) idea of service users as 'everyday makers'.

This framing of the active user has provoked concern from critics, alarmed that all care users must cleave to a particular model of the responsibilised user (Barnes and Prior, 2000; Scourfield, 2007; Barnes, 2008). Barnes has observed:

> It implies a high level of self knowledge and reflexivity; substantial predictability in relation to needs and the circumstances in which they may be met, and a willingness to take on the responsibility for constantly reviewing whether the support and help being given is enabling the achievement of objectives. (2008, pp 156–7)

She notes too that people are required 'to share responsibility for the risk that services will not, in fact, deliver what was anticipated' (Barnes, 2008, p 157). Mahony et al (2010, p 6) make a related point:

> If publics are spoken of and spoken for in a range of personalised grammars and registers, then this challenges the rational/irrational distinction which marks the separation

of public and personal. It implies that public life might be becoming reconfigured around the image of the expressive subject capable of knowing their own interests and being able to effectively articulate them too.

This account sees personalisation as an attempt to impose on health and care service users the same kinds of responsibilisation programmes that have been used in other sectors of the welfare state (Clarke, 2005; Scourfield, 2007; Barnes and Prior, 2009). Ferguson positions personalisation squarely within New Labour's broader neo-liberal agenda of enforced control: 'the notion that the state should play a reduced role in the provision of services and that individuals should take on greater responsibility for their own lives' (2007, p 394). According to Scourfield:

> Direct payments fit comfortably with the project to transform the culture of the public, private and informal care sectors around principles of innovation, risk taking and enterprise. The disability movement's rights discourse, built around notions of empowerment, self-determination and societal change, has been successfully conflated with the New Labour vision to build an enterprise society. (2007, pp 113–14)

Linking to the discussion about citizenship earlier, he goes on:

> This transformation is not simply about the reconstruction of citizens as consumers but the transformation of citizens into both managers and entrepreneurs. New Labour's perspective on citizenship appears to focus less on what the citizen can expect from the state in terms of social rights, and more on how the citizen *should be* – in this case, active, responsible and enterprising. (Scourfield, 2007, p 112, emphasis in original)

This view of the responsible and enterprising citizen appears to be shared by the Conservative–Liberal Democrat Coalition government, with citizens freed to 'run their own lives', but expected to take greater responsibility for their own well-being (Cameron, 2007; Lansley, 2008).

There are obvious links here to the broader governmentality critique, in which individual citizens are seen as becoming self-regulating actors, subject to subtle techniques of discipline and control (Rose, 1996, 1999;

Dean, 1999; Miller and Rose, 2008). As Du Gay (2003, p 675) notes, 'Embedded in these contemporary programmes and strategies for the reformulation of social governance is a particular ethic of personhood – a view of what persons are and what they should be allowed to be', requiring 'autonomy, responsibility and the freedom/obligation of individuals actively to make choices for themselves'. This presumption of independence has provoked concerns from critics of personalisation (Scourfield, 2007, p 120; Barnes, 2008; Land and Himmelweit, 2010, p 24). As Scourfield puts it:

> Choice and independence are powerful concepts but there is more to 'self-determination' and, indeed, 'self-actualization' than simply 'going it alone'. Dependency and interdependency are part of all of our lives, for some more than others. This needs to be acknowledged or there is a real danger that only those who are enterprising and can manage their own affairs will have earned the badge of citizenship. (2007, p 120)

Stuart has argued that concepts such as 'dependence' and 'independence' have particularly cultural resonances and may not be welcomed by black and minority ethnic service users, perceiving 'independent living' as 'a Eurocentric interpretation of independence, where disabled people make decisions independently of carers and family' (2006, pp 5–6).

Tension around how far people are, and ought to be, required to accept a certain type of personhood in order to mesh with the personalisation agenda are likely to become more pronounced as personalisation moves from social care into other sectors. The norm of personalisation established within social care is for a high level of user empowerment with little need for professional oversight to ensure that users act responsibly. It is anticipated that users will have an incentive to use resources more frugally and effectively than the state does on their behalf (Glasby and Littlechild, 2009, p 125). However, there are various sectors in which users are generally perceived to require sanctions to get them to behave appropriately, particularly in relation to labour market entry – with a refusal to integrate into low-wage labour markets characterised as a form of 'subversive citizenship' (Flint, 2009, p 97). This raises the question of how people will make sense of their relationship to the state if placed in control of a personal budget and exhorted to strive for self-actualisation, while at the same time being subject to strictures to enter the labour market on whatever basic terms it is possible to get a job. This is a broader tension that runs through the Right to Control pilots, integrating resources from a range of funds, including Work Choices and Access to Work, aimed at facilitating entry to the workforce for disabled people (DWP, 2008). In relation to Right to Control, when asked why people would choose to spend their personal budget on getting back to work, a Department for Work and Pensions (DWP) civil servant acknowledged the potential for problems: "That is very difficult, challenging. You've got demand-led versus conditionality-led issues, it's about striking a balance."

As a result of these different framings of equity, citizenship and agency, advocates and critics of personalisation tell different stories about social care pasts and futures. One of the recurrent stories relates to the value of collectively funded services such as day centres. It is to those that the chapter now turns, seeing them as emblematic of the tensions within the personalisation agenda.

Day centres

Day centres for older and disabled people are a recurring focus for disagreements between advocates and critics of personalisation. In many localities there is a long-standing process of closing accommodation-based services, which is now being rebadged as a route to personalisation. The dominant storyline in personalisation is that day centres are part of the 'one-size-fits-all' provision offered by a welfare state that is insufficiently person-centred (Leadbeater, 2004; Duffy, 2010). Cottam writes of:

> day-care centres, to which individuals very often have to be bussed, at high cost. Whilst time spent in these largely desolate places might be important relief for carers, those who visit them are unlikely to make any bonds with people who might be able to help them outside the centre, or to strike up more regular friendships, given the distance that day-centres are from people's homes. (2009, p 83)

Despite such framings, day centres are symbolic and actual resources to which service users often cling tenaciously. Yanow highlights the symbolic importance of buildings within policy narratives, seeing them as 'significant carriers of meaning' (2000, p 20). As she puts it, 'one of the roles of the interpretive policy analyst is identifying and learning the meanings of policy-relevant symbolic artifacts [such as buildings] in the "language" of each community' (Yanow, 2000, p 91). In relation to day centres, there is clearly a set of highly diverse meanings, rather than one agreed set of interpretations. There is great difference of opinion on the extent to which the centres themselves are a valued service, which ought to be protected. Extracts from the interviews highlight the different perspectives that people have on their usefulness:

> "People do not flock in their thousands to day services. They do use, when they have the resource, that money to do quite different things."

> "I used to work in day centres.... They aren't great. People are together, but are they engaged, are they progressing?"

> "People are used to having things structured for them. You can see the day centre as a comfortable prison."

> "Some people with direct payments are going to a nice hotel for respite and care, which is cheaper for us, going to Centre Parcs or whatever. People's needs are met in a much more uplifting and creative way – not just going to a grotty place to play bingo."

> "Closing those centres and taking people bowling, swimming and to the local supermarket cafe may be impoverishing life if people are no longer spending time with friends they have made over 30 years."

> "when people are feeling decidedly crap ... sometimes all you need to be able to do is to go to somewhere safe in terms of you know you're accepted ... nobody is going to hassle you ... you can sit and have a cup of tea and a fag and there are people who are around for you.... Rather than being in your own flat on your own ... we need those places. Society isn't welcoming at all to people with mental health [problems] ... it's not like you can pop down your local cafe or McDonalds and hang out ... you need to be amongst your peers."

There is therefore great diversity of opinion about the extent to which these shared spaces are to be valued or rejected. Concerns were expressed by some interviewees that campaigns against the closure of day centres were being led by the service providers (often voluntary-sector bodies), fearful of losing their block grants, rather than by users themselves. Alternatively, there was a sense that the centres were being defended by existing users who lacked the vision to see the creative alternatives opened up by personalisation. A number of interviewees made the point that the arguments being used to protect day centres had strong echoes of those used in favour of keeping disabled people in large residential institutions: "you see they were the same arguments we used about not closing long-stay hospitals. I think it's a morally bankrupt argument really. It's cowardly."

Rather than seeing arguments in favour of day centres as an expression of conservatism or cowardice, however, others have identified the centres as valued spaces in which communities are located (Barnes, 2008). As one service user resisting a day centre closure said, 'They say they want to treat us as individuals but we want to go to the day centre for the interaction and camaraderie' (Morgan, 2010). What appears to be important here is not only the physical and public space in which people can collect, but also the scope for shared thinking and action that is permitted within that space. This may relate to the practical questions of how to pool budgets and purchase shared services. It may also be a place in which more radical challenges to service provision can be explored and planned.

The extent to which day centres continue to enjoy support from users themselves is a crucial issue, but one on which it is impossible to generalise. Data from a Demos study into how people wanted to spend their personal budgets showed that around a third of people continued to want to attend day centres, some or all of the time (Bartlett, 2009). The author notes:

> A slightly surprising finding was the popularity of day care services – two respondents wrote that there were not *enough* day care centres in their local area.... Using day care centres is still a popular way to reconnect with other people. (Bartlett, 2009, p 22, emphasis in original)

However, it is important to note that this survey drew on people who were not currently receiving a personal budget, and asked them what they would want to spend money on in the future if they were.

If people with personal budgets do not want to give up day services altogether, but would rather opt in on a more ad hoc basis, attending on particular days or for particular events, as Duffy suggests (2010), there are concerns about financial viability. Interviewees expressed fears that a few service users choosing to withdraw their funding could lead to the closure of a service that was popular with other users. As one third-sector provider put it: "If people want to go to activities like a day centre occasionally, they won't be there. You can't run a day centre on that basis." According to another interviewee: "Certainly personalisation is a problem because they need a certain capacity to make them effective. If three or four people decide that they don't want these new day care-type services then the whole thing will implode." However, Duffy (2008, p 21) is scathing of the claims that subsidies should continue to be provided to '[c]ertain kinds of congregate provision ... because they won't survive if people have choice about the services they use – this seems a weak argument, particularly given that the rationale for such services is their supposed "efficiency"'.

This dispute highlights the contested legitimacy of cross-subsidisation, discussed earlier. It has relevance not only for people with council funding, but also for those who do not meet the Fair Access to Care eligibility criteria. As one voluntary sector interviewee put it:

> "How can we deliver to those that will never be entitled to an Individual Budget yet use our services ... that's the big fear. You can't run many voluntary-sector organisations on a turnover of five people that come and go especially when they're trying to provide for another 50 that are just simply never going to meet the eligibility criteria."

A report on personal budgets by the mental health charity MIND expressed similar concerns, in the context of a creative arts support project where 'people who use the project do not necessarily have "eligible needs" under the "Fair Access to Care" (FACS) criteria' (MIND, 2009b).

There is disagreement about what will emerge in the absence of day centres. Keohane (2009, p 47) envisages the development of 'new organic collectives'. Certainly, a key part of the social capital element of personalisation is making it easier for people to pool budgets to make choices as groups, rather than as individuals. This may happen on a formal or informal basis, and be spontaneously done by users or facilitated by the local authority. As Tyson outlines:

> What commissioners and others in the local authority will sometimes need to do is to open doors for people who have previously relied on special services. For example a group of friends who are users or former users of learning difficulty day services may want to pool money from their personal budgets to rent a room in a community centre for a party

or a meeting or to hire a five a side football pitch or a coach to go on a trip. They might need someone to take to the leisure centre, community centre, or the coach company for them. There are no doubt a number of ways to achieve this, but one of them is for them to put their money in a pot and ask for assistance to find a support worker to do these tasks for them. (2007, p 21)

A number of interviewees expressed the view that the best encouragement for people to make the most of the personalisation agenda was to see what other people had done as a result of it. As one put it: "Other people get confidence seeing what people do to change their lives."

Some user-led organisations and social enterprises have experimented with alternatives to day centres. One interviewee from a user-led organisation described what such an alternative might look like:

"It could be a community cafe which people use to plan their agendas. Social inclusion is important. It can be a user-run service.... Train people up with skills. People come in and purchase meals, drinks, which provides income for the cafe."

Alternatively, it may be about allowing new spaces to emerge online, for example, via Facebook networks that facilitate the sharing of ideas and support, as well as the pooling of budgets to buy shared services.

However, Roulstone and Morgan (2009, p 334) express concern that the 'enforced collectivity' of the day centre may be exchanged for the 'enforced individualism' of the home, for those who lack the scope to participate in the sorts of self-organising communities that are valorised in the personalisation story. As Beresford puts it:

There is an anxiety that the traditional menu of collective social care services – such as day centres and respite care – will wither away, leaving people adrift in a complex and inadequately regulated market: existing collective services may be closed without adequate alternative support provision being offered in replacement. (2008, p 12)

Concerns that families have about the adequacy of community-based alternatives to day centres were raised by the Mansell review of the DH's Valuing People Now strategy for people with learning disabilities. The report highlighted the continuing need for 'a local base from which people can access different activities' (Mansell, 2010, p 29). The extent to which local authorities will continue to provide, or at least fund, such a hub is uncertain.

Which person?

For people involved in the front line of social care, as service users, practitioners, family members and carers, these are not abstract debates about distant concepts – they are daily concerns about the ways in which services are changing. A theme that emerged from the interviews was that person-centredness was not an unambiguous driver of local policy or practice. In particular, concerns were expressed about how to reconcile the needs of different persons: different types of user group; users and carers; and existing and future users.

The focus on the service user, which lies at the heart of personalisation, suggests that the person is easy to find and to engage. However, the label itself is problematic, as discussed in Chapter 2. As Boxall et al (2007, p 157) point out, 'terms of categorisation tend to be overlooked in critical evaluations of policy as they are often assumed to be unproblematic; this is particularly so in relation to the term "service user"'. The very term is disputed by some (McLaughlin, 2009). Certainly, it is important to recognise that people can occupy multiple roles – user, carer, professional, community member – and that they are not solely defined by their engagement with the state (Barnes and Prior, 2009).

In relation to personalisation and personal budgets, user group labels have been important in the sense that the archetypal direct payment user has been seen as a younger, physically disabled person (Bornat, 2006, p 5). One interviewee warned against trying to 'retrofit' direct payments to older people, for whom they were not designed. Others cited the findings of the IBSEN evaluation that older people were less keen to take on individual budgets than younger people (Glendinning et al, 2008). However, some interviewees expressed concern that this had become a cliché, which had not caught up with the latest evidence. As one put it: "The Alzheimer's Society says that personalisation is essential for people with dementia – they have such chaotic lives that you can't slot them into existing services."

The broader presumption that older people need and want less creative options than younger people has also been contested:

"I think we've tended to see social care for older people to be much more limited in just servicing their care needs and the whole thrust of personalisation is much broader than that. It should be about social engagement, participation, citizenship and all of those things and teasing out what that means for different groups and whether more opportunity for one group is going to mean the same for another. I think it's a debate we haven't really engaged with, I think it's one we hide from."

This comment hints at the challenges encountered in balancing the interests of different user groups in a sector in which 'need' is a key term in determining eligibility for services. Traditionally, older people have been funded less generously than younger disabled people, and been less likely to meet eligibility criteria. As one Age Concern interviewee put it:

"Young people get care plans that involve actually doing things. Social workers won't give you a care plan [for an older person] that includes money to take someone out.... Day care is the only option – unless they manage it themselves, and then you have to reduce the amount of home care that someone gets, but if a person is assessed as needing a certain amount then they need it."

Jeff Jerome, National Director for Social Care Transformation, raised concerns that personalisation should not be seen only as relevant for younger people interested in 'getting a life again', when most people drawing on care and support are dying: often at a late stage of dementia and illness, and hidden away in care homes (Jerome, 2010). This relates to broader questions about how far personalisation will have any meaningful impact on people in residential care settings (SCIE, 2009b; English Community Care Association, 2010). Carr notes that the broader promise of personalisation – that it is 'about better support, more tailored to individual choices and preferences in all care settings' (DH, 2008a, p 5) – 'has equal, if not more, resonance for those living in residential care homes and other institutions, where personalised approaches may be less developed' (Carr, 2010a, p 4). Bowers et al (2009, p 44) have argued that it must be made explicit 'that older people who live in care homes or other supported living arrangements are part of this [personalisation] policy picture'. Help the Aged have developed a 'My Home Life' model of personalisation in care homes to guide good practice (Owen and the National Care Homes Research and Development Forum, 2006).

Equality legislation will make lower levels of funding for older people problematic in the future. This suggests that there will be highly charged political battles ahead as services for younger physically and learning disabled people are cut back and more money goes into older people's care. As one interviewee put it:

> "The budget is not getting larger, it's getting smaller ... that's got to be spread across all adults from 18 to whatever.... What this means is that for those younger adults that have had high care packages, they've had a range of services ... they are going to have to have their services reduced, and that resource has got to be evenly spread based on need across all ages."

For mental health service users, there have been a range of barriers to take-up of personal budgets, including a lack of knowledge among staff and users and the fluctuating nature of some people's mental health (Glasby and Littlechild, 2009, pp 59–60). A MIND guide to personalisation refutes the myth that direct payments are problematic for people with fluctuating needs, arguing that people can build up contingency funds for when they are in crisis (2009b, p 10). However, this may be problematic if local authorities or health authorities are clawing back funds at the end of the financial year.

Some local authorities are separating out funding for crisis services from long-term provision, recognising that the former is not suitable for personalised budget allocations. However, a number of interviewees were keen to assert that in their own sector it was not always easy to establish the point at which people's lives move from crisis to stability. In a domestic violence context, one interviewee commented: "people's lives are always that way, people are fine then there's a crisis and fine again, then there's another crisis". A health service interviewee suggested that, in general, health conditions were less stable and predictable than social care conditions (although there is plenty of evidence that social care needs are also subject to instability and crisis). Within the NHS, Diabetes UK has raised concerns about its applicability for their own members:

> The current literature and the NHS review have identified that Individual Budgets are likely to work best when conditions are stable and predictable. Diabetes is a complex

condition and people with diabetes may experience unplanned healthcare events such as developing a complication which will incur additional healthcare costs.... Diabetes UK would caution against extending Individual Budgets to all aspects of diabetes care. (2008, p 3)

A further issue concerns how far the needs of self-funders and future users can (and should) be accommodated in a system that focuses on the needs of existing users. In the interviews, concerns were expressed about the extent to which risk-aversion among existing service users was calcifying the system and blocking changes that were designed to anticipate future demand. As one social care manager put it: "The problem with engagement is that service users just become a lobby group for existing services. They don't see that they have a role in the solution." A local authority chief executive made a similar point:

> "People speak up for current provision – there aren't enough people who speak up for change. Service users capture the value of the service for themselves and want more of it. We need leading-edge users saying we will do this differently."

According to one local authority social care manager:

> "Engagement with service users means they come and complain – they are a feisty group. If you go from a high cost package to a medium cost package that may be better linked to outcomes for that person, they just see it as a cut."

Such comments hint at one of the paradoxes of the personalisation agenda: it valorises the service user as an 'expert', but also problematises certain kinds of choices – for example, to opt for continuity rather than change. Local authority planners – charged by the Putting People First concordat with making provision for future and unmet need and dismantling collectively funded services to free up funds for personal budgets – have to reconcile such tensions.

Putting People First also requires that local authorities pay more attention to self-funders, those people who do not meet the Fair Access to Care eligibility criteria, estimated to be up to 70% of care users in some areas. Such people may in the future become users of council services when their own money runs low. They provide a guide to what may be chosen in a market, without local authority-imposed constraints. Part of the planning challenge for local authorities is that they do not know much about the needs and preferences of self-funders, the majority of whom never have any contact with the council (Jerome, 2010; IDeA, no date). As part of the Putting People First agenda, local authority commissioners were supposed to be more sensitive to self-funders, but in many areas it seems that these lines of communication are not yet well established. As one local authority manager put it: "Putting People First was supposed to include self-funders, but where is our offer on self-funders? There isn't one." Indeed, rather than being a group of users that councils are attending to more carefully, there are concerns that they may constitute a future drain on resources: "Can we afford to put self-funders through our preventative scheme, when it doesn't save us money?", one local authority manager wondered.

Following a history of invisibility, carers are gaining increased attention in relation to social care reform, as set out in the cross-government Carers Strategy (HM Government, 2008). Carers are entitled to an assessment, and to 'maintain a balance between their caring responsibilities and a life outside caring' (HM Government, 2008, p 9). They may themselves be eligible for a personal budget; carers constitute about a quarter of people receiving direct payments, according to Care Quality Commission figures (CQC, 2010). The potential for conflict between the priorities of users and carers was noted at the time that the legislation extending direct payments to carers was introduced (NCIL, 2000, cited in Glasby and Littlechild, 2009, p 35). It was clear from the interviews that such concerns continue to resonate. For some respondents this was about practical tensions, for example, if service user preferences to spend a personal budget on a varied programme of activities clashed with carer needs for support services to be based in a fixed location on a fixed timetable to fit around other work and family obligations.

Some interviewees expressed a perception that carers have a different, and more conservative, approach to risk than users themselves. As one voluntary-sector leader put it: "Carer groups get worried ... because they can't see any other way that their 50-year-old son could live their life other than bunging them in the day centre twice a week." According to a local authority care manager:

> "Two private learning disability day services have been set up in our area — traditional day centres. They aren't developmental and they aren't personalised, they don't take people anywhere. But parent carers want that model. A lot of parent carers are more concerned about carer relief than

the personalised element. The traditional model gives them security and comfort."

Trade-offs in meeting the needs of users and carers were seen as inevitable. According to one service user: "Choice and control for carers does not necessarily deliver choice and control for disabled relatives, but there has to be a balance there." A commissioner voiced his own uncertainty about where to locate carers in relation to the personalisation agenda: "[W]here do we go with carers and how do we take account of what carers needs are, and should we in personalisation?... [I]s personalisation truly about the person or is it about the person and their families?" An interviewee from the children's sector expressed concern about competing interests: "There is a problem of disability funding being seen as part of the family budget – but this is their money, it's for their lives."

Conclusion

This chapter has examined the arguments made by those who have here been termed the advocates and critics of personalisation. As acknowledged earlier, this is a blunt simplification, but it does provide a useful way to examine the arguments made by those who broadly support the personalisation narrative and those who contest all or some of it. Although some authors have tried to pursue an evidence-based path through the claims and counterclaims made about personalisation, such an enterprise is unlikely to silence debates that have been going on since the early days of direct payments. At issue are interpretations of equality, citizenship and agency, drawing from and sustaining rival framings of welfare histories and likely futures. Responsibility is embraced as the price of greater control within the personalisation narrative, but problematised as 'responsibilisation' by critics of personalisation. There are concerns about how the personal intersects with the social and how the relational and moral aspects of caring are to be fully appreciated. Within the personalisation narrative, the value of social ties is affirmed, but the importance of collectively funded spaces – as sites of social engagement and of joint agency – is contested. In the battles over the closure of day centres, these debates lose their abstract nature and become fights for symbolic and actual resources. Yanow's (2005) work on the policy meanings of buildings and spaces has focused on 'the policy stories that buildings tell'. Day centres can be seen as telling very different kinds of stories to different audiences, only some of which are consonant with the personalisation narrative.

Many of these issues extend beyond the personalisation agenda to theories of the individual and the state, and the relationship between them. Their rehearsal may seem tiresome to advocates of personalisation, frustrated by the slow pace of a reform agenda aimed at transforming people's lives. What was interesting from the interviews, though, was that these were not abstract issues, they continued to pose complex questions for managers, staff and service users, which required unsatisfactory trade-offs or managed uncertainties in front-line practice. The second part of the chapter examined how far person–centredness constituted a clear guide to action for those charged with implementing personalised approaches. It highlighted the difficulty of identifying the relevant person when different users groups have varying needs and experiences, when users and carers have interests that may clash, and when existing users are seen as protecting their own resources at the expense of future users or self-funders.

Under-explored so far is the extent to which personalisation generates tensions and conflicts between service users and professionals, and how these are being experienced and managed. The message of person–centredness clashes with conventional expectations of professional control, and indeed is explicitly designed as a rejection of the 'professional gift' model on which early welfare approaches are seen as being based. If the service user is the hero of the personalisation narrative, the traditional professional seems to be the villain. Yet innovative professionals as advocates, support planners and facilitators are also seen as playing a key part in promoting personalisation, and social workers are expected to be released from stultifying roles in order to develop more meaningful working lives. There are clear questions here about how the relationship between the person and the professional is narrated and transformed in a context of personalisation. These are the focus of Chapter 8.

The personal and the professional

A central theme of the personalisation narrative has been the need to construct a new relationship between service users and staff, resisting conventional norms of expertise and authority. This chapter considers the framing of staff in the personalisation narrative, and how alternative accounts have sought to contest the dominant readings of the professional role. It examines two key claims within the personalisation narrative and the tensions between them: first, that professional expertise must be challenged and the privileged status of professionals resisted to ensure that personalisation is not subverted; and, second, that personalisation requires close collaboration between front-line staff and users based on co-production principles. As in Chapter 7, the discussion focuses on how counter-narratives of personalisation have been articulated and the extent to which oppositions focus on incommensurable claims and values. It does not seek to summarise the literature on the impact of personalisation on professionals and other staff, focusing instead on how the evidence base is contested and problematised by different authors (for a discussion of the evidence base relating to personalisation and the care workforce from authors broadly favourable to personalisation, see Glasby and Littlechild, 2009, pp 165–74; for a more critical account, see Land and Himmelweit, 2010).

The chapter explores the complexities of the staff–user interface within which rival accounts of the impact of personalisation play out. It recognises the key role played by those not usually designated as professionals (care staff, personal assistants) and the emergence of new staff roles (brokers, navigators). It considers the extent to which workers may be acting to embed or subvert the personalisation agenda, recognising the scope for the front line to be a distinctive site of translation and resistance. It concludes by returning to the issue of complexity in staff–user relations. The themes raised in this chapter are not unique to personalisation, nor to the care sector. As Wilson argues, drawing on the work of Wilding (1994):

> Partnership in human services has always been a possible aim for providers, but equally there has always been the possibility of conflict. Teachers join with parents to encourage learning, but they also examine and may fail

the parents' children. In health and social care, professional judgement is backed by sanctions covering wide areas of practice. They may refuse treatment, commit users to mental hospital or take children into care. (Wilson, 1994, p 247)

However, personalisation has at its heart a rejection of the traditional account of the professional–client power dynamic, generating new opportunities for conflict and ambivalence, as well as collaboration. As Foster et al (2006, p 126) put it:

the concept of personalised social care for people with disabilities heralds a new role both for the individual service user and the frontline practitioner. Moreover, the interpretation and implementation of this policy relies substantially on the process and context of frontline practice.

Relocating expertise

As discussed in Chapter 4, the emergence of personalisation within social care has been associated with an assertion of expertise by service users who had traditionally been marginalised and disempowered (Glasby and Littlechild, 2009). The tendency of 'patienthood' and biomedical discourses to diminish agency, particularly for those with disabilities and chronic ailments, has been widely noted (Aronowitz, 1988; Gordon, 1988; Tang and Anderson, 1999). Within mental health services, Baker et al (2008, p 19) highlight the inadequacies of a system in which practitioners were privileged 'as definers of reality'.

A demand that people with disabilities be recognised as 'experts on their own lives' affirmed the importance of legitimating user knowledge, expressed through a range of mechanisms including direct payments to service users (Poll, 2007). The person-centred planning approach was seen as important in the sense that it recognised 'the authority of the service user's voice', rather than the professional's, and focused on 'aspirations and capacities' of the service user, 'rather than needs and deficiencies' (Mansell and Beadle-Brown, 2005, p 20). Conventional accounts of knowledge and evidence were challenged as the authenticity of the user experience became decisive, and forms of informal peer support were valued over professional interventions (Cutler et al, 2007, p 851). Griffiths et al (2009, p 92) note the shift: 'As expertise is increasingly regarded as being constructed as much from self-awareness, achievement and lived experience as from professional or educational background, so there are inevitable implications for the professional–user relationship'.

The relocation of financial control has been seen as a particularly important part of this agenda. Hutchinson et al argue that although direct payments in social care are only a means to the end of more individualised planning and support, there is something distinctive about the payments themselves, namely:

> the changed relationship between the person with learning disabilities and their staff. Instead of being controlled by support staff, direct payments gave people the opportunity to 'be the boss'. This is such a dramatic and complete reversal of roles, and is probably a key to other changes in people's lives. (2006, p 76)

Personal health budgets, now being piloted, give patients the freedom to spend resources on treatments that fit their own assessment of what will help, even if these are not always supported by doctors and conventional standards of evidence-based medicine (Smith, 2010).

This reimagining of the user–professional relationship constitutes a powerful challenge to conventional accounts of roles and status (Ferguson, 2007, p 400; Beresford, 2008, p 12). According to Boyle et al (2006, p ix), 'the role of the professional needs to shift from being fixers who focus on problems to becoming catalysts who focus on abilities'. As one advocate of personalisation from In Control put it, "actually the role of the social worker will become more of a facilitating role … almost like becoming the personal shopper for the individual, but not just in a shopping/buying context, but in the whole community". Hutchinson et al (2006, p 58) describe the role of independent planner and facilitator as 'listening, assisting individuals to dream and express their own voice, supporting family involvement and being skilful about planning and implementation of those dreams'. Elsewhere, the new public service professional brought to life by personalisation has been called a 'Sherpa' (*British Medical Journal*, 2003, cited in Griffiths et al, 2009, p 100).

Personalisation is not unique as a political movement that problematises professional authority. The tension between the expertise of the professional and bureaucrat in contrast to the politician and the citizen has long been acknowledged as an issue within policy analysis (Dewey, 1927; Weber, 1997). More recent critiques of rationalist and technical approaches to policy-making have resurrected older concerns about the anti-democratic nature of policy expertise (Schön, 1983;

Beck, 1992; Fischer, 2009). As Fischer (2009, p 3) puts it, 'Modern life depends fundamentally on trusting experts we don't know – professionals who often move in elite circles socially distant to the lives of everyday citizens and speak languages that can be difficult to understand'. Fischer (2003, 2009) and others who utilise interpretive approaches have argued for new accounts of knowledge and expertise. As Innes (1990, p 32) puts it, 'knowledge is not the exclusive province of experts' (cited in Fischer, 2003, p 222). More broadly, the open source movement has thrived on the 'cult of the amateur', based on the scope for 'user-generated content' to transform services in the public and private sectors (Leadbeater and Cottam, 2007).

This challenge to professional power is also congruent with the moves to consumerism in public services, and the broader acceptance of the public choice account of bureaucracy, discussed in earlier chapters. An ongoing New Labour theme was that services historically were too focused around producer interests (Needham, 2007). Barton (2008) describes how New Labour sought to control the '"untrustworthy" professions', positioning front-line workers as the 'enemy' standing in the way of 'modernisation' (cited in Barnes and Prior, 2009, p 8). Techniques such as performance management and performance-related pay have been seen as necessary to incentivise staff to deploy personalised approaches (Barton, 2008). Thus, personalisation appears well placed to accommodate the managerialism of New Right public service reforms, as well as the anti-elitism of the New Left (Clarke and Newman, 1997).

Co-production

Running alongside this challenge to professional expertise and power within the personalisation narrative is a contrasting account of closer, more collaborative, relationships between staff and users, based on the principles of co-production. According to co-productive accounts of public services, professionals and empowered patients work together to improve services, in a positive–sum game, rather than being placed in a zero–sum relationship in which they battle for authority and status (Leadbeater, 2004; Gannon and Lawson, 2008; Needham, 2008; New Economics Foundation, 2008; Stephens et al, 2008; Needham, 2009; Needham and Carr, 2009).

In this collaborative account, front-line staff are accorded the primary role in delivering public service transformation. Morris and Burford (2009, p 126) borrow the notion of the 'hero practitioner' from Edwards et al (2008), highlighting the key role of the individual front-line worker in relation to family group conferences. This characterisation has a broad resonance in relation to personalisation. A range of recent reports have highlighted the front line as the crucial site of effective practice including: Demos's *Leading from the Front* (Olliff-Cooper et al, 2009); a Localis/KPMG (2009) report, *The Bottom Line: A Vision for Local Government*; Reform's *The Front Line* (Haldenby et al, 2009); and the previous government's *Putting the Frontline First* (HM Government, 2009). The Department of Health (DH) has made clear that 'the service is only as good as the person delivering it' (DH, 2005, p 14). In Darzi's second report, he writes, 'NHS primary and community care services are strongly rooted in their local communities and patients, carers and their families rightly value the personal relationships and continuity of care that they provide' (Darzi, 2008, p 37). Gordon Brown, as Prime Minister, made clear that health was to be seen in terms of a partnership between patients and professionals:

> So if in the last generation progress in health care was seen simply in terms of the doctor administering antibiotics, in the coming generation it will be patients, doctors and NHS staff working together to improve health and manage conditions ... the doctor not just physician but adviser, the nurse not just carer but trainer, patients more than consumers – partners. (Brown, 2008)

The *Putting People First* concordat called for 'the first public service reform programme which is co-produced, co developed, co evaluated' (HM Government, 2007, p 1). The *Personal Health Budgets* document, launching the pilots, also calls for a co-productive approach: 'Personalisation of healthcare embodies co-production. It means individuals working in partnership with their family, carers and professionals to plan, develop and procure the services and support that are appropriate for them' (DH, 2009a, p 23). A recent Demos report also identified the importance of co-production to personalised approaches:

> Writing a truly person-centred care plan with an individual is co-production at its best – the provider working closely with the individual and their family or friends to understand what they are trying to achieve in their lives, and exploring ways this can be done together. (Bartlett, 2009, p 33)

Person-centred planning, self-directed support, individual budgets and initiatives such as Connected Care have been cited as examples of co-production, given the emphasis on people choosing and managing their own packages of care in partnership with professionals (Coulson, 2007; Cummins and Miller, 2007; Parker, 2007; Callaghan and Wistow, 2008).

By emphasising the importance of dialogue and negotiation between front-line staff and service users, co-production can be seen as offering an alternative to confrontational or gatekeeping models where citizens petition staff for access to scarce resources (Needham, 2007). According to Bovaird (2007, p 856): 'the service user has to trust professional advice and support, but the professional has to be prepared to trust the decisions and behaviours of service users and the communities in which they live rather than dictate them'. Citizens are not passive recipients of the 'gifts' of professionals, nor of the meanings projected by policymakers. Rather, as Fischer (2003, p 222) puts it: 'Bringing together professional knowledge and lived experience, citizens and experts form an interpretive community.'

In this account, co-production can be seen as a tool of recognition for the contribution of service users and carers as well as staff, acknowledging their (usually uncosted) input, valuing and harnessing the power of existing informal support networks, and creating better channels for people to shape services (Boyle et al, 2006; Parker, 2007). This form of co-production envisages 'more involved, responsible users' (Leadbeater, 2004, p 59), who are invited to make a greater contribution to the service. Consonant with a broader 'politics of recognition' (Fraser, 2000), this approach can promote increased understanding between multiple stakeholders, ending cycles of hostility (Ostrom, 1996, p 1082).

Co-productive approaches are optimistic about the contribution of professionals to improved services, but do not necessarily seek to preserve traditional professional roles. Leadbeater (2004, p 24) notes that as users take on new responsibilities, the contribution of providers may change as they 'help to create platforms and environments, peer-to-peer support networks, which allow people to devise these solutions collaboratively'. In this sense, co-production is not simply a tool to maintain or re-ascribe professional status. It is expressive of a positive relationship between staff and users, in which the expertise of both is recognised and utilised, rather than assuming that professionals are naturally paternalistic and need to be reined in by newly empowered users.

These two framings – users and staff as adversaries and as co-producers – are deployed side by side within the personalisation narrative, with staff positioned as both barriers to reform and key contributors to its success. The resultant expectation, that relationships are both adversarial and collaborative, can be characterised not as a paradox or an example of incoherent policy-making by the government, but rather as a part of broader efforts by the government to create a dynamic tension between staff and users. It fits with Sullivan's (2009, p 65) claim that some policies can be seen as 'subversive acts' by the government, 'designed with the express purpose of unsettling the established relationships of politicians, the public and professionals in the pursuit of new ones'. It is possible to interpret personal budgets in this way, noting, as Barnes (2009, p 35) does, that 'advocates have explicitly claimed that this is intended to turn traditional service delivery upside down'.

The advantage of this dislocation of traditional staff–user relationships, through the dual narrative of partnership and competition, is that it is hard for critics of personalisation to position it simply as an anti-labour initiative. Trade unions that raise concerns about the ways in which staff terms and conditions may be adversely affected by personalisation can be discredited as failing to embrace the more positive account of staff–user collaboration that co-productive approaches allow. Duffy's (2008, p 15) summary dismissal of trade union concerns can be seen as typical here: 'Service providers within the old social care framework will, quite unnecessarily, see Self-Directed Support as a threat to their jobs.'

Reinventing the social care workforce

The personalisation narrative offers a transformative vision of the social care workforce. For social workers this is framed as a chance to get back to 'what they came into the job for', freeing them from unsatisfactory roles as administrators and gatekeepers and allowing more community-based working. Such a vision was a key element of the *Putting People First* concordat, and was echoed by many interviewees in the discussion of how personalisation was reshaping social work. The report of the government-sponsored Social Work Task Force (2009) set out a vision for raising the status of the profession, involving a new career structure to keep experienced staff on the front line, improved training and a new licensing system. Pilots for independent GP-style practices for social workers were launched by the Labour government and have been extended by the Coalition (McGregor, 2011).

Opportunities for new, more satisfying, ways of working are also held out to other social care staff, including home care workers. In place of 15-minute care visits that fail to preserve the dignity of the service user or the employee, personalisation offers the opportunity to seek employment as a personal assistant – a sector in which job satisfaction has been found to be higher (Glendinning et al, 2000; IFF Research, 2008). Indeed, it was dissatisfaction with rigid home care provision by staff and users that was one of the drivers of personalisation and the expansion of the personal assistant workforce (IFF Research, 2008).

However, just as strong a presumption in the personalisation literature and interviews is that social care staff will try to thwart the reform agenda if they can, failing to recognise its opportunities. In the personalisation narrative, it is social work professionals (social workers in particular) who have presided over the existing system, blocking person–centred approaches through concerns for professional status and conservative attitudes to risk. Comments from the interviews included reflections that "professionals go at the slowest pace they can get away with". The framing of social workers in relation to personalisation is of a profession that "doesn't get it", and is thereby missing out on the potential for an exciting renaissance. The account of professionals attempting to subvert the personalisation agenda draws on evidence showing that social workers may have played a role in reducing the take–up of direct payments, through a conservative interpretation of eligibility criteria and exaggeration of the difficulties (CSCI, 2004; Ellis, 2007; OPM, 2010).

The ambiguous positioning of front-line professionals was evident in interviews with social care managers, who problematise the role of social workers in relation to personalisation – either in terms of being too enthusiastic or not enthusiastic enough:

> "There's a disconnect between local government and social workers, their professional ethos. They don't feel they belong to the local authority…. But they are employed by the local authority so they aren't outside the tent. We want them to be person-centred. But we don't want them telling people to complain against what they've been allocated. We need them to accept the management decision. They don't seem to see that it is a cash-limited budget." (Social care manager, local authority)

> "In terms of social workers who don't get it – that can be in two senses: either in the sense of not wanting to give up their professional expertise, what they were trained for. Or else it can be ones who are promising too much. They need to be clear that the available package is not going up. That's a lot for front-line staff – and indeed managers – to

get their heads around." (Director of adult social care, local authority)

Thus, social workers are framed both as resistors of change, reluctant to give up control, and as excessive enthusiasts, allying themselves too closely with service users and ignoring financial realities. These divergent framings of the workforce and their appropriate roles and relationships draw on different strands of evidence and different interpretations of recent practice. In the face of this, apparent wariness among social workers about elements of the personalisation agenda can be interpreted as either knee-jerk paternalism among professionals who will not allow service users to direct their own support, or as caution among a workforce that fears cost-cutting and reduced care. As Glasby and Littlechild (2009, p 150) observe, 'frontline staff ... can sometimes feel trapped between the empowering rhetoric of direct payments and the severely financially constrained nature of current social care'.

Such ambiguities link to broader controversies about what social workers and other care professionals are for in an era of personalisation. One social care manager set out his vision of what social work training should encompass:

> "[Social workers] need concepts of budget management, brokerage, business interaction, outcomes-based planning. The skill set is not there for social work training. Learning about family dynamics may be important, but it won't help you get a PA for an older person at short notice."

However, this account clashes with Barnes' understanding of the relational and moral aspects of care and the skills they necessitate:

> The skills and qualities required for this are not those of the brokers and support agencies necessary to help service users negotiate terms and conditions and manage a pay roll for their care staff. Rather they are the relational skills, the capacity to engender trust and confidence that, dare it be said, are those that the best social workers, nurses, occupational therapists, day centre and home care workers can demonstrate, and which service users in a wide range of contexts say they value. Such skills are nurtured through dialogic practices that can deliver support through negotiation with service users and those close to them. (2008, p 158)

It is certainly the case that many social workers associate personalisation with an increase in bureaucracy, rather than the scope to 'get back' to a richer community role. A Unison/*Community Care* poll of social care staff from 2010 showed that two thirds of respondents had experienced increased bureaucracy as a result of personalisation (despite Jeff Jerome's claim that the essence of personalisation is to 'reduce process'; cited in Samuel, 2010a). This appears to be due to local authorities duplicating self-assessments and traditional community care assessments because of a fear that legal duties to assess people's needs would not otherwise be met (Samuel, 2010b). As one interviewee put it: "[Social workers] are still having to do the assessing. Their caseloads are not going away. It's not true that they are getting back to their community role." The finding that only half of social workers (49%) felt that personalisation would benefit users (down from 67% in 2009) can be attributed to a perceived failure to deliver on its promises (Samuel, 2010b).

Concerns have also been expressed about the extent to which personalisation will lead to deskilling and deprofessionalisation (Ferguson, 2007). Social work jobs may be lost as staff are employed in more generic roles, staffing call centres or working as support brokers (Beresford, 2008, p 12). Some of these issues are likely to come from broader financial challenges, rather than personalisation per se. The former Director of Strategic Finance for social care within the DH, John Bolton, has suggested that a quarter of the adult social care workforce will need to be cut to meet finance targets, a figure disputed by the Care Services Minister Paul Burstow (Dunning, 2010c). However, it is also the case that the logic of personalisation is to reduce staffing levels, or at least redeploy staff, which raises issues for existing workers in relation not only to their own job security, but also to the extent to which risk is being appropriately managed in relation to personalisation. According to the Association of Chief Executives of Voluntary Organisations:

> There can be little doubt that the implementation of new social markets will create turbulence in the labour market. Some lower level support activity (e.g. home support) may be undertaken in the future on a more casual base and we want to see an increase in the overall amount of self-help and mutual aid activity. (ACEVO, 2009, p 43)

For home care staff, the new vision of work as a personal assistant with higher job satisfaction looks likely to be at the expense of pay, conditions and training, and a broader deregulation of the workforce (Ungerson, 1999; Carr and Robbins, 2009; Low Pay Commission,

2009; Land and Himmelweit, 2010). A 2007 Social Care Institu
Excellence (SCIE) report notes that the flexibility of personal assist
(unsocial hours that can fluctuate a lot, no job description) is key to
the success of many schemes. As Rummery (2006, p 643) puts it:

> the level of direct payments has been set fairly low, which
> means that users can only recruit relatively low-paid,
> unskilled workers, and the very nature of their flexibility
> (which makes them such a success in enhancing disabled
> people's citizenship) means that workers themselves are at
> risk of exploitation and abuse.

Spandler (2004, p 198) suggests that, 'Initiatives such as Direct Payments
may be popular precisely because they have been incorporated as part
of a more general project of destabilizing and weakening the power
of the organized labour movement'.

Such discussions restate the position of staff and users as adversaries,
trapped in zero-sum games, in which, as Rummery (2006, p 643) puts
it, 'one disadvantaged group's citizenship gain is reliant on their being
a group of workers who are themselves at risk of social exclusion
through lack of skills, poverty and low wages'. According to Cambridge
and Carnaby (2005, p 57), it is 'difficult for staff to implement person-
centred approaches when they are poorly paid, often not valued, and
receive poor guidance and training on implementation'. Rummery
notes, however, that such issues are generally concerned with the *process*
of direct payments and could be addressed: 'The rates of payment could
be made higher, enabling disabled people to employ skilled workers
and reducing both users' and employees' vulnerability to exploitation
and abuse' (Rummery, 2006, p 643). Similarly, Pearson (2006, p 44)
has called for unions and policy planners to develop 'sustainable
employment packages for personal assistants, so as to separate the
ethos of direct payments from the privatisation of social care'. This
vision of a care service in which people are given enough money to
train staff appropriately, and observe appropriate employment terms
and conditions relating to holiday pay, sick leave, equalities legislation
and benefits such as payment into a pension, is one that Unison has
also endorsed, clarifying that it is not hostile to personalisation per se
(SPAEN/Unison, 2008; Land and Himmelweit, 2010).

Even with improved pay rates, tensions are likely to endure. Spandler
(2004, p 201) argues, 'the greater the status and training that personal
assistants receive, the more these potentially threaten the balance of
power and control between the recipient and the personal assistant –

exactly what Direct Payments are designed to redress'. SCIE (2007) notes that where a trained cadre of assistants has been developed, it has led to 'development of a new profession which – while arguably providing a more thoughtful kind of care – has not met with approval of all care users'. The discrediting of attempts to limit service user discretion over personal assistants has led Land and Himmelweit (2010, pp 52–3) to observe:

> Some of the benefits claimed for being a direct payment holder sound like those of a 19th-century factory owner, able to hire and fire at will, secure complete working time flexibility and avoid health and safety risk assessments which other employers have to adopt.

Although a register of accredited personal assistants has been suggested by the DH, it was also made clear that limitations on user choice were not acceptable: 'It is important that any local approach does not unduly impinge the ability of people managing their support to make their own decisions about who they choose to employ' (DH, 2008a, p 28). A similar resistance to professionalisation can be seen in relation to brokerage. As O'Brien puts it:

> Requiring Independent Professional Brokerage, in an important sense, sends a message that undermines confidence that people can usually behave decently and sensibly with occasional breakdowns. It also increases complexity and creates expectations of incapacity in people, families, and community members. (Private correspondence, cited in Duffy and Fulton, 2009, p 7)

There is uncertainty, then, about the extent to which it is possible to empower care users while also preserving appropriate levels of pay and status for staff. Clashes between what may be framed a workforce narrative and the personalisation narrative are evident not only in relation to pay and conditions, but also in relation to the location of risk. As discussed in Chapter 7, personalisation has been linked to a range of reforms designed to transfer risk away from the state and on to the service user. However, rather than transferring risk to the user, it may be the case that risk gets stuck at the front line of public services, leaving staff with little protection if things go wrong. There remains uncertainty about how far professionals are (and should be) allowing users to make the 'wrong choices', and who bears responsibility for the implications of their choices. It has certainly provoked concern, for example, from trade unions, about what happens when people run out of their budget, or spend it on the 'wrong' things (Unison, 2009).

There are wider issues relating to safeguarding that are also germane to issues of expertise, professionalism and the role of the family. An interviewee from the children's sector sets out the challenges as professionals perceive them:

> "You've got Fred down the road that's looking after a child that may have complex health needs, maybe a mental health problem, maybe relatively extreme on the autistic spectrum.... He's a good family friend, he understands that child, they get on well, great. But he isn't either a health professional or medical professional or a mental health professional or even someone that's worked in the voluntary sector that's seen these sort of problems come up time and time again. And so it's that issue of, OK, well again how do you spot deterioration in a child's condition, first is a big issue. If there is deterioration will that person know who to go to and equally a bigger concern is well, if he fears that there is harm to that child and he's being paid by the family, is there a conflict of interest in reporting that and will he know how to do it?"

This classic framing of the inadequacies of family- and peer-support mechanisms versus professional expertise remains at the heart of many of the tensions surrounding personalisation. It links to broader debates about family support, and claims that personalisation advocates have tended to be too uncritical about the role of the family. The scope for families to be sites of neglect and abuse, or to be absent altogether for many people, has led to concerns that personalisation should not be too reliant on active family support.

For advocates of personalisation, the potential for families to be abusive is a further argument for personalisation, rather than a reason to limit its scope. As one interviewee put it:

> "Let's look at the evidence. It seems to suggest that people will be abused by people they know in their own homes or in institutional care, rather than living in the community. The flexibility of direct payments allows people to employ people they trust in a way that's not been possible before. So it may be safer. Personalisation has the potential to make

people more evident in the community – if people are in public places they may be less likely to be abused."

Subversion and complexity

Subversion by professionals is an ethically fraught issue, raising broader questions around the extent to which front-line staff have a role to play as resistors of policy innovation. Emerging from the realisation that implementation is always a process of creation and interpretation, policy analysts such as Lipsky (1980) highlighted the significance of the discretion exercised by 'street-level bureaucrats', with a presumption that they tended to modify practices to make their own work life easier. Such coping mechanisms include informal routines for 'mass processing', in order to control the stress and complexity of day-to-day work (Elmore, 1978, pp 249, 251). The work of Maynard-Moody and Musheno (2003) similarly drew attention to the ways in which front-line staff characterise (and caricature) clients in order to simplify decision-making. They found a tendency to 'express disdain for the ungrounded knowledge of politicians, agency officials, and intellectuals', and also to 'assume they know what is best for the client – more so than the upper level policymakers and the clients themselves' (Maynard-Moody and Musheno, 2003, pp 23, 156).

Care professionals are often framed as subversive, either because of a conservative view of risk or because of a desire to protect their own status and jobs – critiques that very much reflect the presumptions that Lipsky made about front-line staff in the late 1970s. Indeed, Ellis (2007, p 405) concludes, 'despite ten years of managerialism, in the course of which professional practice has been routinized and regulated, Lipsky's work is still useful in analysing front line behaviour around direct payments'. Thus, advocates of personalisation have proposed tackling staff resistance through technologies that maximise transparency and user control and minimise front-line discretion. Duffy (2010, p 12), for example, has argued that a resource allocation system enables needs to be defined 'by answering clear and objective questions', implying that staff discretion can be reduced.

However, a number of authors have argued that Lipskyite analyses are of limited value in understanding front-line relationships in the current context. Three limitations of Lipsky's analysis can be identified, requiring new understandings of what it means to be a subversive professional. First, new managerial regimes have transformed the scope that professionals have for exercising discretion and required new relationships with service users. Taylor and Kelly (2006) observe that new performance management frameworks have limited the professional discretion observed by Lipsky, but have also encouraged professionals to act as entrepreneurs, finding new ways to reduce costs and improve quality, thereby creating new opportunities for discretion. Barnes and Prior (2009) note that the traditional, Lipskyite view of the 'street-level bureaucrat' needs to be updated for a context in which workers and users are more constrained than ever before by monitoring and regulation, but are also expected to work together in co-productive relationships as active and reflexive agents.

Second, front-line relationships have become increasingly diverse and stratified and not easily captured in a single model. The traditional binary account of a patient–doctor or client–social worker relationship does not do justice to the varied roles and encounters that exist. Whereas the GP or hospital consultant may be seen as the exemplar of the expert professional, in which status and economic differentials with patients can make collaboration difficult (Wilson, 1994, p 246), other professionals – such as social workers – have a relatively low status (Beresford and Croft, 2004, p 64). According to Boyle et al (2006, p 56):

> One of the peculiarities of modern public services is that front-line staff often share more characteristics with clients than is entirely comfortable for them. In those circumstances, professional status may appear to be all that separates front-line staff from being supplicants themselves because, in practice, the participation that they are asked to extend to clients is often not extended to them.

Reflecting on the low status of social workers, one interviewee observed: "Personalisation is more of a challenge for doctors than for social workers. Social workers are much more likely to get to grips with the personalisation agenda, they are on the same level as their clients."

It is also important to note that there are multiple strata of public service providers who do not fit into a traditional professional category – including care workers, unpaid carers, medical support staff and other ancillary roles that have proliferated since the era that Lipsky was observing. These are often the people with whom service users have the most regular contact, alongside peers, family and friends. As Baker et al (2008, p 27) put it in relation to mental health services:

> Even the most intensive therapeutic interventions represent only a small part of the time that a person spends in struggling with a mental disorder. The vast majority of their

time in company with others comprises family contact, friendship and even informal contact with catering and cleaning staff in hospital.

Whereas the impact of personalisation on professionals has generally been to challenge their expertise, many of these staff already have long experience of having their knowledge undervalued. In an era of expert service users there are uncertainties about how far such staff are further marginalised, given their ambiguous status. Baker et al (2008, p 25) suggest that when controversial service changes are made, 'The people most likely to be challenged by service users are catering and nursing staff – not medical managers, policymakers or politicians'.

It is likely that the proportion of staff taking on non-traditional roles will increase further, generating ever more complex relationships between service users and workers (Ferguson, 2007). Newman and Clarke (2009a, p 62) note that:

> new categories of occupation may be differently classed, raced or gendered from the 'traditional' professions.... Located in new sites, working 'interstitially' between both organisational and professional forms of authority and discipline, these agents typically have mediating roles – doing the work of brokering, negotiating, translating, and assembling the people and practices involved in governing.

Certainly, there are uncertainties over how new roles of brokers and support planners will operate in a context of personalisation, including what skills will be required, to whom they will be accountable and the point at which informal, peer support shifts into formal advice-giving, with potential legal consequences if the advice is deficient. There is a concern that the DH Social Care Workforce agenda has to date neglected hybrid roles such as support planners and continued to take a relatively traditional view of the workforce (DH, 2009d).

The complexity of the new workforce is likely to be reflected in the proliferation of non-traditional organisations providing support and services. User-led organisations are expected to play a major part in transforming provision, and have been supported by the DH. There is great optimism about the scope for social enterprises and mutuals to offer new models of service delivery, but also new sites for the interaction of staff and users. For example, a report from Shaping our Lives et al, predicts, 'service user controlled organisations can be a site where social workers are employed working alongside service users in a hands on way' (2007, p 13). This horizontal view of staff–user relations is clearly distinct from conventional vertical models of power in professional–client interactions. With user organisations acting as the employers of social workers, traditional notions of professional control and discretion may be heavily circumscribed.

The third limitation of the classic Lipskyite view of bureaucratic subversion is its failure to recognise the agency of citizens. As Prior (2009, p 22) notes, drawing on Yanow (2003, p 245):

> [C]itizens are not 'empty vessels' waiting to be filled with the attributes and potentialities prescribed for them by dominant discourses. They respond to policies and engage with practitioners with their own understandings of the situation, their own sense of what would constitute a just or unjust outcome and their own capacities for action, including alternative sources of knowledge. Such understandings and capacities on behalf of the intended subjects of policy introduce a destabilising or unsettling dynamic into citizen and practitioner encounters, which thus involve a negotiation of meanings and a sense of openness about potential outcomes

Thus, the front-line interface may be a site for shared 'meaning-making', rather than the transfer of authoritative and monolithic discourse (Lather, 1991, p 42; Tang and Anderson, 1999, p 86). As discussed in earlier chapters, citizens are not passive audiences, listening to the stories of others; they interact with and shape policy narratives, such that meanings are fluid rather than fixed. There may be 'moments at which users/citizens/residents refuse the place or roles they are allocated – or at least refuse to perform them according to dominant scripts' (Newman and Clarke, 2009b, pp 78–9). Service users and social workers can work together to advance agendas of resistance (Beresford and Croft, 2004, p 65). In relation to personalisation, this could mean campaigning to keep day centres open, demanding better training, pay and job protection for personal assistants, or using the assessment process to get around service rationing.

However, the discussion earlier and in previous chapters highlights the contested nature of these acts of resistance. Prior warns against romanticising subversion in relation to policy change: 'The identification of counter-agency may help to explain why official policy and practice does not always deliver the results as intended; but it does not necessarily imply the presence of radically progressive alternative outcomes.' He goes on:

> [T]his is not intended as a 'heroic' account of policy subversion. Rather, I have tried to show that the conditions for counter-agency are to be found in the internal inconsistencies and ambiguities of the process of governing itself, and that the forms that counter-agency may take are themselves shaped by the particular and differing contexts of public service delivery. (2009, p 32)

Subversion, then, remains inevitable and normatively contested, as it was for Lipsky, albeit in a new managerial context and with greater awareness of complexity and agency in staff–user interactions.

Conclusion

A dominant strand of the personalisation narrative indicates that welfare services to date have been organised at the convenience of service providers (particularly managers and professionals) and that a key aim of reform must be to address this imbalance. One of the contributions of the personalisation story has been to dismiss the notions of information asymmetry that traditionally sustained professional power. A number of commentators on personalisation have argued for it to be the basis on which new collaborative and co-productive relationships can emerge between staff and users. Here, they work together in positive-sum relationships to improve service outcomes, rather than requiring that an improvement in the status of one comes at the expense of another. Thus, contained within the personalisation reforms are accounts of professionals as both barriers to reform and productive collaborators. Staff and users are left to make sense of an agenda that positions them as partners 'co-producing' outcomes and as adversaries battling for status and control.

These dual elements of the personalisation narrative make a slippery target against which counter-discourses – raising concerns about staff pay and conditions or safeguarding – have struggled to be heard. Social workers in particular have been faced with an ambivalent reform context that promises the renaissance of their profession, but also positions them as the major impediment to service improvements. Complaints about social workers were endemic in the interviews – from service users and carers, from local authority staff, and from voluntary-sector providers – although the focus of complaint shifted, with social workers at times being perceived as too willing to take the side of the service user and at other times not willing enough.

Much of this critique draws on Lipskyite accounts of the attempts of street-level bureaucrats to control their work environment so as to minimise uncertainty and stress. However, this account provides only a limited insight into the current public service context in which staff and users are monitored more than ever before, but also expected to be self-actualising entrepreneurs and co-producers. In particular, Lipsky's account fails to recognise the diversity and complexity of front-line relationships, and the agency of citizens themselves, which may entail different outcomes than those envisaged by policymakers or managers. Citizens and staff may sometimes act subversively, deliberately resisting formal policy goals, but they must routinely act as interpreters of policy goals that are ambiguous and shifting. In the face of a personalisation narrative that positions them as adversaries and collaborators, citizens and staff must negotiate new relationships and working practices.

CHAPTER 9

Conclusion: personalised futures

Personalisation constitutes an intriguing topic for anyone interested in public policy: a new policy idea that has rapidly captured the interest of people across the political spectrum and looks likely to be the stimulus for major welfare state reform. This creates a research challenge to identify what is meant by personalisation and what its likely impacts will be. Personalisation does not seem to be coherent or wide-ranging enough to constitute an ideology or indeed a philosophy (despite sometimes being described in those terms), nor is it a broad buzzword in public policy like community and responsibility. It is not a category that bestows roles and identities like citizenship or consumerism. However, it is more than a specific policy programme, like the New Deal for welfare or Sure Start for children and families. Personalisation is best understood as a narrative of public service reform, endorsing a set of relationships and policy goals in a way that is compelling and emotionally resonant, but also multi-interpretable. As it has emerged within social care, and been stretched into other policy sectors, it has been translated into different forms, themselves fluid and contested.

Four themes are looked at in detail in this final chapter. First, the chapter revisits the meaning of personalisation and assesses how far it can be understood as a stable and portable term within public policy. The second section examines the likely policy challenges for personalisation in the future, focusing on social care, where the practical implications are currently most evident. The third section considers the future for personalisation as a system-wide approach to welfare reform, relevant to a range of new initiatives, including personal health budgets and the broader principle of a conditional welfare entitlement. The final section examines the scope for a 'progressive' personalisation, and whether there are nodes in the debate where pressure can be focused to ensure that equity and social justice are valued in the race to personalise.

Assembling personalisation

As the discussions in the previous chapters have indicated, personalisation is not something to be discovered or solved. It is in flux, making it difficult to identify a stable core. Hartley (2007, p 639) reflects on this uncertainty: 'At this juncture, it is difficult to discern whether or not

157

personalisation constitutes the passage of the existing code to a new one, or whether it is simply a bewildering mix – the amorphous shape of things to come.'

It is possible to identify some policy objectives that are core to the personalisation agenda, linked to tailoring services more closely to the needs and/or wants of service users. It is styled as an emphatic rejection of a traditional welfare state in which services were standardised around an average citizen, or shaped only by the agenda of professionals. Chapter 3 identified a range of service reforms that have been characterised as forms of personalisation, or which seem to follow from the same principles. These include self-directed support and individual budgets in social care, personal health budgets and more accessible services in the NHS, individual learning plans for schoolchildren, personal development plans for students, and family intervention projects and personalised conditionality for those using welfare services. However, exactly what constitutes personalisation remains uncertain. As one interviewee put it: "Is passport submission a form of personalisation because you can do it in lots of different ways?" Family intervention projects were seen by some interviewees as a clear case of a personalised programme, tailored to the circumstances of individual families, whereas others felt that the emphasis on compulsion and sanctions was incompatible with the user-as-expert account that underpins personalisation.

Chapter 4 set out the case for approaching personalisation as a narrative of reform, arguing that it is based on five core storylines derived from social care: (1) personalisation works, transforming people's lives for the better; (2) personalisation saves money; (3) personalised approaches reflect the way that people live their lives; (4) personalisation is applicable to everyone; (5) people are experts on their own lives. The storylines are developed through three sources of evidence – formal data, individual testimonies and self-evidence – such that when the formal evidence base proves somewhat elusive, the storyteller can deploy common sense and/or resonant stories about individual transformation to make the case. Reflecting on the enduring potency of narratives, in an era of ostensibly evidence-based policy, Prior and Barnes (2009, p 205) note:

> In spite of attempts to banish the 'anecdotal' from evidence-based policy making, narratives retain their power to enable people to make sense not only of their own lives and circumstances ... but also of collective goals and how these might be realised.

One report on personalisation in the NHS suggested that, while health leaders themselves 'are primarily interested in evidence, not anecdote', stories remain important in inspiring their staff (NHS Confederation/Mental Health Development Unit, 2009, p 18). There is an implicit evocation of hierarchies of evidence here (Glasby, 2011), with a suggestion that only health leaders are able to appreciate the more abstract lessons of formal evidence. However, this distinction is hard to sustain in relation to personalisation, in which it appears to have been the ability of organisations like In Control to tell stories to senior leaders – politicians and civil servants – that drove its adoption. The transformative power of telling the right stories to the right people was a recurrent theme in the interviews that were conducted for this study. As one local authority chief executive put it:

> "We need more storytellers, not more evidence. What will change minds is people telling stories about changed lives. If I was Tsar for personalisation – I would quickly work out how to audit it. Then I would get In Control telling great stories all over the place, not in social care but telling finance directors how much can be saved. I'd go to the LGA, then the professionals."

Stories can be seen as analogous to myths, which permit the silencing of certain aspects of the debate. According to Yanow (1996, pp 193–4): 'Since myths shut off further inquiry, they are difficult to discern and fathom. As they redirect attention, it is hard to see through or beyond them, adding further to public silences.' She goes on: '[P]olicy and organizational myths are typically found when a policy entails incommensurable values – two or more equally valued but incompatible principles embodied within a single policy issue or agency policy or practice' (Yanow, 1996, p 192). Within the personalisation narrative, for example, the notion of win-wins could be defined as one of the policy myths: cost reduction at the same time as service improvement; loss of economies of scale at the same time as more efficient spending; empowerment at the same time as responsibilisation; employment casualisation for staff at the same time as increased job satisfaction. There are silences about the extent to which personalisation might mean achieving something at the expense of something else.

Narratives offer an account of the past as well as the present and future, although in the case of personalisation this engagement with the past is shifting and ambivalent, embracing both continuity with the past and rupture from it. It is unclear whether the personalisation narrative constitutes a rejection of a real past, or an artifice designed to discredit earlier and alternative approaches. As Finlayson (2004, p 154) puts it: 'Tradition is never uniform or natural, it is always the outcome of some prior series of political and social conflicts and struggles that make it look as if "we have always done things this way".' The personalisation narrative draws on a broader New Right critique of the post-war welfare state as monolithic and unresponsive, while also evoking New Left concerns about the tendency of the welfare state to foster inequities and perpetuate discriminatory practices.

Personalisation clearly means different things to different audiences, with implications for its implementation. Peck and 6 discuss implementation as a process through which 'the *whole set* of government and ministerial intentions, institutional and professional commitments, wider public values and so on are taken by the *local networks* of managers and organisations and creatively resolved into *settlements*' (Peck and 6, 2006, p 20, emphasis in original). However, it is too early to talk of a personalisation settlement, if something so fixed is indeed ever apparent in policy terms. Its practical implications remain highly uncertain, as it moves from the fringes to the mainstream. The difficulties of preserving the creativity and often intensive financing of small-scale and pilot initiatives are well known (Nutley et al, 2007; Parr and Nixon, 2009), and seem likely to be repeated in relation to personalisation. Chapter 6 highlighted the messy uncertainties of the front-line experience, and their disconnection from the much cleaner accounts of personalisation given by national policymakers. It is not a question here of merely repairing the disjuncture between policy and practice. As Yanow (2000, p 18) points out: 'Important difficulties ... may no longer be fixed by repairing ambiguous policy language, because in this view not only is language inherently multivocal – capable of carrying multiple meanings – but clients' and others' interpretations cannot be predetermined or controlled.' Ambiguities of the narrative generate uncertainties for policy actors both within and outside government who must translate it for their own context. For them, the gaps and slippages may be experienced not as purposive and functional ambiguity, but as material challenges to the ways in which they encounter welfare services.

Just as uncertain are the normative implications of personalisation. What seems apparent is that 'there are multiple "readers" as well as multiple "readings" of policy and agency "texts"' (Yanow, 2000, p 60). These readers have 'epistemological and ethical differences, not merely differences over priorities' (Pal, 1995, p 202, cited in Yanow, 2000, p 21). The existence of such diverse viewpoints has made it difficult to locate personalisation in a particular ideological space, as Chapters 5 and 7 discussed. However, there are patterns and clusterings in the sorts of arguments that are made in favour of and against personalised approaches, constituting 'contending interpretive communities' (Pal, 1995, p 202, cited in Yanow, 2000, p 21). There is an account of personalisation that links it to the expansion of markets, the use of technology to individualise the welfare state and the transfer of risk on to more 'resilient' individuals. On this basis, it is easy to see personalisation offering a vision of the welfare state that would have appealed to Keith Joseph and a range of other right-wing thinkers. In its emphasis on individual need rather than population need, on individual entitlement rather than risk-pooling and on the needs of the service user rather than the worker, it may be difficult to locate personalisation anywhere but on the right of politics. However, personalisation cannot be reduced to a knee-jerk consumerism or libertarianism, since it makes explicit claims to a richer citizenship based on equity and inclusion. Reflecting on the ambivalent political locus of personalisation, one interviewee noted:

> "If we look back to the roots of direct payments it was the same – there has been an ongoing debate about was it a radical movement from social workers/service users or a dying Conservative government's way of privatising services. Both are convincing."

However, it is important to avoid the conclusion that personalisation is a hybrid in the form of X amounts of consumerist neoliberalism with a Y dose of social democracy and a dash of communitarianism. More convincing is the broader account of policy ideas given by Newman and Clarke, which emphasises assemblage over hybridity, recognising the existence of 'multiple sources, resources and combinations' (Newman and Clarke, 2009a, p 95). Personalisation is not something that can be discovered or defined; rather it has to be assembled by observing its usage and by identifying its location at the intersection of various storylines of policy change. As Roe (1994, p ix) puts it:

> Sometimes what we are left to deal with are not the facts – that is why there is a controversy – but the different stories people tell as a way of articulating and making sense of the uncertainties and complexities that matter to them. (Cited in Yanow, 2000, p 59)

The future for personalisation in social care

Although personalisation was fostered by New Labour, it has continued to be a key theme of policy under the Conservative–Liberal Democrat Coalition government. In January 2011, the Putting People First consortium published *Think Local, Act Personal*, a 'statement of intent' on the future of personalisation, reaffirming the importance of personalisation within the context of the government's broader health and social care reform (Putting People First, 2011). Integration across health and social care services was a key element, alongside increased recognition of the importance of family and community support.

The development of personalisation is being very much shaped by the large spending cuts being implemented in local authorities, leading to job losses and tighter eligibility criteria. There is a danger that the transformative potential of personalisation will be lost as public funding evaporates. Social workers have warned that the cuts are 'ravaging' personalisation, as the amount allocated in personal budgets is reduced (Dunning, 2011). In some local authorities, personal budgets will only be allocated to people with critical need. The combined impact of this may be to stifle innovation. As one social care manager put it: "The creativity around personalisation tends to happen for people with substantial rather than critical need. The trouble with critical is that people are very frail."

Running alongside the immediate budget crisis is the issue of the long-term funding of social care. An independent commission set up by the Conservative–Liberal Democrat government is charged with examining a range of funding options in order to create 'an affordable and sustainable funding system for care and support, for all adults in England' (see http://carecommission.dh.gov.uk). It will determine who can access social care funding, and on what basis, influencing the scope of future personalisation approaches.

One of the anxieties for the future is that personalisation will follow the policy trajectory of community care and care management, themselves once expected to be transformative reforms to empower front-line staff and users. According to one social care manager:

> "There is a risk that this will go the same way as community care. Getting people out of institutions was an excellent idea but you ended up with a structure that has delivered a different form of warehousing which personalisation is meant to address, whether in acute hospitals or sheltered

housing, it's an existence not a life. Personalisation is about enabling people to live a meaningful, quality life."

Another interviewee, from a disability organisation, was cautious about the future because of what had been observed in relation to direct payments:

"I'm a little bit wary because of our experience with direct payments which is that often direct payments have not resulted in people having the choice and control that was originally intended. Because it's been undermined and filibustered by things like unreasonable monitoring processes, local authorities still wanting to have complete control over how people spend their direct payments. That's what worries me about individual budgets and personalisation generally. In fact I feel even more concerned because at least with direct payments we had the legislation and the subsequent regulations and guidelines to fall back on. With personalisation in social care we don't have anything to fall back on because it isn't part of any piece of legislation at the moment."

Other interviewees were more optimistic. As one policy consultant put it: "the genie is out of the bottle and having popped out you can't put it back in ... having given people a glimpse of what's possible with personalisation in terms of the freedoms, the flexibilities and all of that." According to a local authority commissioner:

"even if personalisation fails it's started people on a journey that may be difficult to stop and I hope it's difficult to stop just in terms of the way that services are delivered and the way that we manage those services."

A Demos report looking at how people are likely to spend their social care budgets in the future noted that 'There is some indication that the longer people have a personal budget, the more radical they will become in considering ways of spending their budget money' (Bartlett, 2009, p 27).

Personalisation beyond social care

One of the successes of the personalisation narrative has been its ability to inspire reformers outside social care, adapting its storylines for other sectors of the welfare state. Reflecting on this process, particularly in relation to NHS reform, Beresford (2008, p 17) expressed his bewilderment:

> Why is an inadequately evidenced model from a policy area that is widely recognized to be problematic – social care – being considered as a way forward for a health service that is still seen by most people as one of the greatest achievements of twentieth-century Britain? It is big issues like these which need to be kept under close scrutiny, as cosy stories of a few people's gains from individual budgets are used to sell one of the biggest, least evidenced, reforms to be introduced since the founding of the welfare state.

Similarly, Barnes (2008, p 159) has expressed scepticism about the claims that are being made about the policy reach of personalisation:

> Not only should we be suspicious about any model of social care that purports to offer a common solution to such different circumstances as the needs of isolated older people, young people excluded from school and expectant mothers, we should also be suspicious of doing this and saving money at the same time – haven't we heard this before?

Such criticisms have done little, however, to slow the pace at which personalisation is migrating into health and other sectors. Keohane (2009, p 21) notes the enthusiasm of the Conservative and Liberal Democrat parties for personalisation approaches across public services. Prime Minister David Cameron, for example, has said:

> If we want to make a reality of this post-bureaucratic era ... it's clear to me that political leaders will have to learn to let go. Let go of the information that we've guarded so jealously. Let go of the power that we live to exert. And above all, let go of the idea that "we know best" – that people can't be trusted to run their own lives. (Cameron, 2007)

Liberal Democrat leader Nick Clegg has also pledged his support for personalisation: '[Citizens] want public services which offer more flexibility and diversity – and fit with individual needs and circumstances – rather than being offered on the basis of a "take it or leave it" centrally prescribed format' (Clegg, 2008).

Drawing on technological innovations and new models such as social investment bonds, the Association of Chief Executives of Voluntary Organisations (ACEVO, 2009) has set out proposals for ways in which a range of policy sectors could be reformed according to personalisation principles, including education, welfare to work, criminal justice, transport and international aid and development. Keohane (2009, p 111) has suggested that personalisation could be the basis for introducing vouchers and 'oystercard'-type technology to reform travel and leisure services, voluntary work, criminal justice, recycling, the NHS and the council tax system, recommending that the Census should be redeveloped to gather information 'pertinent to the delivery of personalised services'.

There are a number of issues that will need to be addressed as personalisation stretches into other sectors. First, there are uncertainties over how far the infrastructure for personalisation exists outside the social care sector. Social care has a relatively well-established market of state-, voluntary- and private-sector providers that have grown up over many years. There is certainly nothing analogous in health, and it will take time for new markets to emerge in response to the demands of budget-holding service users. Although the exact terms of the government's 'Big Society' programme are as yet unclear, it appears that more public services will be run as social enterprises and mutuals, at arm's length from the state, which may make it easier for staff and users to work together to develop personalised approaches (Cabinet Office, 2010; Maude, 2010). However, it may also intensify the fragmentation that has impeded joint working, for example, between health and social care, or social care and criminal justice. The development of combined health and social care budgets will require commissioners to work through the complexities of combining means-tested social care monies with health services that are free at the point of use (Audit Commission, 2009, p 34). The reach of personalised principles in health may depend in large part on how far GPs perceive an incentive to promote the agenda in the new commissioning context (DH, 2010b).

New technologies may speed up the spread of personalisation between and its integration into different sectors. Banks are increasingly working with local authorities on smart cards that can be used for personal budgets – and in the future could be expanded into a range of sectors. As one interviewee from the banking sector put it, "We see [prepaid cards] as a major business opportunity, an inexorable trend across the world for more personalised services.... There is huge appetite for this, huge latent demand." Another banker set out his vision of the future, "You could get a card when you are born which caters for your education, your health needs, etc."

A second issue that will need to be addressed encompasses the ethical, relational and collective issues of personalisation. Tensions between individual and collective agency will be evident in health as they have been in social care. Health inequalities remain highly entrenched, as the Marmot Review (Marmot, 2010) set out. Lord Darzi (2008, p 28) envisaged personal health budgets as a tool for tackling health inequalities in recognition that poorer households were more likely to contain someone with a long-term health condition. Flexibility around budgets might enable people to spend money on upgrading aspects of their home that were contributing to ill-health. However, the Marmot Review noted that action to reduce health inequalities would require a focus beyond core health issues into improved life chances for young people, fair employment and sustainable communities (Marmot, 2010, p 9). Devolving responsibility for health to the action or inaction of the individual patient overstates the scope that individuals alone have to tackle ill-health. Diabetes UK (2008, p 8) have argued:

> Having an Individual Budget for the entire care package for a complex, changing and progressive condition such as diabetes, could potentially result in individuals receiving suboptimal clinical care if their budgets run out, or a process of self-rationing in order to achieve all desired goals within budget.

Issues germane to the relational aspects of health care also remain important. For example, new telehealth technologies, such as home monitoring units, may make it easier to tailor the experience of health management to the individual. However, they may also strip people out of a social context in which they receive companionship and care as well as a health assessment.

Third, there are issues relating to who should be given a budget, and on what terms. The interim report of ACEVO's Commission on Personalisation called for primary legislation for 'a "right to control" that applies across a wide range of specified public services, setting out a framework for devolving budgetary control towards individuals across the public service spectrum and across the range of people using services' (ACEVO, 2009, p 29). The report suggested that different levels of control could be devolved to different user groups, based on the following questions:

1. Does the service user want to achieve the same outcome as the public funding in question is being spent to achieve (e.g. employment, good health)?
2. Does the service user have the knowledge, skills and capacity to achieve that outcome if given control over his or her own budget for it? (ACEVO, 2009, p 28)

Thus, they argue:

> An unemployed person who does not really want to get a job should not be given control over their welfare-to-work budget, but might be able to control their social care budget, and should not stop those who do want to work from having a greater say over the support they receive to get back into work (ACEVO, 2009, p 28)

The emphasis on positive incentives for behaviour change links to other ideas supported by the Conservative Party (Cialdini, 1993; Thaler and Sunstein, 2008). However, it may be more difficult in practice to distinguish between those who 'really want to get a job' and others. The extent to which the long-term unemployed are work-shy or are excluded from the workforce by a range of socio-economic barriers has animated welfare debates for centuries, and expecting front-line staff to make the distinction on fair and transparent criteria may be optimistic at best. Personalisation in this account requires professionals to concede just the right amount of authority, depending on the profile of the user. In some sectors it may be possible to identify an expert user, whereas in others the emphasis will remain on the expert professional. The physically disabled person may be offered as the exemplar of the expert user, requiring the professional only as a system navigator. The ex-offender may be placed at the other end of the spectrum, dependent on professional knowledge to develop appropriate plans for a probationary period upon which entitlement to other benefits and support are predicated. In practice, there are many services in which the balance about who owns expert knowledge, and within what parameters, will be shifting and contested. Indeed, a compelling element of the personalisation story is that users are not bounded by sectoral divisions. They are at one and the same time users of a range of services: they are ex-offenders with mental health problems; they are people with a disability who are required (or choose) to seek work. These multiple roles make a spectrum from expert user to expert professional highly problematic.

A progressive personalisation

Despite the issues and concerns that have been expressed in relation to personalisation, it is likely to remain a dominant narrative in welfare state reform in future years – with impacts that are material as well as expressive. Given the trend of politics at the moment – towards a small, low-cost state – it is easy to envisage the co-option of personalisation by a political movement that is antithetical to its potential to advance equity, inclusion, citizenship and empowerment. The reforms look set to transfer greater risk on to the individual, and there are suggestions that moves to individual budgets in a range of services could be a step on the way to greater use of co-payment, building on the model of prescription charges or university tuition fees.

Spandler notes that reforms are always implemented in the context of a wider political landscape that 'can open up – and close down – opportunities for the development of greater strategies for self-determination'. With regard to direct payments, Spandler goes on:

> Direct payments exist within a constraining political culture which ultimately limits the extent to which they might be able to provide the wider benefits advocated by their proponents. Therefore, the extent of their progressiveness may ultimately depend not only on local implementation strategies, but also on these wider forces and, more importantly, how these forces are collectively negotiated, influenced and challenged. (2004, p 205)

Concerns about the way that personalisation is being co-opted have been expressed by Roulstone and Morgan in their discussion of day centre closures. They argue that the deployment of the language of personalisation and self-directed support in relation to closures signals 'the borrowing by the English government of the language of radical disability politics, which makes criticism of its key precepts seem misplaced and "unreasonable"' (Roulstone and Morgan, 2009, p 334). Here personalisation becomes a legitimising tool, separated from the values that originally animated it.

Spandler (2004, p 203) suggests a number of strategies to ensure that individual choice and collective provision – both potentially progressive ideals – can be realised, including the pooling of direct payments, the setting up of consumer cooperatives and greater collaboration between the trade union movement and welfare user movement to improve workforce protection for personal assistants. In relation to personal budgets, it has been widely argued that there needs to be an appropriate infrastructure of information, advice and advocacy to ensure that people can make the most of the choices they encounter, and that those who do not have the support of existing social networks are not further disadvantaged. There also needs to be a much clearer understanding of the mechanisms through which – and the spaces in which – people can come together to pool budgets and make choices that are about more than individualised care.

The reforms offer the opportunity to improve the lives of marginalised groups – for example, those with physical and learning disabilities, children in care and children with additional needs – providing them with stronger advocates or greater scope for self-advocacy (OPM, 2008; Glasby and Littlechild, 2009). Le Grand and others warn against nostalgia for the 'traditional' welfare state, highlighting the scope for already advantaged users to access a disproportional share of resources (Le Grand, 2007; see also Newman and Clarke, 2009a). Yet the mechanisms put in place to foster equity under personalisation and related reforms – brokers in social care, budget-holding lead professionals in children's services, choice advisors in health and education – remain fragile resources, potentially expendable as budgets shrink. Protecting the elements of personalisation that sustain equity as well as individual choice will be a key challenge for progressive reformers.

Conclusion

Debates about personalisation often incline authors to conclude with passionate advocacy or impassioned critique. However, Hartley's (2007, p 637) words on personalised education seem highly resonant for a policy context characterised by ambivalence: 'The application of personalisation … is appropriately riven with imprecision: that is, we must each make of it what we will.' Although the identification and problematisation of a personalisation narrative has been the focus of this book, that narrative is itself shifting and contested. The conclusion of Barnes et al (2005, p 186), following their evaluation of Health Action Zones, is just as pertinent to personalisation: 'many different stories can be legitimately told…. The simple truth is that we cannot answer the question – what difference did [the policy] make – without narrating elaborate stories laden with many qualifications.'

The future shape of personalisation will depend not only on the values that underpin it, but also on the stories that are told about it, and the way that those are integrated into broader governmental narratives about the welfare state. Personalisation can be deployed alongside stories critiquing the post-war welfare state, as offering monolithic services to an 'average citizen' (Keohane, 2009), but can also be weaved into more nostalgic accounts of the welfare state, based on the recovery of its 'real' ethos of collaboration and self-help (ACEVO, 2009). Thus, the personalisation story can be translated in various ways, depending on who is acting as narrator and which other stories are coupled to it (Freeman, 2009).

In an era in which voluntarism and personal responsibility are highly valued, and service cuts will be deep and long-lasting, it is hard not to be pessimistic about the likelihood that personalisation will take progressive forms. The benefits to be accrued from a 'new mutuality' remain highly uncertain (ACEVO, 2009), and may be hard to sustain as local authorities lack the resources to support the voluntary sector. Contemplating this political landscape, it is difficult not to feel concern about the scope for personalisation to leave vulnerable service users and marginalised workers more exposed to risk, and to regret the loss of collective spaces alongside the potential marginalisation of 'logics of care' (Mol, 2008).

Yet, equally, it is hard not to feel some sympathy for campaigners from disability organisations who are encountering the same set of critiques that sought to slow down the implementation of direct payments 20 years ago. As personalisation spreads beyond social care, a new generation of critics are emerging, re-articulating categories of argument that have long been in circulation. Given that a reliable and widely accepted evidence base remains elusive, advocates of personalisation are frustrated by the repeated insistence that they must look for 'evidence that new approaches will work before trying them', demanding instead an alternative path of focusing on 'evidence of what doesn't work and try[ing] to improve practice by doing and reflecting' (Glasby, 2009).

However, problematisation remains an important response to a narrative that is being so widely and apparently indiscriminately applied to welfare state reform. As Howarth (2000, p 135) puts it, 'the strategy of problematization carries with it an intrinsically ethical connotation, as it seeks to show that dominant discursive constructions are contingent and political, rather than necessary'. As the personalisation narrative spreads – gathering together a constituency of support that stretches far beyond disability campaigners – it is important to acknowledge that it is one of many possible stories about welfare pasts and futures.

References

2020 Public Services Trust (2010) *A Brief History of Public Service Reform*, London: 2020 Public Services Trust.

ACEVO (Association of Chief Executives of Voluntary Organisations) (2009) *Making It Personal: A Social Market Revolution: The Interim Report of the ACEVO Commission on Personalisation*, London: ACEVO.

ADASS (Association of Directors of Adult Social Services) (2009) *Personalisation and the Law: Implementing Putting People First in the Current Legal Context*, London: ADASS.

Alakeson, V. (2007) *Putting Patients in Control: The Case for Extending Self-Direction into the NHS*, London: Social Market Foundation.

Aronowitz, S. (1988) *Science as Power: Discourse and Ideology in Modern Society*, Minneapolis: University of Minnesota Press.

Atkinson, R. (2002) 'Narratives of Policy: The Construction of Urban Problems and Urban Policy in the Official Discourses of British Government 1968–1998', *Critical Social Policy*, vol 20, no 2, pp 211–32.

Audit Commission (2006) *Choosing Well: Analysing the Costs and Benefits of Choice in Local Public Services*, London: Audit Commission.

Audit Commission (2009) *Supporting People Programme 2005–2009*, London: Audit Commission.

Audit Commission (2010a) *Protecting the Public Purse 2010*, London: Audit Commission.

Audit Commission (2010b) *Under Pressure: Tackling the Financial Challenge for Councils of an Ageing Population*, London: Audit Commission, www.audit-commission.gov.uk/SiteCollectionDocuments/Downloads/20100218-underpressure-nationalstudy.pdf

Baker, S., Brown, B.J. and Gwilym, H. (2008) 'The Rise of the Service User', *Soundings*, vol 40, pp 18–28.

Baldwin, R. (1995) *Rules and Government*, Oxford: Clarendon Press.

Bang, H. (2005) 'Among Everyday Makers and Expert Citizens', in J. Newman (ed) *Remaking Governance: Peoples, Politics and the Public Sphere*, Bristol: The Policy Press, pp 159–78.

Barber, M. (2007) *Instruction to Deliver: Tony Blair, the Public Services and the Challenge of Achieving Targets*, London: Politicos.

Barnes, M. (2008) 'Is the Personal No Longer Political?', *Soundings*, vol 39, pp 152–9.

Barnes, M. (2009) 'Alliance, Contention and Oppositional Consciousness: Can Public Participation Generate Subversion', in M. Barnes and D. Prior (eds) (2009) *Subversive Citizens: Power, Agency and Resistance in Public Services*, Bristol: The Policy Press, pp 33–48.

Barnes, M. (2011) 'Abandoning Care? A Critical Perspective on Personalisation from an Ethic of Care', *Ethics and Social Welfare*, forthcoming.

Barnes, M. and Prior, D. (2000) *Private Lives as Public Policy*, Birmingham: Venture Press.

Barnes, M. and Prior, D. (2009) 'Examining the Idea of "Subversion" in Public Services', in M. Barnes and D. Prior (eds) *Subversive Citizens: Power, Agency and Resistance in Public Services*, Bristol: The Policy Press, pp 3–13.

Barnes, M., Bauld, L., Benzeval, M., Judge, K., Mackenzie, M. and Sullivan, H. (2005) *Health Action Zones: Partnerships for Health Equity*, London: Routledge.

Barrett, S. (2004) 'Implementation Studies: Time for a Revival? Personal Reflections on 20 Years of Implementation Studies', *Public Administration*, vol 82, pp 249–62.

Barry, D. and Elmes, M. (1997) 'Strategy Retold: Toward a Narrative View of Strategic Discourse', *Academy of Management Review*, vol 22, no 2, pp 429–52.

Bartlett, J. (2009) *At Your Service: Navigating the Future Market in Health and Social Care*, London: Demos.

Barton, A. (2008) 'New Labour's Management and Audit and "What Works" Approach to Controlling the "Untrustworthy" Professions', *Public Policy and Administration*, vol 23, no 3, pp 263–77.

Bawden, A. (2009) 'Dream Teams', *Society Guardian*, 8 July.

Beck, U. (1992) *Risk Society: Towards a New Modernity*, London: Sage.

Ben-Galim, D. and Sachrajda, A. (2010) *Now It's Personal: Learning from Welfare-to-Work Approaches Around the World*, London: IPPR.

Bennett, C. (1991) 'What Is Policy Convergence and What Causes It?', *British Journal of Political Science*, vol 21, pp 215–33.

Beresford, P. (2008) 'Whose Personalisation?', *Soundings*, vol 40, Winter issue, pp 8–17.

Beresford, P. and Croft, S. (2004) 'Service Users and Practitioners United: The Key Component for Social Work Reform', *British Journal of Social Work*, vol 34, pp 53–68.

Bevir, M. and Rhodes, R.A.W. (1999) 'Studying British Government: Reconstructing the Research Agenda', *The British Journal of Politics & International Relations*, vol 1, no 2, pp 215–39.

Bevir, M. and Rhodes, R.A.W. (2003) *Interpreting British Governance*, London: Routledge.

Bevir, M. and Rhodes, R.A.W. (2004a) 'Interpreting British Governance', in 'The Interpretive Approach in Political Science: A Symposium', *British Journal of Politics and International Relations*, vol 6, no 2, pp 130–6.

Bevir, M. and Rhodes, R.A.W. (2004b) 'Interpretation as Method, Explanation and Critique: A Reply', in 'The Interpretive Approach in Political Science: A Symposium', *British Journal of Politics and International Relations*, vol 6, no 2, pp 156–61.

Bevir, M. and Rhodes, R.A.W. (2006) 'Interpretive Approaches to British Government and Politics', *British Politics*, vol 1, no 1, pp 84–112.

Bevir, M. and Richards, D. (2009) 'Decentring Policy Networks: A Theoretical Agenda', *Public Administration*, vol 87, no 1, pp 3–14.

Blair, T. (1998) *The Third Way: New Politics for a New Century*, London: Fabian Society.

Blair, T. (2003) Speech to the Fabian Society, 17 June, London.

Blair, T. (2004) Speech on Public Services, 23 June, London.

Boje, D. (1991) 'The Storytelling Organization: A Study of Story Performance in an Office-Supply Firm', *Administrative Science Quarterly*, vol 36, no 1, pp 102–26.

Bornat, J. (2006) 'Introduction', in J. Leece and J. Bornat (eds) *Developments in Direct Payments*, Bristol: The Policy Press, pp 1–15.

Bosanquet, N. (2008) 'The Health and Welfare Legacy', in A. Seldon (ed) *Blair's Britain*, Cambridge: Cambridge University Press, pp 384–407.

Bovaird, T. (2007) 'Beyond Engagement and Participation: User and Community Co-production of Public Services', *Public Administration Review*, vol 67, no 5, pp 846–60

Bowers, H., Clark, A., Crosby, G., Easterbrook, L., Macadam, A., MacDonald, R., Macfarlane, A., Maclean, M., Patel, M., Runnicles, D., Oshinaike, T. and Smith, C. (2009) *Older People's Vision for Long-term Care*, York: Joseph Rowntree Foundation.

Boxall, K., Warren, L. and Chau, R.C.M. (2007) 'User Involvement', in S.M. Hodgson and Z. Irving (eds) *Policy Reconsidered: Meanings, Politics and Practices*, Bristol: The Policy Press, pp 155–72.

Boyle, D., Clark S. and Burns, S. (2006) *Hidden Work; Co-Production by People Outside Paid Employment*, York: Joseph Rowntree Foundation.

Brindle, D. (2010) 'The Care Minister Will Need Balls of Steel', *Society Guardian*, 29 September.

British Medical Journal (2003) 'Doctors as Sherpas: BMJ Round Table Debate', *The BMJ Patient Issue*, 14 June. Available at: www.bmj.com/content/vol326/issue7402/

Britton, J. (2007) 'Categorising and Policy Making', in S.M. Hodgson and Z. Irving (eds) *Policy Reconsidered: Meanings, Politics and Practices*, Bristol: The Policy Press, pp 61–76.

Brown, G. (2003) 'State and Market: Towards a Public Interest Test', *Political Quarterly*, vol 74, no 3, pp 266–84 (edited version of a speech delivered to the Social Market Foundation, Cass Business School, 3 February 2003).

Brown, G. (2008) 'Time for the Third Act in Public Sector Reform', *Financial Times*, 10 March.

Bruner, J. (1990) *Acts of Meaning*, Cambridge, MA: Harvard University Press.

Bruner, J. (2002) *Making Stories: Law, Literature, Life*, New York: Farrar, Strauss and Giroux.

Bruner, J. (2004) 'Life as Narrative', *Social Research*, vol 71, no 3, pp 691–710.

Burns, S. and Smith, K. (2004) *Co-Production Works! The Win: Win of Involving Local People in Public Services*, London: New Economics Foundation.

Burr, V. (1995) *An Introduction to Social Constructionism*, London: Routledge.

Cabinet Office (1999) *Modernising Government*, Cm 4310, London: HMSO.

Cabinet Office (2009) *Building Britain's Future*, London: HMSO.

Cabinet Office (2010) 'Francis Maude Launches Pathfinder Mutuals', press release, 12 August.

Callaghan, G. and Wistow, G. (2008) 'Can the Community Construct Knowledge to Shape Services in the Local State? A Case Study', *Critical Social Policy*, vol 28, no 2, pp 165–86.

Callon, M. (1986) 'Some Elements of a Sociology of Translation: Domestication of the Scallops and the Fishermen of Saint Brieuc Bay', in J. Law (ed) *Power, Action and Belief: A New Sociology of Knowledge*, London: Routledge, pp 196–233.

Cambridge, P. and Carnaby, S. (2005) 'Introduction and Overview', in P. Cambridge and S. Carnaby (eds) *Person-Centred Planning and Care Management with People with Learning Disabilities*, London: Jessica Kingsley, pp 9–18.

Cambridge, P., Hayes, L. and Knapp, M., with Gould, E. and Fenyo, A. (1994) *Care in the Community: Five Years On*, Canterbury: Personal Social Services Research Unit, University of Kent.

Cameron, D. (2007) 'The Post-Bureaucratic Age', speech, 12 October.

Cameron, D. (2009) 'It is not Enough for Labour to Lose This Election', *Spectator*, 21 March.

Campbell, J. (1997) 'Implementing Direct Payments: Towards the Next Millennium', in S. Balloch and N. Connelly (eds) *Buying and Selling Social Care*, London: National Institute for Social Work, pp 22–34.

Campbell, J. (1998) 'From Breakout to Breakthrough: 25 Years of Legislative Advocacy', in B. Duncan and R. Berman-Bieler (eds) *International Leadership Forum for Women with Disabilities: Final Report*, New York: Rehabilitation International.

Campbell, R.J., Robinson, W., Neelands, J., Hewston, R. and Mazzoli, L. (2007) 'Personalised Learning: Ambiguities in Theory and Practice', *British Journal of Educational Studies*, vol 55, no 2, pp 135–54.

Carr, S. (2008) *Personalisation: A Rough Guide*, London: Social Care Institute for Excellence.

Carr, S. (2010a) *Personalisation: A Rough Guide*, rev edn, London: Social Care Institute for Excellence.

Carr, S. (2010b) *Personalisation, Productivity and Efficiency*, London: Social Care Institute for Excellence.

Carr, S. (2010c) *Enabling Risk, Ensuring Safety: Self-Directed Support and Personal Budgets*, London: Social Care Institute for Excellence.

Carr, S. and Robbins, D. (2009) *SCIE Research Briefing 20: The Implementation of Individual Budget Schemes in Adult Social Care*, London: SCIE.

Cialdini, R. (1993) *Influence: The Psychology of Persuasion*, New York: Quill.

CIPFA (Chartered Institute of Public Finance and Accountancy) (1998) *Community Care Direct Payments: Accounting and Financial Management Guidelines*, London: CIPFA.

CIPFA (2007) *Direct Payments and Individual Budgets: Managing the Finances*, London: CIPFA.

Clarke, J. (2005) 'New Labour's Citizens: Activated, Empowered, Responsibilised, Abandoned?', *Critical Social Policy*, vol 25, no 4, pp 447–63.

Clarke, J. (2010) 'Beyond Citizens and Consumers? Publics and Public-Service Reform', *The NISPAcee Journal of Public Administration and Policy*, vol 2, no 2, pp 37–48.

Clarke, J. and Newman, J. (1997) *The Managerial State*, London: Sage.

Clarke, J., Cochrane, A. and Smart, C. (1987) *Ideologies of Welfare: From Dreams to Disillusion*, London: Hutchinson.

Clarke, J., Newman, J., Smith, N., Vidler, E. and Westmarland, L. (2007) *Creating Citizen-Consumers: Changing Publics and Changing Public Services*, London: Sage.

Clegg, N. (2008) Speech sponsored by the CentreForum, 17 June, London.

Coats, D. (2007) 'Hard Labour? The Future of Work and the Role of Public Policy', in G. Hassan (ed) *After Blair: Politics after the New Labour Decade*, London: Lawrence and Wishart.

Coleman, A. (2007) 'The Developing Discourses of Local Authority Health Scrutiny', *Critical Policy Analysis*, vol 1, no 2, pp 200–16.

Committee of Public Accounts (2003) *Tenth Report: Individual Learning Accounts*. Available at: www.publications.parliament.uk/pa/cm200203/cmselect/cmpubacc/544/54403.htm

Community Care (2010) 'Personalisation: How Well Is It Actually Working?' Available at: www.communitycare.co.uk/carespace/forums/personalisation-how-well-is-it-actually-working-6739.aspx (accessed 1 June 2010).

Concilium (2009) *Social Enterprises Working with Prisons and Probation Services: A Mapping Exercise for National Offender Management Service*, London: Ministry of Justice/Cabinet Office.

Conservative Party (2008) *Prisons with a Purpose*, London: Conservative Party.

Conservative Party (2010) *Invitation to Join the Government of Britain: The Conservative Manifesto 2010*, London: Conservative Party.

Corrigan, P., Jones, T., Lloyd, J. and Young, J. (1988) 'Citizen Gains', *Marxism Today*, August, pp 18–21.

Cottam, H. (2009) 'Public Service Reform, the Individual and the State', *Soundings*, vol 42, pp 79–89.

Cottam, H. and Leadbeater, C. (2004) *Health: Co-creating Services*, London: Design Council.

Coulson, S. (2007) 'Person-Centred Planning as Co-Production', *Research Highlights in Social Work: Co-Production and Personalisation in Social Care, Changing Relationships in the Provision of Social Care*, vol 49, pp 105–18.

Cowburn, M. (2007) 'Ethics, Research and Policy', in S. M. Hodgson, and Z. Irving (eds) *Policy Reconsidered: Meanings, Politics and Practices*, Bristol, The Policy Press, pp 137–54.

Cowen, A. (2010) *Personalised Transition: Innovations in Health, Education and Support*, Sheffield: Centre for Welfare Reform.

CQC (Care Quality Commission) (2010) *The State of Health Care and Adult Social Care in England: Key Themes and Quality of Service in 2009*, London: CQC.

Crosby, N. (2010) *Personalisation: Children, Young People and Families*, Wythall: In Control.

Crossley, N. (2002) *Making Sense of Social Movements*, Buckingham: Open University Press.

CSCI (Commission for Social Care Inspection) (2004) *Direct Payments: What Are the Barriers*, London: CSCI.

Cummins, J. and Miller, C. (2007) *Co-Production, Social Capital and Service Effectiveness*, London: Office for Public Management.

Cutler, T., Waine, B, and Brehony, K. (2007) 'A New Epoch of Individualization? Problems with the "Personalization" of Public Sector Services', *Public Administration*, vol 85, no 3, pp 847–55.

Czarniawska, B. (1988) *A Narrative Approach to Organization Studies*, London: Sage.

Darzi, A., Lord (2007) *Our NHS, Our Future: NHS Next Stage Review: Interim Report*, London: Department of Health.

Darzi, A., Lord (2008) *High Quality Care for All, NHS Next Stage Review: Final Report.* London: Department of Health.

Davey, V., Snell, T., Fernández, J., Knapp, M., Tobin, R., Jolly, D., Perkins, M., Kendall, J., Pearson, C., Vick, N., Swift, P., Mercer, G. and Priestley, M. (2007) *Schemes Providing Support to People Using Direct Payments: A UK Survey*, London: Personal Social Services Research Unit, London School of Economics and Political Science.

Davies, C. (2008) *Reflexive Ethnography: A Guide to Researching Selves and Others*, 2nd edn, London: Routledge.

DCSF (Department for Children, Schools and Families) (2007) *The Children's Plan: Building Brighter Futures*, Cm 7280, London: HMSO.

DCSF (2008) *Family Intervention Projects: An Evaluation of Their Design, Set-up and Early Outcomes: A Research Brief*, London: DCSF.

DCSF (2009) *Your Child, Your Schools, Our Future: Building a 21st Century Schools System*, Cm 7588, London: HMSO.

Dean, M. (1999) *Governmentality: Power and Rule in Modern Society*, London: Sage.

Dearden Phillips, C. (2009) Naked Entrepreneur blog posting, 10 October. Available at: http://nakedentrepreneur.blogspot.com/2009_10_01_archive.html

Department of Health Care Networks (2009) 'Personalisation'. Available at: www.dhcarenetworks.org.uk/IndependentLivingChoices/Housing/Topics/browse/Homelessness1/No_One_Left_Out/Personalisation/

DETR (Department of the Environment, Transport and the Regions) (2000) *The Housing Green Paper: Quality and Choice: A Decent Home For All*, London: HMSO.

Dewey, J. (1927) *The Public and Its Problems*, New York: Swallow.

DfES (Department for Education and Skills) (2005) *Higher Standards, Better Schools for All*, Cm 6677, London: HMSO.

DfES (2007) *Aiming High for Disabled Children: Better Support for Families*, London: HM Treasury/DfES.

DH (Department of Health) (1989) *Caring for People: Community Care in the Next Decade and Beyond*, London: HMSO.

DH (1990) *Community Care in the Next Decade and Beyond: Policy Guidance*, London: HMSO.

DH (1997) *The New NHS: Modern and Dependable*, London: The Stationery Office.

DH (1999) *Saving Lives: Our Healthier Nation*, Cm 1523, London: HMSO.

DH (2000) *NHS Plan,* London: Department of Health.

DH (2001) *Valuing People: A New Strategy for Learning Disability for the Twenty-First Century*, London: DH.

DH (2002) *Planning with People: Towards Person-Centred Approaches*, London: Department of Health.

DH (2004) *The NHS Improvement Plan: Putting People at the Heart of Public Services*, Cm 6268, London: HMSO.

DH (2005) *Independence, Well-being and Choice*, London: HMSO.

DH (2006) *Our Health, Our Care, Our Say: A New Direction for Community Services*, Cm 6737, London: HMSO.

DH (2008a) *Commissioning for Personalisation*, London: DH.

DH (2008b) *Putting People First – Personalisation Toolkit*, London: DH.

DH (2008c) *Putting People First – Working to Make It Happen: Adult Social Care Workforce Strategy – Interim Statement*, London: DH.

DH (2009a) *Personal Health Budgets: First Steps*, London: Department of Health.

DH (2009b) *Contracting for Personalised Outcomes*, London: DH/Putting People First.

DH (2009c) *Safeguarding Adults: Response to Consultation on the Review of the No Secrets Guidance*, London: DH.

DH (2009d) *Working to Put People First: The Strategy for the Adult Social Care Workforce in England*, London: DH.

DH (2010a) 'More Power to the Patient', Press release, 28 June.

DH (2010b) *Equity and Excellence: Liberating the NHS*, Cm 7881, London: HMSO.

Diabetes UK (2008) 'Individual Budgets, Healthcare, Choice and Control', Position statement and briefing paper, London: Diabetes UK.

DiMaggio, P. and Powell, W. (1983) 'The Iron Cage Revisited: Institutional Isomorphism and Collective Rationality in Organizational Fields', *American Sociological Review*, vol 48, pp 147–60.

Dodge, J., Ospina, S.M. and Foldy, E.G. (2005) 'Integrating Rigor and Relevance in Public Administration Scholarship: The Contribution of Narrative Inquiry', *Public Administration Review*, vol 65, no 3, pp 286–300.

Dolowitz, D.P. (1998) *Learning from America: Policy Transfer and the Development of the British Workfare State*, Sussex: Sussex Academic Press.

Dolowitz, D. and Marsh, D. (2000) 'Learning from Abroad: The Role of Policy Transfer in Contemporary Policy Making', *Governance*, vol 13, no 1, pp 5–24.

Dowding, K. (2004) 'Interpretation, Truth and Investigation: Comments on Bevir and Rhodes', *British Journal of Politics and International Relations*, vol 6, no 2, pp 136–42.

Dowson, S. and Greig, R. (2009) 'The Emergence of the Independent Support Broker Role', *Journal of Integrated Care*, vol 17, no 4, pp 22–30.

Driver, S. and Martell, L. (1999) *New Labour: Politics after Thatcherism*, Cambridge: Polity Press.

Duffy, S. (1996) *Unlocking the Imagination: Purchasing Services for People with Learning Difficulties*, London: Choice Press.

Duffy, S. (2005) *Keys to Citizenship: A Guide to Getting Good Support for People with Learning Disabilities*, 2nd edn, Birkenhead: Paradigm.

Duffy, S. (2008) *Smart Commissioning: Exploring the Impact of Personalisation on Commissioning*, London: In Control.

Duffy, S. (2010) *The Future of Personalisation: Implications for Welfare Reform*, Sheffield: Centre for Welfare Reform.

Duffy, S. and Fulton, K (2009) *Should We Ban Brokerage?*, Sheffield: Centre for Welfare Reform/Paradigm.

Duffy, S., Waters, J. and Glasby, J. (2010) *Personalisation and the Social Care Revolution': Future Options for the Reform of Public Services*, Health Services Management Centre policy paper 3, University of Birmingham: Health Services Management Centre.

Du Gay, P. (2003) 'The Tyranny of the Epochal: Change, Epochalism and Organizational Reform', *Organization*, vol 10, no 4, pp 663–84.

Dunning, J. (2010a) 'Ministers to Be Lobbied on Personalisation Development', *Community Care*, 30 June.

Dunning, J. (2010b) 'Personalisation May Force Day Centre Closures in Liverpool', *Community Care*, 30 June.

Dunning, J. (2010c) 'Care Minister Rejects Council Job Cuts Claim', *Community Care*, 14 July.

Dunning, J. (2011) 'Cuts Are Ravaging Personalisation, Say Social Workers', *Community Care*, 28 January.

DWP (Department for Work and Pensions) (2005) *Opportunity Age*, London: DWP.

DWP (2006) *A New Deal for Welfare: Empowering People to Work*, Cm 6730, London: HMSO.

DWP (2008) *No One Written Off: Reforming Welfare to Reward Responsibility*, London: The Stationery Office.

DWP (2010) *Framework Agreement for the Provision of Employment Related Support Services*, London: DWP.

Edwards, A., Apostolov, A., Dooher, I. and Popova, A. (2008) 'Working with Extended Schools to Prevent Social Exclusion', in K. Morris (ed) *Social Work and Multi Agency Working: Making a Difference*, Bristol: The Policy Press, pp 47–66.

Eisenberg, E.M. (1984) 'Ambiguity as Strategy in Organizational Communication', *Communication Monographs*, vol 51, no 3, pp 227–42.

Ellis, K. (2007) 'Direct Payments and Social Work Practice: The Significance of "Street-level Bureaucracy" in Determining Eligibility', *British Journal of Social Work*, vol 37, pp 405–22.

Elmore, R.F. (1978) 'Organizational Models of Social Program Implementation', *Public Policy*, vol 26, pp 185–228.

Elwell, L. (no date) *Partners in Policymaking UK: Information Booklet*. Available at: www.in-control.org.uk/site/INCO/UploadedResources/0528_Partners_Booklet.doc

English Community Care Association (2010) *Personalising Care: A Route Map to Delivery for Care Providers*, London: ECCA.

Evans, T. and Hardy, M., with Shaw, I. (2010) *Evidence and Knowledge for Practice*, Cambridge: Polity Press.

Ferguson, I. (2007) 'Increasing User Choice or Privatizing Risk: The Antimonies of Personalization', *British Journal of Social Work*, vol 37, pp 387–403.

Finlayson, A. (2003) *Making Sense of New Labour*, London: Lawrence and Wishart.

Finlayson, A. (2004) 'Meaning and Politics: Assessing Bevir and Rhodes', in 'The Interpretive Approach in Political Science: A Symposium', *British Journal of Politics and International Relations*, vol 6, no 2, pp 149–56.

Finlayson, A. (2009) 'Financialisation, Financial Literacy and Asset-Based Welfare', *British Journal of Politics and International Relations,* vol 11, no 3, pp 400–21.

Fischer, F. (2003) *Reframing Public Policy: Discursive Politics and Deliberative Practices*, Oxford: Oxford University Press.

Fischer, F. (2007) 'Policy Analysis in Critical Perspective: The Epistemics of Discursive Practices', *Critical Policy Analysis*, vol 1, no 1, pp 97–109.

Fischer, F. (2009) *Democracy and Expertise: Reorienting Policy Inquiry*, Oxford: Oxford University Press.

Fisher, W.R. (1989) *Human Communication as Narration: Toward a Philosophy of Reason, Value and Action*, Columbia: University of South Carolina Press.

Flint, J. (2009) 'Subversive Subjects and Conditional, Earned and Denied Citizenship', in M. Barnes and D. Prior (eds) *Subversive Citizens: Power, Agency and Resistance in Public Services*, Bristol: The Policy Press, pp 83–100.

Foster, M., Harris, J., Jackson, K., Morgan, H. and Glendinning, C. (2006) 'Personalised Social Care for Adults with Disabilities: A Problematic Concept for Frontline Practice', *Health and Social Care in the Community*, vol 14, no 2, pp 125–35.

Foucault, M. (1991) 'Polemics, Politics and Problematizations: An Interview', in P. Rabinow (ed) *The Foucault Reader*, 2nd edn, Harmondsworth: Penguin, pp 381–90.

Fraser, N. (2000) 'Rethinking Recognition', *New Left Review*, vol 3, May/June.

Freeman, R. (2009) 'What Is Translation?', *Evidence and Policy*, vol 5, no 4, pp 429–47.

Gains, F. and Clarke, K. (2007) 'Constructing Delivery: Implementation as an Interpretive Process', *Critical Policy Analysis*, vol 1, no 2, pp 133–8.

Gannon, Z. and Lawson, N. (2008) *Co-Production: The Modernisation of Public Services by Staff and Users*, London: Compass.

Geertz, C. (1973) *The Interpretation of Cultures*, New York: Basic Books.

Giddens, A. (1998) *The Third Way*, Cambridge: Polity Press.

Gilbert, C. (2007) *2020 Vision: Report of the Teaching and Learning in 2020 Review Group*, London: DfES.

Glasby, J. (2009) 'Why People Disagree about Direct Payments and Personal Budgets'. Available at: www.communitycare.co.uk/Articles/2009/05/22/111636/Why-people-disagree-about-direct-payments-and-personal.htm

Glasby, J. (2011) 'Introduction', in J. Glasby (ed) *Evidence, Policy and Practice: Critical Perspectives in Health and Social Care*, Bristol: The Policy Press.

Glasby, J. and Beresford, P. (2006) 'Who Knows Best? Evidence-Based Practice and the Service User Contribution', *Critical Social Policy*, vol 26, no 1, pp 268–84.

Glasby, J. and Dickinson, H. (eds) (2009) *International Perspectives on Health and Social Care*, Oxford: Wiley-Blackwell.

Glasby, J. and Littlechild, R. (2006) 'An Overview of the Implementation and Development of Direct Payments', in J. Leece and J. Bornat (eds) *Developments in Direct Payments*, Bristol: The Policy Press, pp 19–32.

Glasby, J. and Littlechild, R. (2009) *Direct Payments and Personal Budgets: Putting Personalisation into Practice*, Bristol: The Policy Press.

Glasby, J., Duffy, S. and Needham, C. (2010) 'A Beveridge Report for the Twenty-First Century? The Implications of Self-Directed Support for Future Welfare Reform', Paper presented to 'A Beveridge Report for the Twenty-First Century? The Implications of Self-Directed Support for Future Welfare Reform: A 2-Day Think Tank', Health Services Management Centre, University of Birmingham, June.

Glendinning, C., Halliwell, S., Jacobs, S., Rummery, K. and Tyer, J. (2000) 'New Kinds of Care, New Kinds of Relationships: How Purchasing Affects Relationships in Giving and Receiving Personal Assistance', *Health and Social Care in the Community*, vol 8, no 3, pp 201–11.

Glendinning, C., Challis, D., Fernandez, J., Jacobs, S., Jones, K., Knapp, M., Manthorpe, J., Moran, N., Netten, A., Stevens, M. and Wilberforce, M. (2008) *Evaluation of the Individual Budgets Pilot Programme: Final Report*, York: Social Policy Research Unit, University of York.

Gordon, D. (1988) 'Tenacious Assumptions in Western Medicine', in M. Lock and D. Gordon (eds) *Biomedicine Examined*, Dordrecht: Kluwer Academic Publishers, pp 19–56.

Gould, S.J. (1988) *Time's Arrow, Time's Cycle*, Harmondsworth: Penguin.

Gove, M. (2010) 'Written Ministerial Statement to Parliament', 26 July.

Grant, W. (2009) 'Intractable Policy Failure: The Case of Bovine TB and Badgers', *British Journal of Politics and International Relations*, vol 11, no 4, pp 557–73.

Greener, I. (2008) 'The Stages of New Labour', in M. Powell (ed) *Modernising the Welfare State: The Blair Legacy*, Bristol: The Policy Press, pp 219–34.

Gregg, P. (2008) *Realising Potential: A Vision for Personalised Conditionality and Support*, London: DWP.

Griffiths, S., Foley, B. and Prendergast, J. (2009) *Assertive Citizens: New Relationships in the Public Services*, London: Social Market Foundation.

Griggs, S. and Howarth, D. (2002) 'The Work of Ideas and Interests in Public Policy', in A. Finlayson and J. Valentine (eds) *Politics and Post-Structuralism: An Introduction*, Edinburgh: Edinburgh University Press, pp 97–112.

Grit, K. and de Bont, A (2010) 'Tailor-Made Finance versus Tailor-Made Care. Can the State Strengthen Consumer Choice in Health Care by Reforming the Financial Structure of Long-Term Care?', *Journal of Medical Ethics*, vol 36, no 2, pp 79–83.

Gusfield, J. (1976) 'The Literary Rhetoric of Science: Comedy and Pathos in Drinking Driver Research', *American Sociological Review*, vol 41, no 1, pp 16–34.

Habermas, J. (1973) *Legitimation Crisis*, Boston: Beacon Press.

HACT (Housing Associations' Charitable Trust) (2010) 'Up2Us Summary'. Available at: http://hact.org.uk/up2us

Hajer, M. (2005) *The Politics of Environmental Discourse: Ecological Modernization and the Policy Process*, 2nd edn, Oxford, Oxford University Press.

Haldenby, A., Nolan, P., Parsons, L. and Rosen, G. (2009) *The Front Line*, London: Reform.

Hall, P.A. (1993) 'Policy Paradigms, Social Learning, and the State: The Case of Economic Policy Making in Britain', *Comparative Politics*, vol 25, no 3, pp 275–96.

Hartley, D. (2007) 'Personalisation: The Emerging "Revised" Code of Education', *Oxford Review of Education*, vol 33, no 5, pp 629–42.

Hasler, F., Campbell, J. and Zarb, G. (1999) *Direct Routes to Independence: A Guide to Local Authority Implementation and Management of Direct Payments*, London: Policy Studies Institute.

Hayward, G., Hodgson, A., Johnson, J., Oancea, A., Pring, R., Spours, K., Wilde, S. and Wright, S. (2005) *Annual Report of the Nuffield Review of 14–19 Education and Training*, Oxford: Nuffield Foundation.

Help the Aged (2009) *Personalisation in Social Care: Progress in the UK and Abroad*, London: Help the Aged. Available at: http://policy.helptheaged.org.uk/NR/rdonlyres/5CC8D359-0790-4DD1-B8D8-A495558EBA79/0/personalisation_soc_care_060309.pdf

Hewitt, P. (2006) Speech, Fabian Society, 26 April, London.

Hill, M. and Hupe, P. (2002) *Implementing Public Policy*, Sage: London.

HM Government (2003) *Every Child Matters*, Cm 5860, London: The Stationery Office.

HM Government (2007) *Putting People First: A Shared Vision and Commitment to the Transformation of Adult Social Care*, London: HM Government.

HM Government (2008) *Carers at the Heart of 21st Century Families and Communities: A Caring System on Your Side, a Life of Your Own*, London: HM Government.

HM Government (2009) *Putting the Frontline First: Smarter Government*, Cm 7753, London: The Stationery Office.

HM Government (2010a) *The Coalition: Our Programme for Government*, London: Cabinet Office.

HM Government (2010b) *Response to the Report of the Communities and Local Government Select Committee on Supporting People*, London: HMSO.

Howarth, D. (2000) *Discourse*, Buckingham: Open University Press.

Hunter, S. and Ritchie, P. (2007a) 'Introduction: With, Not to: Models of Co-Production in Social Welfare', *Research Highlights in Social Work: Co-Production and Personalisation in Social Care, Changing Relationships in the Provision of Social Care*, vol 49, pp 9–18.

Hunter, S. and Ritchie, P. (2007b) 'Endnote', *Research Highlights in Social Work: Co-Production and Personalisation in Social Care, Changing Relationships in the Provision of Social Care*, vol 49, pp 105–18.

Hurst, G. (2009) 'Undergraduates Should Be Given "Consumer Rights," Says Lord Mandelson', *The Times*, 4 November.

Hutchinson, P., Land, J. and Salisbury, B. (2006) 'North American Approaches to Individualised Planning and Funding', in J. Leece and J. Bornat (eds) *Developments in Direct Payments*, Bristol: The Policy Press, pp 49–62.

Ibarra, H. and Barbulescu, R. (2010) 'Identity as Narrative: Prevalence, Effectiveness and Consequences of Narrative Identity Work in Macro Work Role Transitions', *Academy of Management Review*, vol 35, no 1, pp 135–54.

IDeA (Improvement and Development Agency) (2010) *Adult Safeguarding Scrutiny Guide*, London: IDeA.

IDeA (no date) *Transforming Adult Social Care: Access to Information, Advice and Advocacy*, London: IDeA.

IFF Research (2008) *Employment Aspects and Workforce Implications of Direct Payment*, Leeds: Skills for Care.

Illich, I. (1995) *Limits to Medicine*, London: Marion Boyars Publishers. Originally published in January 1975 as *Medical Nemesis: The Expropriation of Health*.

Illich, I. (2002 [1970]) *Deschooling Society*, London: Marion Boyars Publishers.

In Control (2010) 'Shop4Support'. Available at: www.shop4support. com/s4s/ui/content/CustomNewsPage.aspx?Id=292116

In Control Cymru (no date) *From Policy to Reality*. Available at: www. in-control.org.uk/site/INCO/UploadedResources/0149_Policy_ Reality_English.pdf

Innes, J. (1990) *Knowledge and Public Policy*, 2nd edition, New Brunswick, NJ: Transaction Books.

Izuhara, M. (2003) 'Social Inequality under a New Social Contract: Long-Term Care in Japan', *Social Policy and Administration*, vol 37, no 4, pp 395–410.

James, O. and Lodge, M. (2003) 'The Limitations of "Policy Transfer" and "Lesson Drawing" for Public Policy Research', *Political Studies Review*, vol 1, pp 179–93.

Jasper, J.M. (1998) 'The Emotions of Protest: Affective and Reactive Emotions in and Around Social Movements', *Sociological Forum*, vol 13, no 3, pp 397–424.

Jeffares, S. (2007) 'Why Public Policy Ideas Catch On: Empty Signifiers and Flourishing Neighbourhoods', Unpublished PhD thesis, University of Birmingham.

Jerome, J. (2010) Speech at the In Control Big Event, Liverpool, 15 March. Available at: www.in-control.org.uk/bigevent2010audio

Joseph, K. (1975) *Reversing the Trend: A Critical Re-Appraisal of Conservative Economic and Social Policies: Seven Speeches*, Chichester: Rose.

Kaplan, T. (1993) 'Reading Policy Narratives: Beginnings, Middles and Ends', in F. Fischer and J. Forester (eds) *The Argumentative Turn in Policy Analysis*, London: UCL Press.

Keen, A. (2007) *The Cult of the Amateur: How Today's Internet is Killing our Culture*, London: Crown.

Keohane, N. (2009) *People Power: How Can We Personalise Public Services*, London: New Local Government Network.

Kingdon, J. (1995) *Agendas, Alternatives and Public Policies*, 2nd edn, London: Longman.

Laclau, E. (1996) *Emancipation(s)*, London: Verso.

Laclau, E. and Mouffe, C. (1985) *Hegemony and the Socialist Strategy*, London: Verso.

Land, H. and Himmelweit, S. (2010) *Who Cares: Who Pays?*, London: Unison.

Lansley, A. (2008) 'No Excuses, No Nannying', Speech to Reform, 27 August.

Lansley, A. (2010) Speech to the British Medical Association Conference, Brighton, 30 June.

Lather, P. (1991) *Getting Smart: Feminist Research and Pedagogy with/in the Postmodern*, New York: Routledge.

Latour, B. (2005) *Reassembling the Social*, Oxford: Oxford University Press.

Leadbeater, C. (1988) 'Power to the Person', *Marxism Today*, October, pp 14–19.

Leadbeater, C. (2004) *Personalisation through Participation: A New Script for Public Services*, London: Demos.

Leadbeater, C. and Cottam, H. (2007) 'The User-Generated State: Public Services 2.0', in P. Diamond (ed) *Public Matters: The Renewal of the Public Realm*, London: Politicos.

Leadbeater, C., Bartlett, J. and Gallagher, N. (2008) *Making it Personal*, London: Demos.

Leece, D. and Leece, J. (2006) 'Direct Payments: Creating a Two-Tiered System in Social Care?', *British Journal of Social Work*, vol 36, pp 1379–93.

Leece, J. and Bornat, J. (eds) (2006) *Developments in Direct Payments*, Bristol: The Policy Press.

Le Grand, J. (2007) *The Other Invisible Hand: Delivering Public Services through Choice and Competition*, Princeton, NJ: Princeton University Press.

Lendvai, N. and Stubbs, P. (2007) 'Policies as Translation: Situating Transnational Social Policies', in S.M. Hodgson and Z. Irving (eds) *Policy Reconsidered: Meanings, Politics and Practices*, Bristol: The Policy Press, pp 173–91.

Lewis, J. and Glennerster, H. (1996) *Implementing the New Community Care*, Buckingham: Open University Press.

Lipsky, M. (1980) *Street-Level Bureaucracy: Dilemmas of the Individual in Public Services*, New York: Russell Sage Foundation, pp xi–xv.

Lister, R. (2003) 'Investing in the Citizen-Workers of the Future: Transformations in Citizenship and the State under New Labour', *Social Policy and Administration*, vol 37, no 5, pp 427–43.

Localis/KPMG (2009) *The Bottom Line: A Vision for Local Government*, London: Localis/KPMG.

Lombard, D. (2010) 'Getting in the Know', *Community Care*, 20 May.

London Edinburgh Weekend Return Group (1979) *In and Against the State*, London: Pluto Press.

Lord, J. and Hutchinson, P. (2003) 'Individualised Support and Funding: Building Blocks for Capacity Building and Inclusion', *Disability and Society*, vol 18, no 1, pp 71–86.

Low Pay Commission (2009) *National Minimum Wage Report*, London: Low Pay Commission.

Lundsgaard, J. (2005) *Consumer Direction and Choice in Long-Term Care for Older Persons…: How Can It Help Improve Outcomes, Employment and Financial Sustainability?*, Paris: OECD.

Mahony, N., Newman, J. and Barnett, C. (2010) (eds) *Rethinking the Public: Innovations in Research, Theory and Politics*, Bristol: The Policy Press.

Mansell, J. (2010) *Raising Our Sights: Services for Adults with Profound Intellectual and Multiple Disabilities*, London: Department of Health.

Mansell, J. and Beadle-Brown, J. (2005) 'Person Centred Planning and Person-Centred Action: A Critical Perspective', in P. Cambridge and S. Carnaby (eds) *Person Centred Planning and Care Management with People with Learning Disabilities*, London: Jessica Kingsley Publishers, pp 19–33.

March, J.G. and Olsen, J.-P. (1976) *Ambiguity and Choice in Organisations*, Bergen: Universitetsforlaget.

Marmot, M. (2010) *Fair Society, Healthy Lives: The Marmot Review. Strategic Review of Health Inequalities in England Post 2010*, London: Department of Health.

Marshall, T.H. (1992 [1950]) 'Citizenship and Social Class', in T.H. Marshall and T. Bottomore (eds) *Citizenship and Social Class*, London: Pluto Press.

Matland, R.E. (1995) 'Synthesising the Implementation Literature: The Ambiguity–Conflict Model of Policy Implementation', *Journal of Public Administration Research and Theory*, vol 5, no 10, pp 145–75.

Maude, F. (2010) 'The Conservative Party Will Prove It Can Cope – and That It Cares', *Guardian*, 2 October.

Maynard-Moody, S. and Kelly, M. (1993) 'Stories Public Managers Tell About Elected Officials: Making Sense of the Politics-Administration Dichotomy', in B. Bozeman (ed) *Public Management: The State of the Art*, San Francisco, CA: Jossey-Bass.

Maynard-Moody, S. and Musheno, H. (2003) *Cops, Teachers, Counselors: Stories from the Front Lines of Public Service*, Ann Arbor, MI: University of Michigan Press.

McGregor, K. (2011) Extra GP-Style Social Work Practice Pilots to Be Launched', *Community Care*, 10 January.

McGuire, A. (2010a) *The Role of Third Sector Innovation: Personalisation of Education and Learning Services*, London: Office for the Third Sector.

McGuire, A. (2010b) *The Role of Third Sector Innovation: Personalisation of Health and Social Care and Services to Reduce Reoffending*, London: Office for the Third Sector.

McLaughlin, H. (2009) 'What's in a Name: "Client", "Patient", "Customer", "Consumer", "Expert by Experience", "Service User" – What's Next?', *British Journal of Social Work*, vol 39, no 6, pp 1101–17.

McNeil, C. (2009) *Now it's Personal – Personal Advisers and the New Public Service Workforce*, London: Institute for Public Policy Research.

Means, R., Richards, S. and Smith, R. (2008) *Community Care*, 4th edn, Basingstoke: Palgrave.

Miliband, D. (2004a) Speech to the North of England Education conference, January.

Miliband, D. (2004b) 'Foreword', in C. Leadbeater (ed) *Personalisation through Participation: A New Script for Public Services*, London: Demos.

Miliband, D. (2006a) 'Choice and Voice in Personalised Learning', in OECD (ed) *Schooling for Tomorrow: Personalising Education*, Paris: Organisation for Economic Co-operation and Development Publications, pp 21–30.

Miliband, D. (2006b) 'Putting People in Control', Speech to the National Council of Voluntary Organisations, 21 February. Available at: www.labour.org.uk/index.php?id=news2005&ux_news%5Bid%5D=milibandncvo&cHash=3c0a11dcf0

Miller, C. (2010) Speech at the In Control Big Event, Liverpool, 15 March. Available at: www.in-control.org.uk/bigevent2010audio

Miller, P. and Rose, N. (2008) *Governing the Present: Administering Economic, Social and Personal Life*, Cambridge: Polity Press.

MIND (2009a) *Personalisation in Mental Health: A Literature Review*, London: MIND.

MIND (2009b) *Personalisation in Mental Health: Breaking Down the Barriers*, London: MIND.

Ministers of State for Departments of Health, Local and Regional Government and School Standards (2004) *The Case for User Choice in Public Services*, Joint Memorandum to the Public Administration Select Committee Inquiry into Choice, Voice and Public Services.

Mitchell, W. and Glendinning, C. (2007) *A Review of the Research Evidence Surrounding Risk Perceptions, Risk Management Strategies and Their Consequences in Adult Social Care for Different Groups of Service Users*, Social Policy Research Unit Working Paper, York: Social Policy Research Unit, University of York.

Moe, R. (1994) 'The "Re-inventing Government" Exercise: Misinterpreting the Problem, Misjudging the Consequences', *Public Administration Review*, vol 54, no 2, pp 111–22.

Mol, A. (2008) *The Logic of Care: Health and the Problem of Patient Choice*, London: Routledge.

Moore, D. and Nicoll, T. (2009) *Getting a Blue Life: Personalisation and the Criminal Justice System*. Available at: www.revolving-doors.org.uk/documents/Getting-a-Blue-Life

Morgan, D. (2010) '"Lifeline" for Middlewich Pensioners under Threat', *Middlewich Guardian*, 21 April.

Morrell, K. (2006) 'Policy as Narrative: New Labour's Reform of the National Health Service', *Public Administration*, vol 84, no 2, pp 367–85.

Morrell, K. and Tuck, P. (2010) 'Narrative, Morphology and Tales of Governance', Paper presented to the 2010 Political Studies Association annual conference, Edinburgh.

Morris, J. (1993) *Independent Lives: Community Care and Disabled People*, Basingstoke: Macmillan.

Morris, J. (2005) *Citizenship and Disabled People*, London: Disability Rights Commission.

Morris, K. and Burford, G. (2009) 'Family Decision Making: New Spaces for Participation and Resistance', in M. Barnes and D. Prior (eds) *Subversive Citizens: Power, Agency and Resistance in Public Services*, Bristol: The Policy Press, pp 119–35.

Mossberger, K. and Wolman, H. (2003) 'Policy Transfer as a Form of Prospective Policy Evaluation: Challenges and Recommendations', *Public Administration Review*, vol 63, no 4, pp 428–40.

Mulgan, G. (1991) 'Power to the Public', *Marxism Today*, May, pp 14–19.

Murray, C. (1984) *Losing Ground: American Social Policy 1950–1980*, New York: Basic Books.

NCIL (National Centre for Independent Living) (2000) *NCIL Briefing on the Carers and Disabled Children Bill*, London: NCIL.

NCSL (National College for Leadership of Schools and Children's Services) (2004) *Personalised Learning*, special supplement, Nottingham: NCSL.

NCVO (National Council for Voluntary Organisations) (2009) *Personalisation: Rhetoric to Reality*, London: NCVO.

Neal, S. and McLaughlin, E. (2009) 'Researching Up? Interviews, Emotionality and Policy-Making Elites', *Journal of Social Policy*, vol 38, no 4, pp 689–707.

Needham, C. (2003) *Citizen-Consumers: New Labour's Marketplace Democracy*, London: Catalyst Forum.

Needham, C. (2007) *The Reform of Public Services under New Labour: Narratives of Consumerism*, Basingstoke: Palgrave.

Needham, C. (2008) 'Realising the Potential of Co-Production: Negotiating Improvements in Public Services', *Journal of Social Policy and Society* vol 7, no 2, pp 221–31.

Needham, C. (2009) 'Interpreting Personalization in England's National Health Service: A Textual Analysis', *Critical Policy Studies*, vol 3, no 2, pp 204–20.

Needham, C. (2010) *Commissioning for Personalisation: From the Fringes to the Mainstream*, London: Public Management and Policy Association.

Needham, C. and Carr, S. (2009) *Co-production: An Emerging Evidence Base for Social Care Transformation*, London: Social Care Institute for Excellence.

New Economics Foundation (2008) *Co-production: A Manifesto for Growing the Core Economy*, London: New Economics Foundation.

Newman, J. (2001) *Modernising Governance: New Labour, Policy and Society*, London: Sage.

Newman, J. and Clarke, J. (2009a) *Publics, Politics and Power: Remaking the Public in Public Services*, London: Sage.

Newman, J. and Clarke, J. (2009b) 'Narrating Subversion, Assembling Citizenship', in M. Barnes and D. Prior (eds) *Subversive Citizens: Power, Agency and Resistance in Public Services*, Bristol: The Policy Press, pp 67–82.

NHS Confederation/Mental Health Development Unit (2009) *Shaping Personal Health Budgets, a View from the Top*, London: NHS Confederation/Mental Health Development Unit.

NICE (National Institute for Health and Clinical Excellence) (2006) *Obesity Guidance on the Prevention, Identification, Assessment and Management of Overweight and Obesity in Adults and Children*, London: NICE.

Nutley, S.M., Walter, I. and Davies, H.T.O. (2007) *Using Evidence: How Research Can Inform Public Services*, Bristol: The Policy Press.

O'Brien, J. (2001) *Paying Customers are Not Enough: The Dynamics of Individualised Funding*, Lithonia: Responsive Systems Associates.

O'Brien, J. and Duffy, S. (2009) 'Self-Directed Support as a Framework for Partnership Working', in J. Glasby and H. Dickinson (eds) *International Perspectives on Health and Social Care*, Oxford: Wiley-Blackwell.

O'Brien, J. and Lyle O'Brien, C. (1998) *A Little Book about Person Centered Planning*, vol 1, Toronto: Inclusion Press.

O'Brien, J. and Tyne, A. (1981) *The Principle of Normalisation: A Foundation for Effective Services*, London: Campaign for Mentally Handicapped People.

O'Connor, E.S. (2002) 'Telling Decisions: The Role of Narrative in Organizational Decision Making', in Z. Shapira (ed) *Organizational Decision Making*, Cambridge: Cambridge University Press, pp 304–23.

Oliver, M. (1990) *The Politics of Disablement*, Basingstoke: Macmillan.

Olliff-Cooper, J., Wind-Cowie, M. and Bartlett, J. (2009) *Leading from the Front*, London: Demos.

OPM (Office for Public Management) (2008) *Budget-Holding Lead Professional Pilots: Final Report*, London: OPM.

OPM (2010) *Delivering Personal Budgets for Adult Social Care: Reflections from Essex*, London: OPM in association with Essex Coalition of Disabled People and Essex County Council.

Orr, K. (2005) 'Interpreting Narratives of Local Government Change under the Conservatives and New Labour', *British Journal of Politics and International Relations*, vol 7, pp 371–85.

Ospina, S.M. and Dodge, J. (2005) 'It's about Time: Catching Method up to Meaning – the Usefulness of Narrative Inquiry to Public Administration', *Public Administration Review*, vol 65, no 2, pp 143–57.

Ostrom, E. (1996) 'Crossing the Great Divide: Co-production, Synergy, and Development', *World Development*, vol 24, no 6, pp 1073–87.

Owen, T. and the National Care Homes Research and Development Forum (2006) *My Home Life: Quality of Life in Care Homes*, London: Help the Aged.

Pal, L. (1995) 'Competing Paradigms in the Policy Discourse: The Case of International Human Rights', *Policy Sciences*, vol 18, no, 2, pp 185–207.

Panitch, L. and Leys C. (2001) *The End of Parliamentary Socialism: From New Left to New Labour*, 2nd edn, London: Verso.

Parker, S. (2007) 'Participation: A New Operating System for Public Services?', in S. Creasy (ed) *Participation Nation: Reconnecting Citizens to the Public Realm*, London: Involve, pp 103–12.

Parker, S. and Heapy, J. (2006) *The Journey to the Interface: How Public Service Design Can Connect Users to Reform*, London: Demos.

Parr, S. and Nixon, J. (2009) 'Family Intervention Projects: Sites of Subversion and Resilience', in M. Barnes and D. Prior (eds) *Subversive Citizens: Power, Agency and Resistance in Public Services*, Bristol: The Policy Press, pp 101–17.

PASC (Public Administration Select Committee) (2008) *Public Services and the Third Sector: Rhetoric and Reality*, London: The Stationery Office.

Paton, C. (2008) 'The NHS after 10 Years of New Labour', in M. Powell (ed) *Modernising the Welfare State: The Blair legacy*, Bristol: The Policy Press, pp 17–34.

Patterson, W. (2008) 'Narratives of Events: Labovian Narrative Analysis and Its Limitations', in M. Andrews, C. Squire and M. Tamboukou (eds) *Doing Narrative Research*, London: Sage, pp 22–40.

Paul, K.T. (2007) 'Food for Thought: Change and Continuity in German Food Safety Policy', *Critical Policy Analysis*, vol 1, no 1, pp 18–41.

Pearson, C. (2000) 'Money Talks? Competing Discourses in the Implementation of Direct Payments', *Critical Social Policy*, vol 20, no 4, pp 459–77.

Pearson, C. (2006) 'Direct Payments in Scotland', in J. Leece and J. Bornat (eds) *Developments in Direct Payments*, Bristol: The Policy Press, pp 33–47.

Peck, E. and 6, P. (2006) *Beyond Delivery: Policy Implementation as Sense-Making and Settlement*, Basingstoke: Palgrave.

Phoenix, A. (2008) 'Analysing Narrative Contexts', in M. Andrews, C. Squire and M. Tamboukou (eds) *Doing Narrative Research*, London: Sage, pp 64–77.

Pitt, V. (2010) 'Quarter of Social Care Users Now Have Personal Budgets', *Community Care*, 5 November.

Plant, R. (2003) 'A Public Service Ethic and Political Accountability', *Parliamentary Affairs*, vol 56, no 4, pp 560–79.

Poll, C. (2007) 'Co-production in Supported Housing: KeyRing Living Support Networks and Neighbourhood Networks', in *Research Highlights in Social Work: Co-production and Personalisation in Social Care, Changing Relationships in the Provision of Social Care*, vol 49, pp 49–66.

Poll, C., Duffy, S., Hatton, C., Sanderson, H. and Routledge, M. (2006) *A Report on In Control's First Phase, 2003–2005*, London: In Control.

Pollard, A. and James, M. (eds) (2004) *Personalised Learning, a Commentary by the Teaching and Learning Research Programme*, Swindon: ESRC.

Pollitt, C. (2008) *Time, Policy, Management: Governing with the Past*, Oxford: Oxford University Press.

Porteus, J. (2008) 'Community Housing', *The Times*, 10 June.

Prentis, D. (2010) Speech at the launch of *Who Cares: Who Pays?*, Westminster Central Hall, 23 March.

Pressman, J. and Wildavsky, A. (1973) *Implementation: How Great Expectations in Washington Are Dashed in Oakland*, Berkeley, CA: University of California Press.

Prime Minister's Strategy Unit (2005) *Improving the Life Chances of Disabled People*, London: Cabinet Office.

Prime Minister's Strategy Unit (2007) *Building on Progress: Public Services*, London: Cabinet Office.

Prior, D. (2009) 'Policy, Power and the Potential for Counter-Agency', in M. Barnes and D. Prior (eds) *Subversive Citizens: Power, Agency and Resistance in Public Services*, Bristol: The Policy Press, pp 16–32.

Prior, D. and Barnes, M. (2009) '"Subversion" and the Analysis of Public Policy', in M. Barnes and D. Prior (eds) *Subversive Citizens: Power, Agency and Resistance in Public Services*, Bristol: The Policy Press, pp 191–206.

Purvis, T. and Hunt, A. (1993) 'Discourse, Ideology, Discourse, Ideology, Discourse, Ideology ...', *The British Journal of Sociology*, vol 44, no 3, pp 473–99.

Putting People First (2011) *Think Local, Act Personal*, London: Putting People First Consortium.

Pykett, J. (2009) 'Personalization and De-Schooling: Uncommon Trajectories in Contemporary Education Policy', *Critical Social Policy*, vol 29, no 3, pp 374–97.

QAA (Quality Assurance Agency for Higher Education) (2009) *Personal Development Planning: Guidance for Institutional Policy and Practice in Higher Education*, London: QAA.

Randall, N. (2009) 'Time and British Politics: Memory, the Present and Teleology in the Politics of New Labour', *British Politics*, vol 4, no 2, pp 188–216.

Rawnsley, A. (2010) *The End of the Party: The Rise and Fall of New Labour*, London: Viking.

Richards, M. (2008) *Improving Access to Medicines for NHS Patients: A Report for the Secretary of State for Health by Professor Mike Richards*, London: Department of Health.

Richards, S. (2010) *Whatever It Takes: The Inside Story of Gordon Brown and New Labour*, London: Fourth Estate.

Riddell, S., Priestley, M., Pearson, C., Mercer, G., Barnes, C., Jolly, D. and Williams, V. (2006) *Disabled People and Direct Payments: A UK Comparative Study*. Available at: www.leeds.ac.uk/disability-studies/projects/UKdirectpayments/UKDPfinal.pdf

Riessman, C. (1993) *Narrative Analysis*, Thousand Oaks, CA: Sage.

Robertson, D.B. (1991) 'Political Conflict and Lesson-Drawing', *Journal of Public Policy*, vol 11, no 1, pp 55–78.

Rogers, E.M. (2003) *Diffusions of Innovations*, 5th edn, New York: Free Press.

Roe, E.M. (1994) *Narrative Policy Analysis: Theory and Practice*, Durham/London: Duke University Press.

Rose, N. (1996) 'The Death of the Social? Refiguring the Territory of Government', *Economy and Society*, vol 25, no 3, pp 327–56.

Rose, N. (1999) *Powers of Freedom: Reframing Political Thought*, Cambridge: Cambridge University Press.

Rose, R. (1991) 'What is Lesson-Drawing', *Journal of Public Policy*, vol 11, no 1, pp 3–30.

Rose, R. (1993) *Lesson-Drawing in Public Policy*, Chatham, NJ: Chatham House.

Roulstone, A. and Morgan, H. (2009) 'Neo-liberal Individualism or Self-directed Support: Are We All Speaking the Same Language on Modernising Adult Social Care?', *Social Policy and Society*, vol 8, no 3, pp 333–45.

Rouse, J. and Smith, G. (1999) 'Accountability', in M. Powell (ed) *New Labour, New Welfare State?*, Bristol: The Policy Press, pp 235–56.

Routledge, M. (2010) Speech at the In Control Big Event, Liverpool, 15 March. Available at: www.in-control.org.uk/bigevent2010audio

Rummery, K. (2006) 'Disabled Citizens and Social Exclusion: The Role of Direct Payments', *Policy and Politics*, vol 34, no 4, pp 633–50.

Samuel, M. (2010a) 'The Doubts Remain', *Community Care*, 20 May.

Samuel, M. (2010b) 'Personalisation Losing Favour among Social Workers', *Community Care*, 20 May.

Schofield, J. and Sausman, C. (2004) 'Symposium on Implementing Public Policy: Learning from Theory and Practice: Introduction', *Public Administration*, vol 82, no 2, pp 235–248.

Schön, D. (1983) *The Reflective Practitioner: How Professionals Think in Action*, London: Temple Smith.

Schriffin, D. (1990) 'The Management of a Cooperative Self during Argument: The Role of Opinion and Stories', in A.D. Grimshaw (ed) *Conflict Talk: Sociolinguistic Investigations of Arguments in Conversations*, Cambridge: Cambridge University Press.

SCIE (Social Care Institute for Excellence) (2007) *Choice, Control and Individual Budgets: Emerging Themes*, London: SCIE.

SCIE (2009a) *At a Glance 10: Personalisation Briefing: Implications for Carers*, London: SCIE.

SCIE (2009b) *At a Glance 17: Personalisation Briefing, Implications for Residential Care Homes*, London: SCIE.

SCIE (2009c) *At a Glance 8: Personalisation Briefing: Implications for Housing Providers*, London: SCIE.

Scottish Government (2009) *Personalisation Papers*. Available at: www. socialworkscotland.org.uk/resources/pub/PersonalisationPapers.pdf

Scourfield, P. (2005) 'Implementing the Community Care (Direct Payments) Act: Will the Supply of Personal Assistants Meet the Demand and at What Price?', *Journal of Social Policy*, vol 34, no 3, pp 1–20.

Scourfield, P. (2007) 'Social Care and the Modern Citizen: Client, Consumer, Service User, Manager and Entrepreneur', *British Journal of Social Work*, vol 37, pp 107–22.

Shaping Our Lives, National Centre for Independent Living and University of Leeds for Disability Studies (2007) *Developing Social Care: Service Users Driving Culture Change*, London: SCIE.

Shaw, E. (2008) *Losing Labour's Soul: New Labour and the Blair Government, 1997–2007*, London: Routledge.

Smith, R. (2010) 'NHS Money Given to Patients Could Be Spent on Air-Con, Doctors Warn', *Daily Telegraph*, 22 January.

Social Work Task Force (2009) *Building a Safe, Confident Future*, London: DCSF.

SPAEN (Scottish Personal Assistants Employers Network) and Unison (2008) *Creating and Supporting an Informed Employer and Employee Relationship within the Self Directed Support Sector, Interim Report*, Edinburgh: SPAEN/Unison.

Spandler, H. (2004) 'Friend or Foe? Towards a Critical Assessment of Direct Payments', *Critical Social Policy*, vol 24, no 2, pp 187–209.

Squire, C., Andrews, M. and Tamboukou, M. (2008) 'What is Narrative Research?', in M. Andrews, C. Squire and M. Tamboukou (eds) *Doing Narrative Research*, London: Sage, pp 1–21.

SSAT (Specialist Schools and Academies Trust) (2010) *Personalisation Briefing*, London: SSAT.

Stansfield, J. (2010) Speech at the In Control Big Event, Liverpool, 15 March. Available at: www.in-control.org.uk/bigevent2010audio

Stephens, L., Ryan-Colllins, J. and Boyle, D. (2008) *Coproduction: A Manifesto for Growing the Core Economy*, London: New Economics Foundation.

Stone, D. (2005) *Policy Paradox: The Art of Political Decision Making*, rev edn, New York: W.W. Norton.

Stuart, O. (2006) *Will Community-Based Support Services Make Direct Payments a Viable Option for Black and Minority Ethnic Service Users and Carers?*, London: SCIE.

Sullivan, H. (2007) 'Interpreting "Community Leadership" in English Local Government', *Policy and Politics*, vol 35, no 1, pp 141–61.

Sullivan, H. (2009) 'Subversive Spheres: Neighbourhoods, Citizens and the "New Governance"', in M. Barnes and D. Prior (eds) *Subversive Citizens: Power, Agency and Resistance in Public Services*, Bristol: The Policy Press, pp 49–66.

Sullivan, H. and Skelcher, C. (2002) *Working Across Boundaries: Collaboration in Public Services*, Basingstoke: Palgrave.

Surowiecki, J. (2004) *The Wisdom of Crowds: Why the Many are Smarter than the Few*, London: Little, Brown.

Tang, S.Y.S. and Anderson, J.M. (1999) 'Human Agency and the Process of Healing: Lessons Learned from Women Living with Chronic Illness – Re-Writing the Expert', *Nursing Inquiry*, vol 6, pp 83–93.

Taylor, I. and Kelly, J. (2006) 'Professionals, Discretion and Public Sector Reform in the UK: Re-visiting Lipsky', *International Journal of Public Sector Management*, vol 29, no 7, pp 629–42.

Taylor, M. (2001) 'High Noon for the Centre Left', roundtable discussion with Alibhai-Brown, Y., D'Ancona, M., Barnett, A. and Nairn, T., *Open Democracy*, May. Available at: www.opendemocracy.net/content/articles/PDF/343.pdf

Taylor, M. (2010) Speech at the In Control Big Event, Liverpool, 15 March. Available at: www.in-control.org.uk/bigevent2010audio

Taylor Knox, H. (2009) *Personalisation and Individual Budgets: Challenge or Opportunity*, York: Housing Quality Network (HQN).

Thaler, R. and Sunstein, C. (2008) *Nudge: Improving Decisions about Health, Wealth and Happiness*, Yale: Yale University Press.

Tietel, E. (2000) 'The Interview as a Relational Space', *Forum Qualitative Sozialforschung/Forum: Qualitative Social Research*, vol 1, no 3.

Toynbee, P. (2006) 'Labour Has One Serious Candidate – But It Also Seems to Have a Death Wish', *The Guardian*, 29 September.

Tyson, A. (2007) *Commissioners and Providers Together: The Citizen at the Centre*, London: In Control and Care Services Improvement Partnership (CSIP).

Tyson, A., Brewis, R., Crosby, N., Hatton, C., Stansfield, J., Tomlinson, C., Waters, J. and Wood, A. (2010a) *A Report on In Control's Third Phase: Evaluation and Learning 2008–2009*, London: In Control.

Tyson, A., Brewis, R., Crosby, N., Hatton, C., Stansfield, J., Tomlinson, C., Waters, J., Wood, A. (2010b) *A Report on In Control's third phase: Evaluation and learning 2008-2009, A Summary*, London: In Control.

Uitermark, J. (2005) 'The Genesis and Evolution of Urban Policy: A Confrontation of Regulationist and Governmentality Approaches', *Political Geography*, vol 24, no 2, pp 137–63.

Ungerson, C. (1997) 'Give Them the Money: Is Cash a Route to Empowerment?', *Social Policy and Administration*, vol 31, no 1, pp 45–53.

Ungerson, C. (1999) 'Personal Assistants and Disabled People: An Examination of a Hybrid Form of Work and Care', *Work, Employment and Society*, vol 13, no 4, pp 583–600.

Unison (2009) *Unison Briefing: Personal Health Budgets in the NHS*, London: Unison.

Van Eeten, M. (2007) 'Narrative Policy Analysis', in F. Fischer, G. Miller and M. Sidney (eds) *Handbook of Public Policy Analysis: Theory, Practice and Methods*, London: Taylor and Francis, pp 89–108.

Van Gorp, B. (2001) 'The Implementation of Asylum Policy: Which Frame Dominates the Debate?', Paper presented at the European Consortium for Political Research, 29th Joint Sessions, Grenoble, France, 6-11 April.

von Hayek, F. (1944) *The Road to Serfdom*, London: Routledge & Kegan Paul.

Wainwright, H. (1994) *Arguments for a New Left: Answering the Free-Market Right*, Oxford: Blackwell.

Waldegrave, W. (1994) 'The Reality of Reform and Accountability in Today's Public Service', in N. Flynn (ed) *Public Finance Foundation Reader: Change in the Civil Service*, London: CIPFA, pp 81–8.

Walker, J., Donaldson, C., Laing, K., Pennington, M., Wilson, G., Procter, S., Bradley, D., Dickinson, H. and Gray, J. (2009) *National Evaluation of the Budget Holding Lead Professional Pilots in Multi-Agency Children's Services in England*, London: DCSF.

Wanless, D. (2003) *Securing Our Future Health: Taking a Long-Term View: Final Report*, London: Department of Health.

Weber, M. (1997) 'Rational Legal Authority and Bureaucracy', in M. Hill (ed) *The Policy Process: A Reader*, London: Prentice Hall, pp 323–7.

Weick, K.E. (1995) *Sensemaking in Organizations*, London: Sage.

White, C., Warrener, M., Reeves, A. and La Valle, I. (2008) *Family Intervention Projects – an Evaluation of Their Design, Set-up and Early Outcomes*, London: DCFS/CLG.

White, H. (1981) 'The Narrativization of Real Events', in W.J.T. Mitchell (ed) *On Narrative*, Chicago: University of Chicago Press, pp 249–54.

Wilding, P. (1994) 'Maintaining Quality in Human Services', *Social Policy and Administration*, vol 28, no 1, pp 57–72.

Willard, C. (1996) *Liberalism and the Problem of Knowledge*, Chicago, IL: University of Chicago Press.

Williams, F. (2001) 'In and beyond New Labour: Towards a New Political Ethics of Care', *Critical Social Policy*, vol 21, no 4, pp 467–93.

Williams, R. (1975) *Keywords: A Vocabulary of Culture and Society*, Glasgow: Fontana.

Wilson, G. (1994) 'Co-Production and Self-Care: New Approaches to Managing Community Care Services for Older People', *Social Policy and Administration*, vol 28, no 3, pp 236–50.

Wolman, H. (1992) 'Understanding Cross National Policy Transfers: The Case of Britain and the US', *Governance*, vol 5, no 1, pp 27–45.

Wright, P. (1985) *On Living in an Old Country: The National Past in Contemporary Britain*, London: Verso.

Yanow, D. (1996) *How Does a Policy Mean? Interpreting Policy and Organizational Actions*, Washington, DC: Georgetown University Press.

Yanow, D. (2000) *Conducting Interpretive Policy Analysis*, London: Sage.

Yanow, D. (2003) 'Accessing Local Knowledge', in M.A. Hajer and H. Wagenaar (eds) *Deliberative Policy Analysis: Understanding Governance in the Network Society*, Cambridge: Cambridge University Press, pp 228–46.

Yanow, D. (2004) 'Translating Local Knowledge at Organizational Peripheries', *British Journal of Management*, vol 15, pp 9–25.

Yanow, D. (2005) 'Built Space as Story: The Policy Stories That Buildings Tell', *Policy Studies Journal*, vol 23, no 3, pp 407–22.

Yanow, D. (2007) 'Interpretation in Policy Analysis: On Methods and Practice', *Critical Policy Analysis*, vol 1, no 1, pp 110–22.

Zarb, G. and Nadash, P. (1994) *Cashing in on Independence: Comparing the Costs and Benefits of Cash and Services*, London: BCODP.

Index

learning pathways 40, 41
learning plans 40
Lendvai, N. 82–3
Lewis, I. 59, 74
Lewis, J. 68
Liberal Democrats 2, 165
  see also Coalition government
lifestyle-related health factors 35
Lipsky, M. 150, 155
Littlechild, R. 49, 50, 66, 70, 77, 107, 145
Liverpool, day centre closures 106
local authorities 37, 38, 68, 69, 92, 95
  adult social care 32–3
  clawing back funds 102, 131
  market-shaping 94–7
  and providers 96
  resource allocation system 33, 88, 100, 101
  and risk 103
  and self-funders 132–3
  spending cuts 100–1, 162
  support planning 90–1, 92
  Transforming Social Care Grant 32, 70, 97, 105–6
local housing allowance 38
long-stay hospitals 67
Lord, J. 71

M

macro-financing 100
Mahony, N. 121–2
mainstreaming personalisation 104–9
Major, J. 77
managerialism 77, 140
Mansell, J. 67, 68, 71, 128–9
market failure 103
marketisation 118, 119
market-shaping 94–9
Marxism Today 77
maternity services 36
Maynard-Moody, S. 150
McLaughlin, E. 26
means testing 116
mental health problems 34
mental health service users 31, 33, 36, 67, 131, 151–2
mental health services 138
micro-financing 99
Miliband, D. 39, 40, 75
Miller, C. 107
MIND 127, 131

Moe, R. 20
Morgan, D. 126
Morrell, K. 18, 49–50
Musheno, H. 150
mutuals 152, 165
My Home Life guide 130–1

N

narrative 4–5, 21–2
narratives of personalisation 4, 7–8, 22–4, 47, 159–60
  common-sense rationale 50, 51, 52, 53, 55
  justification, storylines 48, 55–6
    applicable to everyone 53
    it works 49–50
    reflects the way people live their lives 52–3
    saves money 50–2
    users are the experts 53–6
  self-evidence 49–50, 51, 55
  time framings 57
    continuity and discontinuity 57–60
    cycles and arrows 60–3
    slowness and speed 63
narratives of policy 16–22, 56
national curriculum 41
National Health Service *see* NHS (National Health Service)
National Indicator 130: 32
National Performance Review (Clinton) 20
Neal, S. 26
needs assessment 68, 88, 146
Netherlands 71
New Labour 2, 60, 73–80, 122, 140
  education 39–40
  employment 38–9
  equity 114
  health service 35
  housing 38
  responsibilisation of citizens 122
New Local Government Network 59
New Times 77, 78
Newman, J. 16, 109, 152
NHS (National Health Service) 35–6, 81, 159, 166
  individual budgets 36, 116, 131–2
  reform of 36, 164, 165
  topping up 116
  see also personal health budgets